Praise for *The Habit of Excellence*

'An extraordinary read for any leader. Through a thoughtful
analysis of leadership at every level in the British Army,
The Habit of Excellence offers invaluable insights for
understanding the ecosystem in which you lead, and
maximising your effectiveness. Truly brilliant'
General Stanley McChrystal, author of *Team of Teams*

'*The Habit of Excellence* offers proven tools and strategies
drawn from the British Army's centuries of leadership
experience, showing how you can drive higher
performance in your own teams. Most importantly,
this excellent book challenges popular assumptions
about British Army leadership, revealing what
makes it the "gold standard"'
Matthew Syed, author of *Rebel Ideas*

'A *terrific* book – one that is full of insights and lessons that
will be of enormous value to leaders in all fields! I was
privileged to witness the strength of British Army leadership
first-hand, serving alongside British forces during the Cold
War and in Bosnia, and then commanding British forces in Iraq,
Afghanistan and throughout the greater Middle East.
Lt Col Langley Sharp distils and describes very effectively
the impressive elements that exemplify the leadership of
our most trusted ally and partner'
General David Petraeus, former Director of the CIA

'In the complex and stressful world in which we live, strong
and inspiring leadership has never been more needed.
It's sadly too rare a commodity but we all know when we are
in the presence of it. This very readable book uncovers
the skills and qualities that have made Sandhurst a byword
for effective leadership. Whatever your profession or occupation,
learn what allows people to respect you, to follow you, to trust
you. I could not recommend this exceptional book more'
General The Lord David Richards, former Chief of the
Defence Staff

'Lt Col Sharp's forensic study of how leadership in the British Army is identified, nurtured and exercised is a primer for those serving. In particular, I commend his exposition of the vital relationship between commissioned and non-commissioned officers. I also believe this book is of much wider value in any walk of life that requires teams to be built and common purpose to be achieved'
General Sir Mike Jackson, former Chief of the General Staff

'Most organisations teach leadership as a complement to professional skills. At Sandhurst, it is the professional skill and that's why Sandhurst graduates are in demand not just in the military but in civilian life too. However, what this book demonstrates above all is that, while good leadership techniques can be learned and must evolve to meet the needs of the modern era, great leadership is fundamentally a question of character. We are fortunate indeed that the British Army still recruits and inspires those who meet that enduring test. This book is a handbook for them and for those aspiring to be great leaders everywhere'
Lord Mark Sedwill, former Cabinet Secretary and National Security Adviser

The Habit of Excellence

Why British Army Leadership Works

LIEUTENANT COLONEL
LANGLEY SHARP

Centre for Army Leadership

BUSINESS

PENGUIN BUSINESS

UK | USA | Canada | Ireland | Australia
India | New Zealand | South Africa

Penguin Business is part of the Penguin Random House group of companies
whose addresses can be found at global.penguinrandomhouse.com.

First published 2021
001

Set in 12/14.75pt Bembo Book MT Pro
Typeset by Jouve (UK), Milton Keynes
Printed and bound in Great Britain by Clays Ltd, Elcograf S.p.A.

The authorized representative in the EEA is Penguin Random House Ireland,
Morrison Chambers, 32 Nassau Street, Dublin D02 YH68

A CIP catalogue record for this book is available from the British Library

ISBN: 978-0-241-50750-6

Follow us on LinkedIn: https://www.linkedin.com/company/penguin-connect/

www.greenpenguin.co.uk

To the families and loved ones of soldiers past and present,
without whose sacrifice we could not do the job we do

For one swallow does not make a summer, nor does one day;
and so too one day, or a short time, does not make a
man blessed and happy.

Aristotle, *Nicomachean Ethics*[1]

We are what we repeatedly do. Excellence,
then, is not an act, but a habit.

William Durant, *The Story of Philosophy*[2]

Contents

Preface

We were twenty minutes out from the Normandy drop zone when I looked up and noticed the words opposite me, scrawled inside the fuselage of the Dakota aircraft.

> Jock Hutton
> Operation Overlord
> Ranville
> 5/6 June 1944
> Night Drop

Exactly seventy-five years earlier, Jock had made this journey, in this same aircraft, one of the first wave of British soldiers to set foot in France on the day the battle to liberate it began. With 13th (Lancashire) Parachute Battalion, he was part of the 18,000-strong Allied airborne assault that paved the way for the success of the D-Day landings, capturing key positions behind the Normandy beaches, including Pegasus Bridge. Now, in 2019, the last survivor of his battalion, Jock sat at Duxford airfield, waiting to be lifted to Ranville to repeat the jump he had made behind enemy lines in 1944, as a nineteen-year-old private soldier.[1]

Ahead, in the plane that carried his name, we were nearing our drop, the first of a series of jumps to commemorate one of The Parachute Regiment's most famous battle honours, and one of the British Army's most significant operations. Beside me, from 16 Air Assault Brigade, were my fellow Commanding Officers, including Lieutenant Colonel Matt Taylor and Lieutenant Colonel Mark Swann, two of my closest friends. Written on to the aircraft around us were the names of those who had jumped in 1944: the founding generation of our regiment, who set the standard and defined the global reputation The Parachute Regiment enjoys today. In my mind were the 650 soldiers of the 1st Battalion (1 PARA): the men and women I commanded and had the honour and privilege to represent on that day.

That day, 6 June 2019, brought home what being a leader in the British Army has meant to me, across a career that now covers more than two decades. The deep bonds of kinship and loyalty with those you serve and have grown up alongside. The requirement to be a custodian of traditions and standards that were forged generations before you, and will live long after you. The duty to represent the very best of your people, your regiment and your service.

I knew none of this twenty years earlier, when I arrived at Sandhurst, the Army's officer training academy, in the expectation that I would stay in the Army for a handful of years at most. I do not come from a military background: my dad has worked his whole career as a self-employed cleaning contractor and my mum as a psychological therapist. I didn't grow up dreaming of being a soldier or becoming a paratrooper. But once I had joined the Army, buoyed by a sense of adventure and challenge, I discovered the seductive, almost addictive quality of a profession that isn't a job, but a way of life. The Army can be hard to live with, especially for the families who sacrifice so much to enable their loved ones to serve, but for many it is even harder to live without.

The demands the Army makes on its people explain much of its proud and distinctive leadership culture. While combat operations are only a small part of any Army career, it is to fight and, for some, to lead soldiers in battle that most have ultimately joined; to do work that has an unmistakable purpose, to defend the nation, its freedoms and values. That duty is sought, but also carries with it a burden: a responsibility to protect and serve those around you, to uphold the standards of those who came before you, and to pass them on to the generations that will follow. It is this combination of pride, purpose and people – that juncture of past, present and future – which defines to me what it means to be a leader in the Army.

Army leadership is also shaped by the breadth of experiences that make up any military career. From my first tour as a platoon commander deployed to Fermanagh, Northern Ireland, to a NATO peace support operation in Macedonia, to Afghanistan immediately following 9/11, and multiple subsequent tours both there and in Iraq, my time in the Army has taken me to many different places, put me in a variety of leadership roles, and exposed me to the contrasting approaches of numerous military and civilian partners. I learned as much about leadership when planning the training programme for 17,000 Armed Forces personnel during the 2012 Olympics as I did commanding a company in Helmand Province the following year, and as I had years earlier from observing the work of my corporals as a novice platoon commander.

Every tour teaches you, every command challenges you in new ways, and every ally and partner brings something different from which you can learn. In over twenty years, there have been few days when I have not encountered something that has inspired, helped or taught me: the leadership of a private soldier still in their teens, the advice and guidance of a late-entry officer, the courage and professionalism of a US Marine Corps officer, or the fighting spirit of our loyal Afghan partners.

In an organisation that is deeply committed to leadership, on operations that demand it in spades, you become immersed in the subject – stimulated by the example of others and constantly challenged to rethink and evolve your own approach. The Army provides a career-long education in human nature, the power of leadership, and the extraordinary lengths to which people who share a common purpose and identity will go in service of their mission. It reinforces my belief that leadership is not about the heroic exception or one-off action, but the habitual practice of doing what is right, difficult and necessary every single day to build a team, look after the people in it, and work towards the next objective.

For the past two years it has been my privilege to take on another role, as head of the Centre for Army Leadership (CAL), the guardian and conscience of a leadership tradition that stretches back 360 years, and the body tasked with ensuring this evolves and adapts to meet the challenges of the future. The CAL is still a young organisation, but its highly capable and committed team, drawing on expertise from across the Army, both military and civil service, provides an institutional core that has never previously existed, one that is fostering a more active dialogue on leadership between the Army and the civilian world. The Army has much to teach about leadership, but also plenty to learn. This book is part of that ongoing process of knowledge exchange and reflection.

Like most who serve in it, I am proud of the British Army, of its work and the role it plays in society: representing our nation, defending our interests and providing career and life opportunities for so many. Captain Den Starkie, who led 1 PARA alongside me as my Regimental Sergeant Major, puts it best. 'I was dragged up, in what I would best describe as a bit of poverty for my first thirteen years. In 1996 I joined The Parachute Regiment, which ultimately became my family. And now I am stood here as a commissioned officer.' That is the Army at its best: a chance to serve, an opportunity to grow, and a family that will be with you for life.

But the Army is not perfect, and not without its many problems and flaws. As an organisation of over 100,000 people, it reflects the society it recruits from, both its strengths and its shortcomings. And as a disciplined and hierarchical institution with a strong culture, and one which demands high performance, the scope for misinterpreting what good leadership looks like will always exist. These are problems the Army acknowledges and, as the book will explore, some of the most serious failings of recent times have been the spur for changes in how its leaders are trained and developed through their careers. The Army is still in the process of moulding the leadership cohort and culture it needs: one which has the operational advantage of being truly diverse, in which the institution's Values and Standards are intrinsic principles for each individual, and where the leadership of soldiers is encouraged, developed and acknowledged as much as that of officers.

Like every organisation, the Army faces a future in which the pace of social, technological and geopolitical change appears to be ever accelerating, in a world that seems increasingly complex. Leadership will be the defining factor in its ability to meet these challenges and continue to fulfil its enduring purpose. As it faces this future, the Army has the benefit of a solid core of over three centuries of tradition and experience in the art, science and practice of leadership. That is the basis on which this book has been written, drawing on a history that shows the long-standing principles that define Army leadership, and how these have continued to evolve in a constantly changing context. As I was reminded, sitting on the Dakota, the lessons of that history are all around, often within touching distance.

Jock Hutton passed away in August 2020, at the age of ninety-six. The 75th anniversary commemoration was the last jump of a pioneering career and extraordinary life. His generation may be fading into memory, but their example burns bright, an inspiration to my generation of Army leaders, as it will be for those who follow. His story epitomises British Army leadership: a tradition and a duty whose history never loses its relevance, but whose evolution and development is never complete. It is a constant work in progress, a living story whose next chapter is forever in the process of being written.

Introduction

When war broke out in August 1914, Roland Bradford of the Durham Light Infantry was a young second lieutenant, a junior officer in command of a platoon of thirty soldiers. By November 1917, he had responsibility for a brigade of approximately 4,000 and was the youngest general officer in the Army, at the age of just twenty-five. Only weeks after being promoted to this command, he was killed at the Battle of Cambrai, fatally wounded by fragments from a shell that landed near his brigade headquarters.[1] He was one of four Bradford brothers to see active service during the First World War, one of the three who did not survive it, and one of the two to be decorated with the Victoria Cross, the Army's highest commendation for valour, awarded after an action in which he stepped forward to command a battalion that had taken heavy casualties under machine-gun fire, in addition to his own.[2]

His story is remarkable not just for its precocious achievements, but for his understanding of Army leadership and the leader's role. Notes he jotted down over a century ago reveal an appreciation of the art of leadership that stands the test of time.

> Leadership – ability to make comrades follow you. Within power of everyone to become a Leader. Ability to appreciate requirements of human nature [. . .] Power & ability to set example to subordinates. Knowledge. Determination & intensity of purpose. Optimistic and enthusiastic. Look after men's comfort and welfare [. . .] Justice. Friend as well as leader. Fitness & Endurance. Courage. Cheerfulness.[3]

Of a subject that has been talked and written about for centuries within the Army, there can be few more aptly succinct summaries of the key qualities and requirements. Brigadier-General Bradford understood that leadership is a fundamentally human endeavour, one that rests on the ability to understand people and inspire them through personal example. He recognised that it is a universal pursuit, not one limited by rank or experience. And he knew that it is, at its heart, about service: leaders meet the needs of their people so that they, in turn, can serve those of the collective mission. All these aspects of leadership are universal to any profession or area of life, but the distinctive nature of the military experience exemplifies them and brings them to the fore.

Leadership is the lifeblood of the military, the human force that propels every part of an army's work, from training to deployment. The business of the military – the profession of arms – depends by its nature upon extremes. Every soldier accepts the responsibility, when required, to go to war, to fight, and to enter combat situations where they may need to take life or give their own. This undertaking, intrinsic to the Army's primary purpose to protect the nation, requires people and teams with extraordinarily high levels of discipline, morale and cohesion. None of that can exist or be sustained without leaders capable of nurturing individuals and moulding collective motivation and identity. More than any other factor, the Army's operational effectiveness stands or falls, based on the quality of its leadership.

The British Army has a particular need for leadership and also a distinctive perspective on it. That is partly based on history, with over three centuries of practical experience and institutional memory of both success and failure. It also arises from an organisational structure that relies almost entirely on promotion from within: the Army's senior leaders have all risen from the most junior ranks, underlining the paramount importance of leadership development. In addition, the Army is an institution that contains multiple layers of leadership and different kinds of leaders. Commissioned officers, who hold the legal authority to command soldiers and order the use of deadly force, work alongside non-commissioned officers (NCOs), soldier leaders with their own rank structure and distinct role. Tactical leaders drive the Army's operational work, organisational leaders co-ordinate its complex machinery, and strategic leaders work to set its current and future direction.[4] Leaders in the Regular Army are supported by those in the Army Reserve, who combine their service with civilian careers. Most importantly, the Army is an organisation that is led at all levels, with the leadership of soldiers and corporals at the tactical level as important in its own context as that of officers on the General Staff, the central body of the Army's senior leadership.

The lessons of British Army leadership that this book will outline are the product of centuries of evolution. Much connects the leaders of today's Army with those from previous generations. Their work continues to be a human endeavour, defined by the relationships forged between leaders and followers. It is still conditioned by the enduring influence of the regimental system, the administrative structure of the Army that organises its forces according to function and geography, into regiments and corps with distinctive histories and identities. It remains an art: to balance the needs of a mission, the team that must deliver it, and the individuals in that team. And it is informed by values such as courage, discipline and integrity that were not formally codified until the turn of the twenty-first century, but would have been equally recognisable to an officer or NCO of the eighteenth century.

Equally, there have been many areas of growth and development. While leadership in the Army might once have been perceived as the natural product of social class, public school education and individual style, today the guiding belief is that leaders are made, not born, and that it is the Army's responsibility to develop them.[5] The modern Army regards leadership as a matter of professional knowledge, established principles and shared Values and Standards, which provide the basis for developing every officer and soldier as a leader throughout their career. It believes leadership must be a collective responsibility, as influential at the bottom of the rank structure as it is at the top, in an operating environment that increasingly puts the onus on the independence of small teams with junior leaders. And it recognises that while leadership may sometimes be manifested by acts of individual courage and heroism, most importantly it is a habit, the ability to do the right thing and make the difficult decision every single day: an accumulation of countless small choices, interventions and demonstrations that set the example required to uphold standards and drive performance.

For much of its history, leadership was something the Army and its people were more comfortable doing than seeking to define or interrogate on a conceptual level.[6] That has changed in recent decades, as the emergence of a doctrinal approach has seen the Army work to codify the principles that underpin its work in all areas and establish an institutional view. Following the publication of warfighting doctrine in the late 1980s, and of formal Values and Standards in 2000, the Army published its first leadership doctrine in 2016. The following year, the Centre for Army Leadership (CAL) was established, with the mission to champion leadership excellence and keep the Army at the forefront of its theory and practice.

This book has therefore emerged from a period in which the Army has undertaken significant work to develop its perspective on leadership. While numerous accounts have related the personal experiences of British Army leaders, and explored its leadership at particular points in history, no previous work has provided the institutional view on British Army leadership, what makes it effective and how it is done.[7] What follows seeks to fill that literature gap, and provide an insight into leadership in the British Army that is relevant to professionals in all fields, at any stage of their career. Much as the Army's leadership philosophy covers a spectrum from soldiers still in their teens to generals with decades of experience, it is hoped that the lessons in this book will be of equal relevance to senior executives and emerging leaders alike.

While certain aspects of the Army experience are distinctive to those serving in the military, most of its lessons have a universal relevance. The book will explore questions that are fundamental to leadership in any area of life: how to build trust and cohesion, achieve a balance between control and delegation, and deliver results in the face of adversity. It will show how the Army trains leaders capable of thriving in the chaos and confusion of the battlefield; how it builds teams filled with leaders that can remain effective under pressure, in all environments; and how its command philosophy empowers the most junior people on those teams to become leaders whatever their age, rank or experience. For any organisation that is committed to maximising the effectiveness of its teams and unlocking the potential of its people, the book distils centuries of the Army's experience in developing the leadership that defines its ability to fight and win.

What follows will blend the practical and the conceptual, outlining the frameworks and methods that Army leaders are taught, and illustrating through examples how leaders have used these ideas to navigate the challenging environments of military operations. While its primary focus is on the theory and practice of leadership in the Army today, it will draw on examples from history that underline the enduring nature of many key principles. The book is the product of the CAL's research, drawing on extensive collective experience from across the Army and seeking, as far as possible, to be representative.

It begins with an overview of how the Army's leaders and leadership have developed since its establishment following the Restoration of King Charles II in 1660, tracing how they have evolved in line with changes in society, major events in its own history, and a long, gradual process of professionalisation. The second chapter explains the distinctive context in which the Army's leaders must operate, in a profession that includes the use of lethal force, a strictly hierarchical command structure, and an organisation that blends the needs and technology of the twenty-first century with long-standing traditions and regimental identities. An understanding of this history is important to appreciate how the Army's approach to leadership has emerged as the product of centuries of continuity and change, and to understand why elements that may appear artefacts of tradition, such as the regimental system, remain tangible contributors to cohesion, fighting power and leadership today.

Based on this context, the book considers the key components of modern British Army leadership and follows the structure of the Army's Leadership Framework to explore in successive chapters what the Army's leaders are and what roles they fulfil, what leaders must know in order to carry out their responsibilities, and what they do in practice to develop individuals, build teams and achieve the mission they have been set. The second half of the book then explains how these fundamental tenets of leadership are put into practice by the Army's officer and soldier leaders, respectively, and in the context both of peace and war. As these chapters will explain, the interplay between these different styles of leadership, and the contrasting environments in which Army leaders must operate, are all-important.

Officers cannot lead without NCOs, any more than the Army can succeed in war if its units have not been properly trained and developed by their leaders during peacetime.

The book concludes by looking to the future faced by the Army and its leaders, and how the enduring principles of Army leadership may need to evolve to respond to an environment of emerging threats, technologies and social trends. That focus on the future reflects that Army leadership is constantly developing, as it has throughout its history. An institution like the Army, which exists by democratic consent, must continually evolve in order to represent the society it exists to defend, and equip itself for a shifting threat landscape. Tomorrow's Army will need more leaders from diverse backgrounds, and individuals with skills and outlooks that may look very different from the soldiers and officers of previous generations.[8] It will need to develop as a Whole Force that combines the skills and experience not just of Regular Army soldiers and officers, but also reservists, civil servants and defence contractors.

The Army's approach to leadership has also developed in response to notable past failings that revealed deficiencies in its culture, values and operational procedures: cases that the book will touch on, including the death of Baha Mousa in Army custody in 2003 and the death of four soldiers at Deepcut Barracks between 1995 and 2002. These events led, respectively, to a renewed focus on training and education in the Army's Values and Standards, and an overhaul of how every Army instructor is trained for the vital leadership role of developing recruits and future leaders.

Leadership is a familiar and extensively discussed subject, but one whose importance is ever growing in the contemporary context. The Army faces a fast-evolving threat landscape driven by social, economic, environmental and technological change, just as every business is having to adapt rapidly to the changing needs of its customers, the changing expectations of investors and employees, and the speed at which competitors can emerge. In the same way as the Army must now equip itself for an environment in which technology can empower adversaries with minimal resources to launch attacks from anywhere in the world, companies face a market in which their business models are vulnerable to competitors that can grow more rapidly than ever, with cheap and accessible technology that allows them to reach customers and acquire market share more readily than before. When the operating environment feels more volatile and the future more uncertain than ever, the quality of leadership becomes an area of solid ground in which every organisation can and must invest to support its growth, resilience and impact.

Based on the British Army's unique experience and distinct perspective, this book has been written to promote debate, discussion and reflection, helping every organisation develop its leadership and every individual to grow as a leader.

The Army is committed to giving each of its people the opportunity and the support to become the best leader they can be. We hope what follows can play some small part in helping you to achieve the same.

1.   In History and Changing Society

In his memoir of service in the Peninsular War (1807–14), fought against Napoleonic France's invasion of Spain and Portugal, Sergeant Joseph Donaldson of 94th Scots Brigade offered a portrait of his commanding officer, Lieutenant Colonel Thomas Lloyd.

> So harmoniously did he blend the qualities of a brave, active, intelligent officer with those of the gentleman and the scholar, that the combination fascinated all ranks [. . .] [He] endeavoured to encourage, not to terrify – if there was a single spark of pride or honour in the bosom, he would fan it to a flame . . . By the measures he took, he made every individual interested in his own honour and that of the regiment; and I believe that every man in it loved and honoured him. So successful were his efforts, that he brought the regiment into a state of order, cleanliness and discipline, which could never have been obtained by any other means.[1]

Writing about an individual who lived and died over two centuries ago – killed commanding his battalion at the Battle of Nivelle in 1813 – Donaldson captured many of the characteristics that embody the best of British Army leadership in any generation. His description of a leader rich in human qualities resonates as a model of leadership equally applicable to the modern business environment as it was to the military in the Napoleonic era. It underlines that the most important elements of leadership are timeless. Then as now, leadership is best understood as a human endeavour whose central concerns are to influence the individual and mould the collective in service of the ultimate mission: 'a combination of character, knowledge and action that inspires others to succeed,' as defined by Army Leadership Doctrine.[2]

There is an enduring character to Army leadership that explains much of its institutional strength. Everyone who joins the Army to become a leader is also joining a tradition – of the organisation as a whole, and of their regiment in particular – that stretches back for decades and centuries. Consciously and subconsciously, they are influenced by the leaders around them, who in turn have been shaped by those who came before them: a continuum that links leaders in the era of drones and big data with those who operated in the age of the flintlock musket.

Tradition is a cornerstone of Army leadership, but not an anchor. Alongside enduring continuities are areas that have been subject to constant and dramatic change through 360 years of history: the way the Army selects and develops its leaders, the relationships between leaders and followers, the perception of who is qualified to lead, and the question of what methods they should use. The history of Army leadership is one that reflects a slow process of professionalisation, moving from a traditional mindset that held leadership to be innate to individuals of privileged social and educational backgrounds, and was suspicious of attempts to codify and teach it, to the modern belief that it can be taught, must follow common principles, and is the business of every individual in the Army, from private soldiers to four-star generals.[3]

The Army's theory and practice of leadership has developed to reflect an institution that has undergone multiple transformations, from the tiny force of 5,000 established following the Restoration in 1660 and drawing on the remnants of Oliver Cromwell's New Model Army, to the military that stretched across the British Empire from the Caribbean to India during the eighteenth and nineteenth centuries, the millions-strong machine that would fight in the World Wars of the twentieth century, and the post-1945 Army whose role has ranged from managing colonial withdrawal to short offensive wars, counter-terrorism campaigns (including in Malaya, Kenya, Cyprus and Borneo), long-term interventions (from Bosnia to Iraq and Afghanistan), and operations to provide military aid to civil authorities. As the size and role of the Army has fluctuated over time, it has also been shaped by the wider context of change in society. Through its history, the Army's leaders have had to adapt to the changing mores and expectations of the people it recruits and the society it exists to defend, as much as to evolutions in the business of warfighting and military affairs.

The foundations of Army leadership that this book will explore are not novel creations, but modern manifestations of these evolutions: outcomes of thinking, controversies, hard-fought arguments and hard-won lessons spanning more than three and a half centuries. These legacies are the basis of the Army's unique perspective on leadership, one that is as steeped in history as it is focused on future needs. To understand how the Army operates today as an organisation with leadership at its core, it is essential to understand the history of its leadership, and how this has reflected the changing society the Army works for and exists within. This chapter will provide an overview of that history, tracing a centuries-long story of professionalisation that stretches from the eighteenth-century era of heroic leadership and officers as 'military proprietors' to the disciplinarian age of Wellington, the reforming urge of the Victorian and Edwardian eras, the shock of change and civilianisation during both World Wars, and the modern Army's emphasis on doctrine, delegated authority and the democratisation of leadership.[4]

1660–1852: Purchase, honour, discipline

The identity and role of the Army's leaders in its early years was shaped by the circumstances of its creation, most notably the political unease surrounding the idea of a standing army, spurred by the recent memory of the Civil War and the brief period of direct military rule under Cromwell's Protectorate. Following the restoration of King Charles II in 1660, to which the modern history of the Army dates, the lack of political will to create the visible infrastructure of a standing army (such as sufficient barracks to house its troops), or to fully fund its operations, concentrated power in the hands of individual officers. The Crown appointed and partially funded colonels to create regiments for which they then took almost complete responsibility, in everything from clothing and accommodation to training and pay.[5] Officer commissions were largely obtained through purchase: young men would buy or be bought an Ensigncy or Cornetcy (first commissioned rank in infantry and cavalry regiments) and then continue to pay their way up the ladder, acquiring ranks of progressively greater value, whose final sale would form their pension on retirement. This system of officers as 'military proprietors', which would last in various forms until the outlawing of purchase in 1871, created a skew in the Army's leadership ranks towards men of independent wealth who could manage their commission as a form of investment.[6]

Such a state of affairs provided reassurance to those who remained concerned about the existence of a standing army. 'Has it not always been with good reason urged that our liberties are in no danger from our standing army because it is commanded by men of the best families and fortunes?' the Whig Prime Minister Henry Pelham contended in 1744.[7] It also conditioned the style of leadership: an aristocratic model that prized physical courage, personal honour and leadership by example. As a brigade commander in the War of the Spanish Succession, a twelve-year campaign to stave off French accession to the Spanish throne, the Duke of Argyll was renowned for leading from the front. One account of an action in 1706 noted that he 'was himself the second or third man who, with his sword in hand, broke over the enemy's trenches', while another observer recorded in 1708 that he:

> [. . .] exposed his person in such a manner that he had several musket shots through his wig and clothes. It was not from an overheated valour which runs into all places merely to show a contempt for it, but that might animate the troops to imitate his example and to perform those miracles which [. . .] [seem] to have been expected from them.[8]

Even though, in practice, the Army's leadership in the eighteenth century was not of uniform social origin – aristocrats mixing with 'members of the middling and lesser gentry', the cost of commissions varying considerably according to the status of a regiment, and around a third being awarded without payment – there was collective aspiration towards a certain style of heroic leadership. '[The] prevailing *culture* of the officer corps was predominantly aristocratic in tone, based as it was upon a pre-Enlightenment honour code with quasi-medieval trimmings,' the historian Alan Guy has suggested.[9]

Less is recorded in this period of NCOs, the Army's soldier leaders, with personal accounts of life in the ranks not becoming prevalent until the nineteenth century as literacy levels improved. However, the writings of Captain Thomas Simes, who produced widely read military textbooks between the 1760s and 1780s, offer some insight into their role and standing.[10] The aristocratic leaning of the officer corps meant that much of the administration and management of the regiment was left in the hands of NCOs. 'He is to have the care of the men of his squad, and to be answerable for their soldier-like appearance; to instruct them in their several duties, and teach them the respect and obedience they are to pay to superiors,' Simes wrote of corporals, junior NCOs. For sergeants, the senior NCOs, discipline was a core concern, as it remains today.

> [When] negligence appears amongst those under his command, he should exert his authority over them; and insist upon an implicit obedience in order to reform them; nor is he to conceal from his officer any of their bad conduct; on the contrary, he is to report them, *by which he will be feared by the bad, and be beloved by the good.*

In summing up how corporals and sergeants were to be chosen, Simes touched on themes that are still pertinent to modern NCO leadership, from high personal standards to the ability to be a parent figure to their soldiers.

> They should be men remarkable for their expertness in performing every part of the manual exercise and firings, manoeuvres, marchings and wheelings [. . .] [they should] give their instructions with clearness and firmness; they should be mild in disposition [. . .] a stranger to hatred and a friend to the recruit.

As the role of NCO leaders emerged, officers' perceptions of their soldiers began to diverge, leading to a sharpening divide in leadership styles and attitudes as the eighteenth century wore on. Some treated their men with an attitude of contempt and despair. Lieutenant Colonel John Blackader, whose Army career spanned

1689 to 1712, complained that, 'Armies which used to be full of men of great and noble souls, are now turned to a parcel of mercenary, fawning, lewd, dissipated creatures; the dregs and scum of mankind.'[11] Such attitudes conditioned the prevalent use of corporal punishment as a form of discipline, including incidences of flogging that could run into thousands of lashes, and hot-iron branding of deserters and those who had shown 'bad character'.[12] These punishments and the beliefs that supported them were long-lasting, most famously championed by the Duke of Wellington, who said he had 'no idea of any great effect being produced on British soldiers by anything but the fear of immediate corporal punishment'.[13]

But they did not go unchallenged. Sir John Moore, whose career began during the American War of Independence and ended with his death in command of British forces in Spain during the Peninsular War, was one who favoured encouragement over punishment. He believed that the dismissal of an incompetent officer would be more effective as a corrective to indiscipline than the flogging of fifty soldiers.[14] The 'humanitarian movement' that he represented would not gain the upper hand until the second half of the nineteenth century, but it began a long process which shifted the prevailing style of Army leadership from the restrictive control and punitive discipline of soldiers towards an approach that seeks to motivate and empower – captured by the modern concept that leaders should be servants to their people, and the Mission Command philosophy that encourages responsibility to be delegated where possible to the lowest level, allowing junior leaders the freedom to act based on what is in front of them, within the bounds of the intent they have been given by their commander.

Despite the high regard in which Moore was held, it was Wellington who emerged as the dominant military leader of his era, his legend and influence assured by victory over Napoleon at Waterloo in 1815, and continuing to be felt long afterwards. Summarising the condition of the Army in 1837, General (later Field Marshal) Viscount Wolseley wrote that, 'The lieutenant colonels commanding regiments were mostly old men who had seen service in the great French war [. . .] Their views of the British soldier, and of the best way of dealing with him, were those of the Duke of Wellington.'[15] As has frequently been the case in the history of the British Army, it would take the shock of war and the experience of failure to bring about meaningful change in attitudes and approach.

1853–1914: Reform and professionalisation

In contrast to the relatively staid decades that followed Waterloo, the period between the death of Wellington in 1852 and the beginning of the First World War in 1914 was one of marked evolution in the organisation of the British Army, which brought the professionalism and capability of its leaders sharply into focus.[16] Change was driven by a combination of disastrous failures on the battlefield, with the experiences in the Crimean War (1853–6) and later the Second Anglo-Boer War (1899–1902) both prompting significant periods of reform. It also reflected developments in society: the increasing sophistication of the civilian professions, the growth of public schools as a dominant source of new officers, and the evolution of more paternalistic attitudes emphasising the social obligations of the upper classes. All contributed to a changing face and style of Army leadership.[17]

Failings of leadership and professional knowledge were highlighted by experiences in Crimea, a campaign beset with problems over transport, supply and medical care bringing political attention on to the Army and how it was led. 'The system by which an army should be provisioned, moved, brought to act in the field and the trenches, taught to attack or defend, is non-existent,' lamented Lord Panmure, who became Secretary of State for War in 1855. 'We have no means of making general officers or of forming an efficient staff.'[18] In the search for answers, the spotlight quickly moved to the purchase system. A Royal Commission appointed by Panmure in 1857 to examine it returned a disdainful conclusion concerning its influence on the Army's leadership capability.

It is contended that it is vicious in principle; repugnant to the public sentiment of the present day, and equally inconsistent with the honour of the military profession and with the policy of the British Empire. The system it is moreover affirmed produces ill effects on the constitution of the Army, and impairs its efficiency by giving an undue pre-eminence to wealth, discouraging exertion, and depressing merit.[19]

What followed was an extended period of reform, including changes to how the Army trained, educated and promoted its leaders. In the long aftermath of Crimea, notable developments in these areas included: the establishment of a Staff College in 1858, to provide specialist training to staff officers; the introduction of examinations for applicants to Royal Military College Sandhurst and as a prerequisite for promotion in ranks up to lieutenant colonel; and eventually, the abolition in 1870 of the purchase system.[20] From 1873, commanding officers were required to submit annual reports on their subordinates, assessing their performance and suitability for promotion – a forerunner to the system that exists today in military and civilian leadership.[21] These changes sought to address specific military shortcomings, but also followed and reflected the increasingly sophisticated organisation of civilian professions in the mid-nineteenth century, evidenced by the formation of the General Medical Council in 1858 to produce an accredited list of qualified practitioners, and the granting of a Royal Charter in 1845 to the Law Society, establishing it as an independent body to govern and regulate its profession.[22] The desire for a more thoroughgoing approach to the education, training and promotion of Army officers reflected the emerging expectation that the members of a profession be appropriately and demonstrably qualified.

As more structure was built around the officer profession, the attitudes of its members were also changing. 'Paternalism [. . .] was increasingly in vogue,' the historian Edward Spiers had written of the period 1868–1902.

The concept of a gentleman had changed during the nineteenth century, with the suppression of the duel and the greater emphasis upon Christian virtues – the unselfishness, thoughtfulness and sense of *noblesse oblige* which were intrinsic aspects of [the emerging] ideal of a Christian gentleman.

Such ideas were a staple of education at the public schools which were becoming the dominant source of officer cadets in the Army: the source of over 60 per cent of Regular Army officers by the end of the century, according to Spiers.[23] In the second half of the nineteenth century, they began to permeate the Army, as reformers championed a more enlightened approach to leading soldiers – an approach that owed much to the paternalist ethos. In his *Soldier's Pocket Book*, a guide first published in 1869, Lieutenant Colonel (later Field Marshal) Garnet Wolseley wrote that officers 'must make themselves loved as well as respected. In our intercourse with the rank and file, we must make them realise that all our interests are identical, causing the latest-joined recruit to feel that success is of as much real moment to him as it can be to the general.' He preached a style of leadership that could hardly have been more different from the model of Wellington, advocating that officers should consider the well-being of their soldiers: 'You should study their prejudices, learn their individual characters, and by a knowledge of their respective sensitiveness, guard against wounding their feelings.'[24] This developing approach also acknowledged the reality of a changing social context. Senior officers increasingly recognised that 'a voluntary army could not compete for recruits in the labour market unless the men were dealt with fairly and honestly, with due attention to their wants and grievances.'[25] In the regiments of the late Victorian Army, libraries, savings banks and charities to support the families of soldiers became regular features.

Wolseley's advice reflected the 'industrial paternalism' that was the tenor of contemporary employer and worker relations, in which business owners more readily recognised their responsibilities to their employees, without giving up the conviction that they were best qualified to make important decisions on their behalf. An obituary of the noted nineteenth-century Danish industrialist Carl Christian Burmeister recorded:

Towards his workmen he was an extraordinarily humane employer and he very early established a well-organised sick-benefit association

and old age provision fund for the workers. But he stood on the old
paternalist standpoint and wanted [. . .] the employer to be the father
and master of the workers. With trade unionism he never learned to
sympathise.[26]

The Army and its leadership were the subject of consistent reform
in the later nineteenth century, both formally in terms of structures
and informally as regards attitudes.[27] But such change was not looked
upon kindly in all quarters. Traditionalists such as the Duke of Cambridge, the Army's Commander-in-Chief from 1856 to 1895, believed
that the urge to professionalise represented a menace to the strength
of the Army and, in particular, the primacy of the regimental system
in the training and development of the Army's leaders. He consistently voiced his opposition to reforms, including the creation of
Staff College ('a man who will stick to his regiment will learn his
profession in that regiment much better than in any college'[28]); the
growing emphasis on officer education ('I fear, gentlemen, that the
army is in danger of becoming a mere debating society'[29]); the idea of
merit-based promotion, and even to the adoption of khaki uniforms
('I should be sorry to see the day when the English Army is no longer
in red. I am not one of those who think it is at all desirable to hide
ourselves too much'[30]).

The new requirements also encountered apathy and resistance among
those affected by them. 'Many officers, unfortunately, look upon these
examinations as merely so many irksome bars to promotion,' a report
by the Director-General of Military Education concluded in 1894. The
Akers-Douglas committee, which reported on the state of officer education in 1902, found that: '[The] junior officers are lamentably wanting
in Military knowledge, and what is perhaps even worse, in the desire to
acquire knowledge and in zeal for the Military art.'[31]

The shattering defeats in the early months of the Second Anglo-
Boer War emphasised how much work remained to be done,
prompting a fresh round of public criticism of the Army's leaders and
their professionalism. 'The abolition of purchase was supposed to
make the nation master of its Army [but] [. . .] expensive habits,
mostly connected with amusement of one kind or another, have made

the Army a close corporation just as in the old purchase days,' a leader in *The Times* complained. This prompted letters of agreement from within the Army, including one stating, regarding a typical cavalry regiment, that the emphasis on hunting and polo 'acts most detrimentally upon the efficiency of officers, who have neither time nor inclination for the serious study of their profession, which has become a vital necessity nowadays'.[32]

The faltering professional ethos of the British Army in the nineteenth century stood in stark contrast to some of its European peers, notably the Prussian Army. Following its shattering defeat to Napoleon in 1806, it had embarked on a reorganisation that included the creation of a General Staff: a central organising body that would be responsible for planning and administration, and also seek to raise the quality of command and leadership across the Army by creating a centrally trained body of staff officers to be distributed throughout, and acting as 'the brain of the army [. . .] an effective planning and controlling instrument for military operations'.[33] The increasingly large-scale, industrial character of warfare meant that reliance on the 'individual genius' of generals such as Wellington and Napoleon was no longer seen as sufficient: 'it was already apparent to the thoughtful that something else would have to be developed to meet the growing problem of generalship in the modern technological state,' the military historian Walter Millis summarised.[34]

This realisation had dawned more slowly in the British Army, which did not seek to achieve a form of equivalence until the aftermath of the Second Anglo-Boer War.[35] 'Unlike the other great nations, we had never established any thinking department for the British Army,' the Liberal Secretary of War Richard Haldane, principal architect of the subsequent spate of reforms, told Parliament in 1906. Such a capability, he argued, would have equipped the Army's leaders in South Africa with structured plans and tactics, 'instead of having to devise ways and means as they went along'.[36] The reforms he led from 1906 to 1912 sought to address this deficiency: establishing a General Staff responsible for training, military operations and war planning; instigating an overhaul of training, overseen by Major General Douglas Haig; and reorganising the Army into an expeditionary force ready to fight a war in continental Europe, and a territorial force for the purpose of home defence.[37]

By the time war was declared in 1914, the Army's professional capacity had been transformed from its condition at the turn of the century.[38] It had produced its first official manual – the *Field Service Regulations* – outlining the institutional approach to warfighting; implemented operational planning for a continental war, down to the detail of shipping soldiers and horses to France; and created a common approach to training at all levels.[39] All this was tied together by the General Staff, which provided the professional underpinning for such a concerted approach to organisation and future planning.[40] In the long-running contest between the amateur tendency of Army leadership and the professionalising imperative, professionalism had taken a dramatic step forward.

1914–45: Mass mobilisation and the civilian influence

The two World Wars of the twentieth century saw the British Army mobilise in larger numbers than at any previous or future point. In its last major continental war, the Army's manpower had peaked in 1813 at a little over 250,000.[41] A century later, the Regular Army stood at close to the same level, numbering 247,432 when war was declared in August 1914. By the time of the armistice, four and a half years later, the total British strength had reached close to 3.5 million.[42] The Second World War saw a similarly dramatic, though slightly smaller, expansion: from a regular strength of 259,000 in 1939 to over 2.9 million in 1945.[43] The nature of mass mobilisation had a dramatic effect on the Army. The huge influx of civilians as soldiers, NCOs and officers brought with it leaders from different social and educational backgrounds, it introduced experience and expertise from different professions, and it necessitated a significant overhaul of the Army's approach to the selection and development of leaders, as it scrambled to facilitate two huge periods of expansion in its fighting power. From a newly formalised approach to training people in leadership, to the use of psychometric testing in selection, the demands of large-scale industrial war helped bring about new ideas and approaches that would have a lasting effect on Army leadership.

In the First World War, mass mobilisation had a significant impact on the demographic of the Army's leaders. Officers needed to be found to replace fatalities at the front, and to command the huge number of units that were being created in the 'New Army' forged by Lord Kitchener's famous recruitment drive.[44] Widening the net for officer recruitment was the only answer, and of the 229,316 commissions awarded during the war, many went to individuals who were hardly represented in the pre-1914 officer corps: soldiers promoted from the ranks and men from professional backgrounds, including clerks, shopkeepers, teachers and tradesmen.[45] By the closing years of the war, this process of forced enfranchisement had effected a dramatic change on the demographic of officer leaders, with approximately 40 per cent in 1917–18 coming from a working-class or lower-middle-class background.[46]

This new breed of officer often brought valuable experience and perspective from civilian life. 'The New Army leaders, a large number of whom were practical business men with no time for obsolete customs [. . .] brought critical and well-trained minds to bear on every aspect of the war, and won not only our respect, but our admiration,' wrote Sergeant John Lucy of the 2nd Royal Irish Rifles.[47] Class prejudice still persisted, however, and not all were so welcoming to the 'temporary gentlemen' who filled the ranks of the wartime officer corps. The poet Robert Graves, who had been commissioned into the 3rd Royal Welch Fusiliers in August 1914, sneered at the 'Manchester cotton clerks' who had become officers in the latter stages of the war, writing that 'the latest arrivals from the New Army battalions were a constant shame to the senior officers', and citing among other infractions 'table manners at which Sergeant Malley stood aghast'.[48]

Mass mobilisation was also bringing women into the Army in non-nursing roles for the first time. The formation in 1917 of the Women's Army Auxiliary Corps (WAAC) would see over 50,000 women serve in support roles, including 9,000 in France.[49] Paving the way for the conscription of women in the Second World War, when over a quarter of a million served in the Auxiliary Territorial Services alone, the mobilisation of women was widely regarded as momentous. The establishment of the WAAC, its founding Chief Controller Dr Mona Chalmers Watson believed, was 'an advance of the women's movement [. . .] and a national advance'.[50]

The *Manchester Guardian* was effusive, with an editorial commenting:

> Throughout two and a half years of a war that taxes our manhood to its uttermost, tradition has decreed that thousands of soldiers fit for more active service should do work that is well within the compass of women. That tradition is ended, and with its passing the face of the British Army is altered for all time.[51]

At the front, the volume of new leaders, and the rapid promotion of young officers into senior command posts to replace those killed or wounded, meant new systems of leadership training and education were needed. Temporary officers received the best approximation of a public school education that wartime necessities would allow, which from February 1916 comprised a crash course within Officer Cadet Battalions in which 'the stress was on developing leadership and the cultivation of initiative and self-confidence' and the tone was 'intended to be that of Sandhurst or Woolwich or of the best public schools'.[52] Additional training was also instituted for officers whose wartime careers had compressed a progression of decades into a handful of years, with some junior officers of 1914 being required to command battalions and even brigades into the middle and later years of the war.[53]

In October 1916, General Sir Douglas Haig, Commander-in-Chief of the British Expeditionary Force (BEF), ordered the establishment of a Senior Officers' School for battalion commanders. The content of the course suggests a conception of leadership that was fast evolving. With regard to their soldiers, participants were asked to consider the question, 'How am I going to make the most of them, and how are they going to make the most of me?' They were encouraged to work closely with their junior leaders: 'It is a good plan to consult your section commanders when you have any scheme on foot.

Sometimes you get valuable ideas from them, and when they know that they have, so to speak, a share in the business, they will go all out to make your plans successful.'[54] And they were taught six principles of effective leadership: courage, knowledge, demeanour, fairness and justice, civility, and 'hard work combined with imagination'.[55]

As the emergence of the Senior Officers' School demonstrates, the exigencies of war had helped to bring about a more systematic approach to defining and teaching the principles of Army leadership. 'Before the war the leader obtained leadership by the light of nature [. . .] no help was given,' believed Brigadier-General H. M. W. Watson.[56] The prevailing assumption had been that leadership was something acquired primarily through the osmosis of a public school education, and the 'qualities of character' imbued by experience acquired on the rugby or cricket field.[57] Now a more professional approach was starting to be adopted: leadership as a subject of dedicated study rather than a series of traits that individuals were assumed to have acquired along the way.[58]

The experience of war, and the temporary civilianisation of the Army, also led to greater recognition of the shortcomings of drawing leadership talent from such a limited source. The typical Regular Army officer in the First World War 'showed extraordinarily little real knowledge of his fellow citizens whom it became his duty to lead', Sir Hugh Elles, shortly to become Director of Military Training, reflected in 1929. 'We were too close a corporation. We moved too much in one stratum of society.' Attempts to change this were made in the interwar period. A 1923 committee chaired by Lord Haldane – architect of the pre-war reforms – recommended that more officer cadets be recruited from the rank and file, and from state secondary and grammar schools. It also sought to raise the number of university graduates commissioned, which had stood at just 17 in 1922.[59]

The short-term impact of these proposals was limited – the proportion of Sandhurst cadets educated at public school remained steady at over 80 per cent in 1920, 1930 and 1939 – but the intent was significant, underlining a recognition that the Army needed to extend the franchise of its leadership ranks.[60]

This process was given further impetus by the circumstances of the Second World War, and the challenge of populating an officer corps that had once again expanded significantly in size. After initial struggles, a significant overhaul of the selection process was undertaken, replacing the traditional interview process with the War Office Selection Boards (WOSBs), which drew on German Army practice to deploy a range of personality and psychological assessments. The combination of written tests, interviews and 'leaderless' tactical exercises across a three-day period bears strong resemblance to the selection process for officer cadets used by the Army today, and marked a shift towards a more scientific and inclusive model of leader selection. The development of the WOSB process was steered by a group of psychiatrists and psychologists recruited to advise the War Office, one of whom later recalled that, '[One] aim [was] getting more people in the ranks to aspire to commissions and to get rid of any residual beliefs that commissions were only for the "posh" or for the Sandhurst Stereotype. The WOSBs were informed by a meritocratic philosophy.' As with the more organised approach to leader development on the Western Front, the demands of industrial-scale war were compelling the Army to professionalise critical areas of its approach to leadership, instituting processes that in shape and intent would be enduring.

The Army did not suddenly emerge in 1945 with a newly professional approach to leadership, but the shock of its two largest conflicts and its rapid reconfiguration as a millions-strong fighting force had led both to introspection and innovation. Necessity had compelled the Army to experiment with new methods of selecting, training and developing its leaders, bringing systematic and scientific approaches into areas where instinct, assumption and experience had previously dominated.

In parallel, there was growing recognition that the traditional trappings and distinctions of the Army's rank structure were becoming outmoded in an era of less instinctive deference. 'The wide difference between the accommodation, food, and general amenities of officers and other ranks on board ship is frequently mentioned, sometimes with great resentment that such a state of affairs should be allowed in this democratic age,' commented an internal report on Army morale from 1942.[61]

In this context, there was growing recognition of the need for leaders to do more than rely on hierarchy, discipline and command authority to achieve their will. Writing in 1940, the military theorist Basil Liddell Hart argued that leaders 'must provide creative ideas from which a positive faith can be generated. To get the best out of men it is not enough to tell them that they must be ready to die in the last ditch. They must be given a new vision of the future and a new hope.'[62]

1945–present day: Demobilisation, doctrine and decentralisation

Since the cessation of hostilities in 1945, the British Army has fought in few traditional land wars: only the Korean War (1950–54), the Falklands War (1982), the Gulf War (1990–91) and the Iraq War (2003) can be counted as 'regular' conflicts that have pitted it directly against the Armed Forces of one or several nation states. Much more frequently, the Army has found itself engaged in numerous 'irregular' conflicts, defined by the US Army as 'a violent struggle among state and non-state actors for legitimacy and influence over the relevant populations'.[63] From the operations mounted across the receding British Empire in the post-1945 period – including in Malaya, Kenya, Cyprus and Aden – to the long-running Operation BANNER in Northern Ireland, and deployments between 2001 and 2014 in Iraq and Afghanistan, the Army's principal commitments since 1945 have been in the form of counterinsurgency, peace support and peace enforcement.[64] This has significantly shaped the modern evolution of British Army leadership, driving two developments in particular: the decentralisation of leadership responsibility towards small units and junior commanders, and the development of institutional doctrine to support the growth of a professional, universal leadership culture.

Decentralised command was far from a novel development in the post-1945 era. The Army's first formal warfighting manual, *Field*

Service Regulations, set out in 1905 a principle that holds true in the
contemporary Army: 'centralised intent and decentralisation of execution'. As it outlined, 'when it is impossible, as must often be the
case, to issue more than very general instructions, the attainment of
the object aimed at must be left to the initiative and intelligence of
[subordinate] leaders.'[65] The significance of the post-war years was
how operational circumstances consistently reinforced this idea
through experience. The small colonial wars of the early Cold War
years provided an object lesson in irregular warfare and the emphasis
it demanded on small teams, effectively and independently led.

In Malaya, where the Army was deployed to combat the long-
running guerrilla campaign of the Malayan National Liberation
Army, leaders whose primary experience was in regular warfare
foundered in the early stages of a very different conflict.

Richard Clutterbuck,[66] an officer with the Royal Engineers who
served in Malaya, wrote:

> Initially, because of their previous training and experience, senior
> army officers were inclined to launch their units into the jungle in bat-
> talion strength – either in giant encirclement operations when a camp
> was known to be in the area, or in wide sweeps based on no informa-
> tion at all.

Lieutenant General Sir Harold Briggs, who arrived in 1950 as Director of Operations and brought new focus to the campaign,
recognised the need for a change in approach. Of senior commanders, he told a journalist: 'They'll have to reconcile themselves to war
being fought by junior commanders down to lance-corporals who
will have responsibility to make decisions on the spot if necessary
[. . .] Flexibility of operations in the jungle must be the keynote.'

An idea that helped to deliver success in the jungle warfare of
Malaya has continued to hold true in the decades that followed, from
the streets of Northern Ireland to the desert of Helmand Province.
In operational theatres that bear little outward similarity, Army
teams have faced the common requirement to work in conditions of
ambiguity, in which civilians and adversaries occupy the same space,
and a situation can escalate in an instant from calm to violence. The

connecting thread is the need for critical operational decisions to be made at the point of contact, by individuals who may be junior in rank and experience, but who are also closest to the detail of complex and fast-moving situations. It is for this reason that Operation BANNER was often referred to as a 'corporals' war', one in which the most important decision makers were frequently the Junior NCO leaders commanding a section of eight soldiers on patrol or at a checkpoint.[67] The prominence of junior commanders has continued to grow in the decades since, personified by the US Marine Corps General Charles C. Krulak's definition in the 1990s of the 'outcome strategic corporal': NCOs who play a critical role in operations 'whose outcome may hinge on decisions made by small unit leaders, and by actions taken at the *lowest* level'.[68]

This growing emphasis on decentralised command, the importance of decision making at all levels of the military hierarchy, and of every soldier being empowered to lead, has been supported by the development of institutional doctrine. While formal principles had been written and disseminated since the days of the *Field Service Regulations*, historians have tended not to regard the British Army as a doctrinal military for most of its history, emphasising the long-standing focus on learning through experience and individual style.[69] This changed in the 1980s, with reformers including Field Marshal Sir Nigel Bagnall, Chief of the General Staff (CGS) from 1985 to 1988, establishing a role for doctrine within the British Army that has grown in scope and significance since.[70]

Central to this was a command philosophy – Mission Command – that gave definition and depth to the decentralised approach. *Design for Military Operations: The British Military Doctrine*, published in 1989, stated:

> To conduct a battle of manoeuvre successfully, commanders at all levels must react rapidly and decisively to what will be an evolving situation. Initiative and boldness will be at a premium and over-direction by superiors must be avoided. Orders should [. . .] define the commander's concept and purpose but leave the execution to the commander directly responsible.[71]

With its new emphasis on decentralisation, the Army mirrored changes in the business world. In the technology industry, the late 1980s also saw the beginnings of what would become agile software development, an approach emphasising the independence and agility of small development teams over monolithic project plans. One influential article from 1986 stated:

> Companies are increasingly realising that the old, sequential approach to developing new products simply won't get the job done. Instead, companies in Japan and the United States are using a holistic model – as in rugby, the ball gets passed within the team as it moves as a unit up the pitch.[72]

That was influential in the subsequent development of the 'scrum' approach to agile development, which has become the dominant approach today.[73] The description of the scrum methodology by its originators – 'To tackle an opportunity, the organisation forms and empowers a small team, usually three to nine people [. . .] [which] includes all the skills necessary to complete its tasks. It manages itself and is strictly accountable for every aspect of the work'[74] – is one that any Army leader would recognise as a close parallel to effective use of Mission Command and the onus it puts on the independence, initiative and leadership of small teams.

Codified in the context of the late Cold War, the Mission Command philosophy has proved its enduring relevance across a wide variety of operational conditions in the three decades since. It has become intrinsic to the Army's modern approach to leadership, an approach that, when applied effectively, acts as a force multiplier for trust within teams, swiftness of decision and action, and the empowerment of leaders regardless of rank, age or experience. It accords with the military theorist J. F. C. Fuller's definition of doctrine as 'the central idea of an Army': both simple enough to be widely transmitted and understood, but also sufficiently rich and sophisticated an approach to be adaptable across the full spectrum of circumstances Army leaders will encounter.[75] Mission Command – which will be discussed more fully in Chapter 3 and illustrated throughout this book – can be as challenging to implement as it is effective when deployed. Its significance as a doctrinal concept owes much to its ability to promote self-reflection and debate among leaders. 'Bagnall recognised that [. . .] there was a need to conceive a military doctrine which taught people not what to think but how to think about going to war and warfighting,' wrote his successor-but-one, Field Marshal Sir Peter Inge.[76]

The Army has always been an organisation in which leadership has been paramount – but for most of its history that happened through a combination of instinct, the influence of individual example, and accident. The Army was proud of its leadership tradition and capability, but less certain about how to define its ingredients or explain how it came about. The process of codifying its approach to leadership represents one of the most important recent developments in the long, gradual professionalisation of the Army's approach to command and leadership. 'The reinvention of the British Army since 1989 as a doctrinally-based organisation is as profound a revolution as any experienced in its [. . .] history,' the historian Professor Gary Sheffield has suggested.[77] Since the era of the Bagnall reforms, that process has included the establishment of the Development, Concepts and Doctrine Centre within the Ministry of Defence in 1999, the codification of the Army's Values and Standards the following year, the publication of the Army Leadership Doctrine in 2016, and the creation of the Centre for Army Leadership in 2017 to champion Army leadership excellence.[78]

Today's Army leaders have a robust foundation of doctrine to guide how they think about and practise leadership: from codified Values and Standards that are a reference point for expected behaviour, to a leadership model that encourages a constant balance between the needs of the task, team and every individual, as well as a spectrum of leadership styles from transactional leadership (control, process and incentive oriented) to transformational leadership (encouraging and inspiring people to achieve the desired ends).[79] These principles do not just live on the page, but are taught and instilled through leadership development that spans the whole careers of serving officers and soldiers.

The work to professionalise the Army's approach to leadership is ongoing, part of a wider continuum that stretches back through centuries of British Army history: from the establishment of the first officer training college, Royal Military Academy Woolwich, in 1741, to the creation of Staff College in 1858, the many improvements made to officer education in the nineteenth century and the innovations that arose from the necessity of both World Wars. Army leadership continues to evolve as it has done through over 360 years of development, blending fundamental ideas that connect leaders across centuries of change with new approaches that reflect the modern context and the requirement for leadership to be a universal responsibility – common to every serving soldier. It is a living, constantly evolving concept: formed by its traditions but not bound by them; proud of its long history but equally conscious of the many chapters yet to be written.

2. Challenges of Army Leadership and Uniqueness

'[Although] the rights of the individual are important, there are times in the military when those rights must be subordinated for the collective good. Military life is different. It is not like going to the office or the factory.'[1] General Sir Charles Guthrie, Chief of the Defence Staff when he made those comments in 2001, encapsulated one of the basic realities and essential tensions for the military in its wider social context. The Army – in common with all the Armed Forces – must in many ways reflect and represent the society from which it recruits, and whose security and defence is its reason for being. Yet that necessity cannot override the reality that the Army is an organisation often several steps removed from most areas of civilian life. The institution and those who serve in it are asked to take on responsibilities involving combat, mortal danger and the use of lethal force. Soldiers are required to accept the contract of unlimited liability, accepting the risk to their own life inherent in carrying out their duties. In their work they will sometimes encounter agonising moral dilemmas around life and death: their own, their comrades', their enemies' and those of the civilians who are increasingly enmeshed in modern urban warfare. Together, these challenges amount to a particular set of requirements that shape the practice of Army leadership.

These realities underpin what has been variously termed as the Army's right, duty or need to be different, and to use sometimes extreme means in the service of extraordinary ends.[2] The Army requires the scope to train, manage and deploy its people in the best interests of national defence and the individual well-being of every serving soldier. This entails making demands, accepting risks and imposing discipline in ways that would feel alien or unacceptable in many working environments. It must do this while fulfilling its wider duty as the organ of a democratic society whose elected

representatives govern and fund it, whose laws it follows and whose
ethical expectations set the baseline for what is and is not regarded as
acceptable behaviour, including in the extreme circumstances of
combat and war. As later chapters will explain, the Army's Values
and Standards are the principal tool for reconciling this need to be
different with the duty to defend British society in ways that retain
its trust and implicit consent.

This healthy, sometimes marked, tension between civil and military also helps to explain the relevance of the Army as a source of
leadership insight. In many important ways, Army leadership reflects
and draws upon parallel expertise from the civilian world. The challenges of developing a strategic response to social and technological
change, motivating multi-generational teams with contrasting needs,
harnessing organisational culture and upholding high standards are
all those that would be recognised by any business, charity or public
sector organisation. The Army is as much in competition for talent as
any major employer, and must be as conscious of not preparing to
fight the last war as companies are of not becoming shackled to
legacy products or services.

Yet the nature of its work also means that leadership in the Army
is undertaken in consistently challenging conditions that create
unusual requirements. To succeed, its leaders must prepare soldiers
for the extreme circumstances they may encounter, and for the realities of using lethal force. They must bond teams together with a
cohesion that will enable units to work effectively even amid the
chaos, fear and confusion of combat. They must provide the ethical
example required to make decisions that can arise in the distorting
context of war. And they must operate while respecting the strict
chain of command that defines the Army, and also going beyond it –
recognising that the duty to lead is shared across all ranks, not limited
to those with command authority. The Army's leaders must meet
these needs in peace and war, on operations and during training,
whether engaged in combat, providing civilian support or deployed
on operations that require the two in parallel.

To understand the lessons of Army leadership, it is first necessary
to understand some unusual elements of the Army experience, and

the challenges these create for leaders. There are three areas of context that define and are distinctive to Army leadership: the nature of a profession that involves combat and the use of lethal force; how leadership and management intersect with the idea and exercise of command; and the location of leadership within the regimental system, one which fosters a deep sense of ethos and tradition, but which also challenges leaders to balance loyalty to the regiment with their obligations to the Army as a whole.

The profession of arms

General Sir John Hackett, who enjoyed one of the more varied and distinguished British Army careers of the twentieth century, provided perhaps the most enduring description of the military as a profession. 'The function of the profession of arms is the ordered application of force in the resolution of a social problem,' he said in the first of a lecture series at Cambridge University in 1962. He defined the bearing of arms as a profession, on account of its being:

> [. . .] an occupation with a distinguishable corpus of specific technical knowledge and doctrine, a more or less exclusive group coherence, a complex of institutions peculiar to itself, an educational pattern adapted to its own needs, a career structure of its own and a distinct place in the society which has brought it forth.[3]

By meeting these criteria, he concluded, it was in many ways analogous to society's most recognised professions: medicine, law and the clergy.

In developing his thesis, General Hackett – a cavalryman who commanded a parachute brigade at the Battle of Arnhem (where he was near fatally wounded); an Arabic speaker who wound down the British military presence in Palestine; and a student of Saladin who in retirement became a Visiting Professor of Classics – drew widely on historical references, from the martial culture of Sparta to the armies of Renaissance Italy and the military organisation of pre-revolutionary

France. He was feeding into a growing debate of the mid-twentieth century about the professionalism of the military and the nature of the military as a profession. His lectures followed the influential arguments of the American political scientist Samuel P. Huntington, whose 1957 book *The Soldier and the State* sought to counter perceptions that the military was less of a profession than its civilian equivalents. '[The] professional character of the modern officer corps has been neglected,' he wrote. '[The] public, as well as the scholar, hardly conceives of the officer in the same way that it does the lawyer or doctor, and it certainly does not accord to the officer the deference which it gives to civilian professionals.' Huntington's contention that the 'modern officer corps is a professional body and the modern officer a professional man' rested on what he regarded as the three defining elements of any profession: the expertise on which it rested, which must have an intellectual as well as a practical element and rely on professional education; the responsibility to perform or provide a service 'which is essential to the functioning of society'; and a corporateness whereby the profession's members have a shared sense of identity and commitment that acts both as a bond and as a force for self-regulation.[4]

Some have disputed the categorisation of the military as a profession, querying whether soldiers have the necessary autonomy, specialist skillsets or integrated role within society to warrant the label.[5] But the idea of the profession of arms has become ingrained within Armed Forces around the world.[6] It is used to teach soldiers and officers about the unique nature of their work, and it provides a starting point to understand the distinctive elements of the Army as an organisation and the leadership required within it. Ultimately, the challenges and uniqueness of the Army relate not to its status as a profession, but to the nature of that profession: the requirement to bear arms and the practical, moral and psychological ramifications of doing so.

First and foremost, this relates to unlimited liability, the abiding factor that distinguishes the Armed Forces from any civilian profession. 'You offer yourself to be slain,' General Hackett bluntly summarised during an interview given in 1985. 'This is the essence of being a soldier. By becoming soldiers, men agree to die when we tell them to.'[7] This principle is fundamental to the military covenant that expresses the mutual obligations existing between the State and those who serve in the Armed Forces. As a document that formalised this hitherto unwritten contract in 2000 stated:

> [Every] soldier is a weapon bearer, so all must be prepared personally to make the decision to engage an enemy or to place themselves in harm's way. All British soldiers share the legal right and duty to fight and, if necessary, kill, according to their orders, and an unlimited liability to give their lives in doing so.[8]

Leaders must prepare their people for the realities of bearing arms and the unlimited liability that follows. That soldiers have volunteered to serve does not mean that an understanding of the risks involved, the psychological burden of bearing arms, or the moral dilemmas that arise on the battlefield can be taken for granted. It is the responsibility of leaders to illustrate these realities and help their people to be ready for them. The nature of the profession of arms lends additional urgency to many key requirements of leadership. The ability to foster team morale, shared identity and high standards of discipline is not just important – as in any professional context – but something on which lives may ultimately depend. That responsibility can create an unusual burden on Army leaders. This exists in all areas of professional life, where leaders must weigh momentous decisions that affect people's jobs, livelihoods and, in extremis, the survival of their organisation. But it can be heightened in the context of the profession of arms, and how this is manifested for the Army in particular.

As a force primarily designed to operate on land, the Army's people are most exposed to warfare as a human endeavour and a contest of wills, rather than systems or technology. 'Land conflict is a human activity, between individuals and groups of individuals,' as the Army's Land Operations doctrine states. 'Land forces [. . .] are complex organisations, requiring moral as well as structural cohesion and deep hierarchies of command [. . .] [They] are particularly reliant on high quality leadership, education and training at all levels.'[9] Leaders, from the senior officer who gives an order to the junior NCO who will be tasked with leading their team to carry it out, have an acute sense of the consequences of every action and decision. There is a deep sense of obligation that comes with the knowledge that you are responsible for ensuring the safe return of every soldier to their family and loved ones.

As Huntington outlined, the profession of arms stands apart from medicine and the law because it is primarily responsible not to an individual patient or client, but to society as a whole. An officer, he said, must be 'guided by an awareness that his skill can only be utilised for purposes approved by society through its political agent, the state'.[10] In other words, while undertaking the unique and challenging duties of the profession of arms, soldiers must never lose sight of their overriding duty: to defend society by the organised use of force, without resorting to measures that will be perceived as unacceptable by that society.[11] This entails one of the most challenging aspects of Army leadership: to manage the application of violence and lethal force while keeping to a strict ethical code that avoids moral or legal transgressions, whose boundaries war and combat inevitably bring into view. To do so, leaders must endeavour to set a strong ethical example, closely monitor the behaviour of their people, and intervene decisively when they see either an ethical breach or a situation that might easily lead to one.

Those requirements can be challenging, especially in combat conditions, when soldiers must face mortal danger, physical and emotional exhaustion, and an enemy that may not fight by the same rules. As the late Professor Richard Holmes, one of Britain's most distinguished military historians and a long-serving Territorial Army officer, argued, 'the character of military life makes soldiers especially vulnerable to particular sorts of lapse', requiring leaders with the moral courage to draw and hold ethical lines in the sand. He highlighted the example of Sergeant Adam Llewellyn of the Princess of Wales's Royal Regiment, who suffered appalling burns in Iraq in 2005 from a petrol bomb thrown into his vehicle by a child. 'The spectacle of the brave and popular Llewy stumbling through the blazing heat of an Iraqi summer with his clothes burnt away and curtains of smoking skin hanging from his body shocked many of those who saw it.' As Professor Holmes recounted, this was a moment in which the intervention of the battalion's leaders made a critical difference to ensuring the shock and distress of the situation did not become a precursor to retribution.

> A hard-headed company commander, backed by a well-respected company sergeant major . . . made it absolutely clear to the boys that no lapses would be tolerated. But, believe me, it would not have taken much of a blind eye or subtle wink for there to have been split lips, broken heads or worse.[12]

By its nature, the profession of arms takes its members into extreme circumstances that test their courage, cohesion, moral compass and stamina to the limit. In doing so, it demands of leaders that they meet a range of responsibilities, from ensuring the welfare and well-being of their people to meeting the expectations of their regiment and upholding the reputation of the Army as a whole. In this regard the duties of the professional Army leader are not so very different from civilian professions – rather, they are magnified. In the crucible of combat, the margin for error dwindles to nothing, and lives depend on the ability to think clearly, decide quickly and communicate effectively. Ethical dilemmas around life and death are not unique to the profession of arms, but are given additional complexity and urgency in situations when weapons are being carried on both sides, and lives may need to be purposefully taken.[13]

This explains the heavy emphasis that the Army places on leadership development, ensuring that every leader has a conceptual, practical and historical understanding of their role, the theories that underpin it, and the skills required to perform it. The unique nature of the profession of arms requires that these ideas be ingrained to the level of habit and instinct, ready for the moment they will be most needed. As Chapter 9 will discuss, this means much of the most important work done by Army leaders happens during peacetime, in the barracks environment and on training exercises. Soldiers must be prepared for extreme operational circumstances they may never ultimately encounter, which creates an additional set of leadership challenges about how to demand high standards when the stakes appear to be low.

The professional knowledge required of Army leaders is constantly expanding. As warfare, the weapons used to wage war, and the information environment that surrounds it continue to evolve, the need for continuous learning and professional development only increases. Modern Army leaders need to understand the changing technology of war, the changing shape of both physical and virtual battlefields, and the social and political expectations that surround both combat and peacekeeping operations. The profession of arms demands of its leaders that they are constantly developing and enhancing their understanding of what it takes to fight and win.

Command, leadership and management

As with any military, the British Army depends to a significant extent on respect for hierarchy, an established process for adhering to orders, and the individual and collective willingness to maintain discipline. Such structures and systems are designed not to restrict but to enable, providing a framework within which leaders can think for themselves, act on their initiative, and consider the need to challenge or disregard, when appropriate, the order they have been given. The contemporary British Army wants – and needs – every soldier to be a thinking soldier, in operational conditions that increasingly bring the decision making of junior leaders to the fore. In this context, the Army recognises that operational success depends not on the willingness of soldiers to blindly follow the orders of their superiors, but to interpret their intent and decide how best to implement it. In this way, the formal structures of command within the Army intersect with the consistent practice of leadership by individuals who may hold no formal authority. Both are necessary, the one guaranteeing responsibility and accountability, and the other creating necessary freedom for creativity and initiative. To appreciate how the Army works, it is important to understand command and leadership as distinctive and interlinked concepts, and how they relate, in turn, to the practice of management.

Definitions of leadership in the Army have frequently focused on its core function of influence and persuasion. 'I said that leadership was concerned with getting people to do things. What I meant was getting them "to do things willingly",' summarised General Hackett.[14] Leaders may gain such consent through a combination of their personal example, the way they serve their people, and the relationships they build with them. 'No wonder every man in the Battalion thinks such a lot of him,' Private Giles Eyre, who served with the 2nd King's Royal Rifle Corps during the First World War, wrote of his commanding officer. 'Ever careful of the men's comforts, thoughtful for their well-being, foremost in action, always accessible. The ideal C.O. [. . .] able to call on his men for any effort required of them.'[15] As this description implies, leadership is a human endeavour whose practice is highly personal. There are many ways to lead, and the effectiveness of a leader is better judged by the impact they have on people than the particular style they use.

By contrast, command is a defined, highly specific form of authority that can only be granted. Command is the legal and constitutional position to which Army officers and some NCOs (for example, corporals who serve as section commanders) are appointed, granting them authority over the forces they will direct.[16] It is the Army's primary mechanism of assigning responsibility and ensuring accountability. A commander may not control everything that happens within their scope of command, but they are responsible for it and know they will be held accountable. Command is the position an individual holds, denoted by rank, and it is the authority they exercise in practice. Army doctrine states that this applies to three principal areas: responsibility for decision making, control of forces and resources within the scope of a command, and the exercise of leadership.[17] As Kevin Gentzler and Ken Turner of the US Army Command and General Staff College have summarised: 'An effective commander: provides answers when required; manages processes when necessary; and leads collaboratively when needed.'[18]

A good commander will demonstrate effective leadership, which is not to say the two are interchangeable. Officers and corporals command by law but lead by consent. The way they utilise the command

authority that accompanies their rank will determine whether or not
they earn recognition as a leader in the eyes of their people. The
Army's handbook on command, leadership and management makes
this clear: 'commanders are not leaders until their position has been
ratified in the hearts and minds of those they command.'[19] A commander may achieve their objective on a given day, but they will fail
as a leader if they do not develop credibility and build trust with their
unit through their actions. In his research into life at the regimental
level of the British Army in the later twentieth century, the anthropologist Dr Charles Kirke encountered one such example, a platoon
commander:

> [. . .] described to me as a man who always knew what he wanted,
> could deal with his men firmly but fairly, and was a good soldier. He
> shone in the eyes of his superiors. He remained distant from his men,
> however [. . .] For most of his period as their platoon commander
> they did everything he told them to, but when he finally needed them
> to 'go the extra mile' for him, they left him in the lurch and he had an
> embarrassing failure in front of his chain of command.[20]

As this suggests, an individual can appear to be excelling in the
business of command while failing as a leader – not building the
bonds of trust that augment the power of rank with the strength of
followers' consent in their leader.

The distinction between command and leadership is important,
making clear the separation between the existence of a chain of command, and the inspiration, example and galvanising force that leaders
provide. Fundamental to the Army's concept of leadership is that it
should be something embodied and exercised across all ranks, as much
the domain of the youngest private soldier as the most senior general.
This has become especially important in the modern operating environment, which brings the need for Mission Command to the fore. As
the former Dutch Army General Peer de Vries has written:

> [. . .] 'new' wars are fought mostly on the level of small units which
> means that junior soldier[s] [. . .] have to bear the brunt of moral
> decision making. Furthermore, these small units operate in relative

isolation, as generally speaking there is only a limited number of troops in an extended area of operations.[21]

At a time when command authority is liable to be stretched or distant, the Army cannot afford for its leadership capabilities to be narrowly based. It requires an understanding and a willingness to embrace leadership that spans the entire chain of command, including soldiers with no rank.

Both leadership and management – which the Army defines as 'the allocation and control of resources (human, material and financial) to achieve objectives'[22] – are considered facets of command, though leadership must also exist independently of it. While the copious literature on the subject often seeks to distinguish and differentiate between the three,[23] the Army prefers to consider how they interrelate, delivering training that focuses on command, leadership and management as an integrated series of concepts. As the military historian and management expert Stephen Bungay has written: 'The three types of activity overlap, which is why it is easy to confuse them. Indeed, at any point in time, a single individual might be doing all three.' In his description, the trinity describes 'types of work, not types of people'.[24]

Like all organisations, the Army faces its share of problems in all three categories, requiring its people to excel at the personal exercise of influence that represents leadership, the responsible use of authority that constitutes command, and the diligent organisation of resources that is management. By stressing the distinct functions and complementary nature of these three requirements, it avoids the ambiguity that can exist between leadership and management, and encourages the exercise of leadership at all ranks, beyond those with command authority. This holistic view of the three concepts explains how the Army is able to balance the benefits of a strict hierarchy with freedom for small units and individuals, offering the combination of control and flexibility, planning and initiative that modern military operations demand.

The regimental system

If the profession of arms and the balance between command, leadership and management are common features of Armed Forces around the world, the regimental system is something peculiar – at least in the depth of its culture – to the British Army. While this book refers throughout to the Army as a whole, it is also essential to recognise the abiding role and influence of its regiments, the administrative groupings into which soldiers enlist and officers are commissioned: their functional and spiritual home within the Army. Regiments effectively operate as decentralised bases of administration and organisation, with their own distinctive identities, histories and cultures. A soldier and officer's primary experience of the Army will be through their regiment, which conditions their understanding of what it means to serve and lead. They learn from the officers and NCOs who have been brought up in the same regimental environment and tradition, shaping a clannish culture that by definition sets itself apart from its peers. 'If [he was] an armoured soldier [. . .] a man joined the Royal Armoured Corps: this was, so to speak, his nation,' wrote General Sir David Fraser of his experience as a junior officer during the Second World War.

> But within the nation were many tribes, called regiments [. . .] Each regiment had its own name, place in the Army List, cap badge, customs, likes and loathings. A man absorbed these, and the regiment was his family, a source of support in a world often alien and alarming.[25]

As discussed in the previous chapter, in its early days the Army hardly existed or operated as a functional institution beyond its regiments. The balance between centre and periphery has shifted considerably since then, but despite their frequent reorganisation and consolidation, regiments retain a strong sense of their individual identity and continue to foster deep, tribal bonds of loyalty and affiliation.

That ability to influence and foster cohesion has been critical to the fighting power of the British Army throughout its history. 'One should think of the Privates of the 2nd Scottish Rifles [. . .] as men of many varied types, with numerous different facets to their characters, but held together by toughness of spirit, strong discipline and, most important of all, fierce loyalty to the Regiment,' Lieutenant Colonel Sir John Baynes wrote in his study of morale and courage in the First World War, focusing on the 2nd Cameronians (Scottish Rifles) at the Battle of Neuve Chapelle in 1915 – which saw a battalion of 900 reduced to a strength of just 150 after six days of fighting. 'This last quality cannot be overemphasised – it is essential to realise that it was the strongest single influence on the lives of everyone in the battalion.' As he concluded:

> [. . .] if anyone wants to know what was the quintessence of the morale of the pre-1914 Army – what was the rock of its foundation – then the answer is the Regiment. Everything else was important, but if the actions of the soldiers of the Scottish Rifles at Neuve Chapelle are to be explained in a few words one can only say that they did it for the Regiment.[26]

Regiments exercise this power through multiple layers of influence on those who join them: an emphasis on history and tradition, carrying a legacy that demands to be matched; a distinctive identity and a way of doing things that sets standards to uphold; and the feeling of one-upmanship that inevitably follows from comparing your own regiment's history and achievements to those of others, a sometimes unhelpful side effect of the system's ability to inspire such strong feelings. Historically, regimental identity has also been geographical: the Cardwell reforms of 1868–74, which tied regiments to sub-districts, sought to replicate the Prussian model of drawing soldiers together from the same towns and villages to increase cohesion and common understanding.[27] Although this had limited success in practice, it did establish local pride in regiments, many of which continue to bear proudly their place names and to recruit, where possible, from their area.

All these factors – made tangible by symbols ranging from the regimental colours to the cap badge, to the events to mark the anniversaries of battle honours – contribute to the sense of loyalty and identity that connect many soldiers and officers to their regiments, often forging a deeper affiliation than with the Army as a whole. This can be measured in how soldiers have responded to the many rounds of reorganisation and consolidation that the regimental system has seen since the late nineteenth century. After it was amalgamated in 1881, the 92nd Highlanders staged a full-dress mock funeral, burying a coffin containing the regimental number they were being forced to surrender, accompanied by a gun salute and piper's lament.[28]

The regimental system creates a unique context for leadership in the Army. It means, for example, that a junior commander not only has responsibility to their own team within the wider team of their company, squadron or battery, but as part of an institution within the institution. It requires that leaders understand both the Army's leadership doctrine and the specific application of these principles in the context of their regiment. Regimental identities are fundamental to every officer and soldier's knowledge, development and practice as a leader. The culture and expectations of the regiment are as important as the personality of the individual and the principles of the institution in moulding the kind of leader someone will be.

The regimental system can benefit the work of leaders as much as it shapes their approach to leadership. The cohesion, sense of tribalism and common understanding that it nurtures are factors that every leader can harness to collective benefit. They provide a baseline of culture and cohesion that leaders can mould into the specific climate of their unit, knowing that they are not bringing together a disparate group but one that is starting from common ground – often the sense of aspiration that inspired people to join that regiment in the first place, and which creates the impetus to continually achieve and outperform what is expected.

The importance of regiments within the Army reflects an idea put forward by the authors of *Tribal Leadership*: that the success of any organisation arises from the culture and leadership of the tribes (groups of 20 to 150 people) that form it.[29]

> Tribes are the building block of any large human effort, including earning a living [. . .] In companies, tribes decide whether the new leader is going to flourish or get taken out. They determine how much work gets done, and of what quality. Some tribes demand excellence for

everyone, and are constantly evolving. Others are content to do the minimum to get by.

In the book's five-stage model – from Stage 1, which brings people together in mutual antipathy, to Stage 5, which defines the most innovative and idealistic teams – most well-functioning regiments would sit at Stage 4: 'When groups get to this point, they see themselves as a tribe, with a common purpose. They commit to shared core values and hold one another accountable.' In addition, a Stage 4 tribe 'always has an adversary – the need for it is hard-wired into the DNA of this cultural stage [. . .] For Apple's operating systems engineers, it's Microsoft. Often, it's another group within the company.'

This combination of common identity, values and the desire to be better than both peers and competitors describes the best of the regimental system well. As a tribe of tribes (with the component battalions, companies and platoons each having a distinctive ethos of their own), regiments are cultural touchstones as much as administrative groupings. And their power to galvanise is deepened by the history and legacy embedded in the regimental system. From the Grenadier and Coldstream Guards (which can trace their lineage back to the regiments that first formed the British Army in 1660), to others more recently formed (which can lay claim to some of the British Army's most famous actions and achievements), regimental identities carry a particularly strong resonance and convey a powerful sense of responsibility to uphold that tradition and continue its legacy.

The regimental system is a defining feature of the British Army, one that brings challenges as well as benefits. As highlighted by the purchase system, which in practice entailed an internal market in which some regimental commissions were much more highly valued than others, there has always been a tendency to consider some regiments more or less fashionable than others – a pecking order still articulated through the Order of Precedence at major parades, led by the Household Cavalry and Royal Horse Artillery.[30] In the Army of a century ago, some regiments were also guilty of seeking to prevent their people from engaging with the wider Army as its institutional structures for training and development grew. 'Why do you want to leave the Battalion?' a company commander in the Suffolk Regiment demanded of one officer who had applied to attend Staff College in 1910. 'The Regiment should be good enough: only wasters go away.'[31] While such attitudes are largely a thing of the past, the regimental system remains an asset that needs to be carefully managed to avoid its strengths becoming problems. Tribalism can easily slip into parochialism, internal cohesion can limit the ability to engage externally (within what is technically the same organisation), and friendly competition can become corrosive disparagement.

It is the role of leaders to ensure that the Army benefits from its proud and distinctive regiments without suffering the unintended consequences of untrammelled sub-cultures. As an officer in The Parachute Regiment, one with an unmistakably strong ethos and pride, I was always aware of the need to nurture the identity that has been a hallmark of our historical success, without letting it spill over into institutional arrogance. Fighting power in the modern Army rests not on individual regiments ploughing their own furrow, but a one-team ethos across different cap badges, Arms and services, which accords due respect and recognition to the contribution that each makes. The balancing act for leaders is to ensure that the inter-regimental rivalries that are a feature of the system do not amount to the damaging situation of divided cultures. This challenge is nothing new for the Army or its leaders. The regimental structure is a facet of the British Army that has persisted through huge changes, retaining its power to galvanise and inspire even as it has had to repeatedly adapt to new forms. It creates a unique environment for leaders that both equips them with the power afforded by an underlying culture and legacy, as well as challenging them to balance their responsibilities to that community with their duty to the institution they represent.

The art of influencing and inspiring people to achieve what is needed defines leadership in all areas of life. The Army is no different in this, but its leaders also face distinct challenges and carry unusual advantages. To their benefit is the sense of duty and loyalty that binds together those who serve, something deepened by the nature of the regimental system. Among those who have volunteered to serve, and in many cases competed to earn a place in their regiment of choice, leaders do not need to manufacture any sense of commitment to the cause. They do, however, need to prepare those people for the unique nature of a profession defined by the use of violence and lethal force. Cohesion may come more naturally, but it is also needed in greater measure. Ethical example is not incidental, but fundamental to ensuring that challenging missions are not just achieved in practice, but in accordance with the Army's Values and Standards. Professional knowledge is not just helpful, but imperative to ensure leaders are prepared for the rigour and complexity of operations in the modern operating environment.

The Army does not just demand more of its leaders, but that more of its people become leaders. It can only succeed if the leadership culture stretches across all ranks, ages and levels of experience: from the largest grouping to the smallest unit. Modern British Army leadership, the subject of the next chapter, is entirely predicated on the idea that the need for leadership is universal. It is the business of every individual, not simply those with rank, seniority and experience. Success depends on everyone being able to lead.

3.   Modern British Army Leadership

'Do not let us be mesmerised by what worked in past wars; it will not work again. We must take off our hat to the past and roll up our sleeves for the future.' This was the sentiment of Field Marshal Bernard Montgomery, writing in 1954 about the role of science and technology in future warfare. It could equally have been articulated by any military strategist of the preceding century or the decades since: all have faced the constant demand to adapt to modernity, changing social mores and new technology. In the final posting of his career, as NATO Deputy Supreme Allied Commander Europe, Montgomery was focused on the role of nuclear weapons, the growing prevalence of air power ('the dominant factor in future war') and the corresponding need for improved mobility in land forces.[1] For his predecessors of the early twentieth century, the guiding considerations had been the development of the tank, the machine gun and the logistical infrastructure of road, rail and telegraph. His modern successors are increasingly occupied by the challenges posed by artificial intelligence, cyber and information warfare, and autonomous vehicles.

Like every military, the British Army must constantly assess changes in its strategic, operating and threat environment, adapting its own structures and capabilities, recognising how those of adversaries are changing, and acknowledging how existing assets and assumptions could be neutralised or turned to enemy advantage. The challenge of ensuring that the Army is equipped to deter, contain and contest the constantly evolving threats to national security underpins a constant process of review and reorganisation. This work of modernisation is continuous and must move at the same speed as the environment that surrounds it – providing an agile response to the questions of how, by whom and with what war is being waged, and will be in the future.

The development of Army leadership has been a parallel process of change built on essential continuities. The idea of artificial intelligence would have been alien to a leader of Montgomery's generation, but the work of responding strategically, organisationally and operationally to a changing social and technological context was deeply familiar. Figures such as Montgomery, Patton, Napoleon and von Clausewitz remain popular and valuable references of leadership insight because, while the context they operated in might have little direct bearing on today, their ideas and experiences reflect enduring truths about warfare, leadership and how to organise and deploy fighting power. They provide important reminders about the unchanging realities of warfare and leadership in war, even as these adapt to reflect new technological and geopolitical circumstances. Carl von Clausewitz, the Prussian general whose unfinished treatise *Vom Kriege* ('On War') has influenced generations of soldiers, was one who emphasised this balance. 'Clausewitz likened [war] to a chameleon that takes the [colour] of its surroundings,' his translator, the military historian and Army officer Professor Sir Michael Howard, summarised. 'While warfare may seem to change, it remains as Clausewitz defined it, just as the chameleon, whatever [colour] it adopts, remains the same animal still.'[2] Similarly, modern armies and army leaders are a reflection of both radical change and enduring fundamentals.

Modern British Army leadership epitomises this duality. Its core tenets and practices would be familiar to any generation of former officers and NCOs, and have been shaped by the aggregation of their experiences and example. But over the last three decades, these ideas have been updated, codified and professionalised to ensure that the Army's leadership is both sufficiently capable in its means and broad-based in its reach to meet the distinctive challenges of the modern operating environment. It is only comparatively recently that the full weight of experience, example and institutional memory has been brought to bear, making the lessons consistent and accessible: turning leadership from an often individualist pursuit into one that is collectively understood as a shared responsibility, based on agreed theory and practice. What distinguishes modern Army leadership is not so much its fundamental principles, which are enduring, but the professional and institutional nature of how these are now taught, understood and applied.

As part of this evolution, a Leadership Review in 2015 identified a combination of historic strengths in the British Army leadership tradition, as well as some distinctive flaws.[3] Among the findings, it concluded that the Army's approach to leadership remained too officer-centric to encourage leadership development at all ranks; that there was too much focus on delivering the task, regardless of whether achieving the objectives had involved good or bad leadership behaviour; and that there remained a reluctance to establish doctrine as the basis of effective leadership. The latter was a familiar criticism, echoing Field Marshal Erwin Rommel's barb that: 'The British write some of the best doctrine in the world; it is fortunate their officers do not read it.'[4] Indeed, the Leadership Review specifically rejected the 'suspicion that doctrine will restrict individual style and innovation by creating an archetype'.[5]

Modern Army leadership is founded on the premise that, today more than ever, complex circumstances demand clear guidance about how leaders of every rank might act. 'There is no place in today's Army for the gifted amateur,' General The Lord Richards wrote in 2010 while serving as Chief of the General Staff (CGS). 'The land operating environment is just too dangerous and too complicated to make it up as we go along.'[6] Out of that has come an acceptance of the importance of doctrine, the professional body of knowledge governing how Armed Forces conduct operations, blending past experience and example to provide method for today's soldiers and insight into the future challenges they may face. This doctrine ranges from strategic philosophies to detailed tactical practices, providing a guide for soldiers and officers to the military profession, as Archbold does to the criminal Bar, or Erskine May to parliamentary procedure.[7] As Chapter 1 outlined, since the mid-1980s the British Army has begun to embrace doctrine and to place it at the heart of its approach to warfighting and leadership.

The Army Leadership Doctrine that was developed following the 2015 review, to sit alongside existing doctrine on Land Operations, provided the first comprehensive reference point for the Army's leadership philosophy, principles and methods. It was written to complement rather than replace regimental approaches to leadership, which reflect their specific needs, context and histories. Under the capstone of the leadership doctrine, many regiments continue to codify their own specific ethos, whether that is the Household Cavalry's identity as 'The Trusted Guardian', upholding 'the highest standards, fit for our Monarch',[8] or 16 Air Assault Brigade's Pegasus Ethos and its underlying creed: 'As British Airborne soldiers we place the mission, and our comrades, before ourselves.'[9]

The establishment of a leadership doctrine in 2016 reflected the needs of an Army that, including reservists, had become less than half the size it was in 1989.[10] When the fighting force is smaller, and technological superiority relative to adversaries cannot be guaranteed, there is an even greater premium on the quality of people and leadership. Even as technology plays a more prominent role, it is ultimately the people controlling it who provide the agile edge and point of difference. The British Army has not always been able to rely on large budgets or ideal equipment, but has and continues to pride itself on the ability of its soldiers and leaders as sources of excellence. In the increasingly technological, multidimensional and contested contemporary operating environment, the timeless abilities to think clearly, act ethically and lead confidently are as important as ever, if not more so. The imperative is to develop leaders capable of navigating the battlespaces of today and tomorrow: 'leaders who thrive and improve in chaos and ambiguity'.[11]

To achieve this, modern Army leadership doctrine and training focus on philosophical and practical principles that equip people to deal with whatever they encounter. They encompass the three elements of fighting power – the physical, moral and conceptual – and a framework that explains what Army leaders are, what they know and what they do: leadership as an expression of character and habit, a profession grounded in knowledge, and a series of defining responsibilities.[12] Underpinning this framework are critical aspects of doctrine that are sources of extensive study in their own right.[13] Three of the most important will be discussed here: values-based leadership, Mission Command and servant leadership. They are respectively the moral and ethical grounding of Army leadership, its agile implementation and the service mindset that underpins it. To understand modern

Army leadership it is first necessary to appreciate these fundamental ideas, how they came into being and what they represent.

Values–based leadership

Those who volunteer to serve in the British Army make personal commitments and sacrifices that are not mirrored by any civilian profession. Through the principle of unlimited liability, they consent to knowingly risk their lives in the service of their comrades and, ultimately, the nation. They acknowledge that certain personal freedoms will be given up for the sake of that service. They sign up to serve in combat situations of severe stress and danger that may necessitate the use of lethal force, and which will frequently pose moral and ethical dilemmas that must be resolved in the moment. Ultimately, they accept the duty, when required and lawfully directed, to close with and kill an enemy.

The nature of this service requires deep bonds of trust between those who undertake it, and continued legitimacy in the eyes of people on whose behalf it is carried out. Both the intrinsic and external layers of trust on which the Army so depends are maintained by its Values and Standards: the principles, benchmarks and behaviours that every soldier and officer is required to embody. As *Soldiering: The Military Covenant* stated:

> [. . .] grave responsibilities mean that military effectiveness cannot be based on functional output alone; unless an Army is focused on higher ethics, it risks moral bankruptcy. This is vitally important because a morally bankrupt force, even if effective, risks alienation from the community it serves.[14]

Soldiering, which was published in 2000, emerged from a period in which the Army's ethical behaviour had come into serious question. 'By the 1990s, to many critical observers the Army's everyday values seemed to include racism, sexism and homophobia,' General The Lord Dannatt, CGS from 2006 to 2009, wrote in his history of the Army since 1945.[15] As he recounted, in 1993 the Army upheld its ban on homosexuality, which would not be lifted until 2000; the following year, the Household Cavalry's first black recruit, Mark Campbell, left the regiment following persistent racial abuse, precipitating an inquiry by the Commission for Racial Equality. Allegations of bullying and harassment would later be substantiated by the independent review into the deaths of four private soldiers at Deepcut Barracks between 1995 and 2002, which led to wide-reaching changes in the training and care of young recruits.[16] 'The Army was in urgent need of an ethical shake-up,' Lord Dannatt concluded.[17] Its leaders at the time recognised the need not only to correct flagrant breaches of morality, discipline and behaviour, but for the Army to better reflect the society it both represented and recruited from.

It was in this context that the Army's Values and Standards were codified for the first time and published, also in 2000. These represent 'constant, non-discretionary principles that define the behaviours expected of all members of the British Army, whatever the circumstances'.[18] The Values and Standards are the moral principles of the Army as an institution, determined not in isolation but as a reflection of its role within UK law and society: to protect the nation and take responsibility for the application of lethal force on its behalf, while acting both within the law and in accordance with the ethics and expectations of society. To fulfil its function as the legitimate organ of a democratic society, the Army must conform with society's laws, morality and ethical foundations, as it engages in operations well beyond the experience of most citizens. The Values and Standards are the primary tool for achieving this, ensuring that every member of the British Army understands what is expected of them, the responsibilities they carry and the boundaries they must work within. They mirror similar practice across large organisations in both the private and public sectors. The NHS is governed by a Constitution that sets out the rights of patients, staff and the public, with values that include 'working together for patients', 'commitment to quality of care' and 'compassion'.[19] While every office holder in public life (including elected representatives, civil servants, local government officials and the courts and probation services) is subject to the seven Nolan

Principles: selflessness, integrity, objectivity, accountability, openness, honesty and leadership.[20]

In the decades since they were formalised, the Army's six Values and three Standards (Figure 1) have become a core element of the training and assessment of all soldiers and officers. That they were newly expressed did not make them new ideas. Principles such as courage, loyalty, discipline and integrity have been fundamental to Armed Forces of every stripe throughout history. The significance was in their institutionalisation, creating an unambiguous moral and behavioural core for all to share, one intended to shape attitudes, inform decisions and mould teams. Values and Standards form part of the benchmark in the mandatory annual testing for all Army personnel, and are a golden thread through all career and leadership development courses. Whenever soldiers are being taught about their job or assessed on their performance, the Values and Standards are used to demonstrate the bottom line of what is expected . . . they provide individuals with institutional solid ground on which to base their most difficult decisions. Corporal Robert Chamberlain, a junior non-commissioned officer (JNCO), who faced the dilemma of whether to report a fellow corporal for a potentially serious breach of their rank and responsibilities, knowing the ostracism he might face from his peers as a result, recalls how the Values and Standards provided an important handrail. 'It's a statement in the handbook under courage: doing the right thing on a difficult day. It's a cheesy line, but it's literally the situation that we faced. It was difficult to do, but we needed to have the moral courage to go forward and report that issue.'

Encouraged through training and consistent leadership example, the Army's Values and Standards create the habits that are essential to operational effectiveness and decision making in challenging circumstances. They provide the shared understanding and intuitive trust that enable soldiers and officers to serve effectively together in extreme conditions, when there is no time to question those to the left and right of you. By showing respect, integrity, loyalty and selfless commitment in small, everyday ways, individuals develop the habitual behaviours that will help them in the most testing moments on operations, when they must make instant decisions around use of lethal force and management of risk. It is the Values and Standards that prepare soldiers for such situations, underpinning capabilities and understandings that cannot simply be wished or ordered into being at the moment they are most needed.

The Values and Standards also underpin one of the Army's strengths, that it brings together people from all walks of life and every corner of the globe, uniting many who would not normally work alongside each other in civilian life. In some cases the Army offers opportunity, structure and example to those who have never experienced these things. To do this effectively it must create bonds of trust and understanding between people who have not grown up together but must rely on each other in demanding, sometimes chaotic circumstances. The Values and Standards make that possible. They create a common ground on which leaders can build trust, togetherness and the intuitive leader–follower relationships that military operations require. As a shared code, they ensure that Army leadership is grounded in common values, rooted in the ethics and law of the nation, rather than those of the individual leader.

This does not happen in isolation or without deliberate leadership. The straightforward expression of values does little to either promote desirable behaviours or underpin morality. 'It's a waste of time to

Values
Courage
Discipline
Respect for Others
Integrity
Loyalty
Selfless Commitment

Standards
Lawful
Acceptable Behaviour
Totally Professional

Figure 1: The British Army's Values and Standards

articulate ideas about values and culture if you don't model and reward behavior that aligns with those goals,' Patty McCord, who was Chief Talent Officer at Netflix for over fifteen years, has written.[21] Worse than being meaningless, values that exist in a vacuum of moral leadership can be actively harmful.

As Professor Philip McCormack, formerly an Army senior chaplain and its professional lead on ethics, has suggested, military values can exist alongside the most extreme inhumanity and immorality. The Schutzstaffel (SS) had a guiding value − *Meine Ehre heißt Treue* ('My Honour is Loyalty') − as it administered the murder of millions in Nazi death and concentration camps.[22] The soldiers of the US's Charlie Company, 1st Battalion, 20th Infantry Regiment, who murdered hundreds of unarmed civilians during the My Lai massacre of 1968, had been overtaken by a distorted sense of loyalty to each other, 'a private moral world with its own social pressures'.[23] Taken on their own terms, values can become distorted, re-interpreted to justify immoral or criminal behaviour, and used to pressure people into behaviour they would not otherwise condone − whether as participants or consenting bystanders. The review into the death of soldiers at Deepcut, which concluded that the Army had failed institutionally to identify sources of risk to those soldiers, found that an appeal to loyalty had been used to try and dissuade one soldier from bringing forward a complaint about a training sergeant alleged to have engaged in persistent physical and verbal abuse. 'He told me that [. . .] if I still wished to make a complaint against him, I should know it would affect my career. He said that the [regiment] was like a close-knit family and I could become known as the one who got a Sergeant sacked.'[24]

Values alone are insufficient to ensure morality. This relies upon leadership that puts these principles into a practical context that can inform behaviour and decision making at all ranks. Values-based leadership illustrates appropriate behaviour, through a combination of example and intervention; and it demonstrates that an operational decision can only be justified if it is not only expedient, but also moral and lawful. Ultimately, it shows how soldiers can and must apply the Values and Standards in their everyday work: why these words on a page are defining moral principles that must be embraced by every serving soldier, both to deliver operational success and to uphold the integrity and reputation of the Army.

It is the role of leaders to exemplify and teach the Army's Values and Standards, making the morality that is required a tangible and liveable concept against which performance can be measured and individuals held to account. As a sub-unit and unit commander, my first question to soldiers who appeared in front of me on a disciplinary charge would always be whether they thought they had breached any of the Values and Standards, a printed copy of which was displayed on my desk. And my second question was whether or not their behaviour had passed or failed the Service Test, a benchmark which asks, 'Have the actions or behaviour of an individual adversely impacted or are they likely to impact on the efficiency or operational effectiveness of the Service?'[25] The Service Test, which applies to individuals of every rank, concisely reinforces the link between the Values and Standards and the ability of a unit and its people to do the job that is being asked of them.

Values-based leadership is not just a necessary means of instilling the Army's behavioural principles and setting them in their wider ethical context. It is also fundamental to modern Army leadership as it navigates a complex operating environment, as challenging morally and ethically as it is strategically and technically. 'We live and fight in a goldfish bowl,' General Sir Nick Carter, then CGS, wrote in the 2017 edition of the Land Operations doctrine.[26] This captures a number of the challenges inherent in contemporary warfare, from the constrained nature of operations that must often be conducted in dense urban environments, to real-time public scrutiny of those operations, a complex legal context, and the awareness of enemies who seek to exploit all of these factors to achieve operational advantage. The modern battlefield represents a mixture of enduring and novel challenges. It is virtual as well as physical, flooded with information and misinformation, and sits within an increasingly fragmented geopolitical context – with blurred boundaries between war and peace, state and non-state actors. Further complexity is added by technology, and moral questions about how and when to use equipment such as unmanned vehicles and missiles.

Overall, as the MOD's assessment of the operating environment
in 2035 concluded, the battlespaces of the future will have five defining characteristics: congested, cluttered, contested, connected and
constrained.[27] The British Army must continue to adapt to these
changing conditions, without letting them set the terms of its moral
and ethical behaviour. It is the latter that needs to be imposed on the
former – using the Army's Values and Standards to shape both strategic objectives and tactical implementation. As the character of war
changes, introducing new technical and moral challenges, the importance to the Army of values-based leadership has never been greater.

Mission Command[28]

The defining advantage of values-based leaders is their ability to
build trust, which in turn transforms the scope and effectiveness of
leadership in action. In any military operation, whether on the battlefield, in training or supporting civilians, trust is the galvanising
force. As US Army Lieutenant General Robert L. Caslen wrote, in
terms that would be recognised by Armed Forces across the world:
'trust is both the fuel that drives the Army and the glue that holds it
together.'[29] When decisions must be made rapidly and with imper-
fect information, and action taken in the face of risk and danger,
high levels of trust are a prerequisite for success. Leaders must trust
that followers are capable of interpreting then implementing their
intent; and followers that leaders are making decisions that support
their needs and safety, alongside those of the mission. While those
of equal rank must trust in each other, confident in the capabilities
of the soldiers to their left and right. Without these layers of vertical
and horizontal trust, communication breaks down, confidence ebbs
and mission success is threatened.

Modern Army leadership is predicated on the belief that leaders
should not rely on their rank and command authority to achieve
their objectives. Instead, they must do so by earning the trust of their
followers through a combination of their personal example, integrity and the relationships they build. Meaningful leadership does not

exist without leaders who can demonstrate trust in their people and earn the trust of those followers in return.

A leader's ability to build trust in this way is manifested and tested through Mission Command, the British Army's command philosophy. This requires that officers relinquish centralised control of command, and instead take a more directive, delegatory approach, 'founded on the clear expression of intent by commanders, and the freedom of subordinates to act to achieve that intent'.[30] This approach holds that only the overall intent − the mission − should be fixed by commanders; the means to achieve it must be flexible and will depend on the judgement and experience of the commander on the ground. Indeed, that commander should be given as much room for manoeuvre as the situation reasonably allows. As then General Sir Nigel Bagnall, whose doctrinal reforms of the 1980s helped to formally introduce Mission Command to the British Army, wrote: 'The mission should leave the subordinate commander as much freedom of execution as possible and should contain only those constraints essential to co-operation with other units.'[31]

Mission Command is designed to help operations proceed with speed, agility and self-direction across the chain of command. In principle, it minimises the inflexibility and information asymmetry of traditional command-and-control, where the continuous recourse to higher authority creates friction and delay that can undermine operational effectiveness. Under Mission Command, subordinate commanders are trusted to use their initiative and make judgement calls based on their visibility and awareness of a fast-moving situation. With the trust of their commanding officer, they gain the confidence to act as they see fit and proceed as best meets the needs of the mission and the people around them. In this system, commanders work independently but not autonomously − their freedom to operate is directed and limited by the nature of the overall intent, the resources allocated to them, and their position within the chain of command. They are expected to work within the intent of superiors at least two levels above them, and to ensure their directions are resourced and understood at least two levels below.[32] This 'vertical integration', alongside 'horizontal' understanding of what needs to be done among those of equivalent rank, is what ensures a balance between unity of effort and freedom of action.[33]

As a historically German philosophy, with its roots in Prussian *Auftragstaktik* ('mission orders'), the British Army came relatively late to Mission Command as formal doctrine. While the essential precepts of decentralised command are present in early field manuals, and senior commanders were exponents during the Second World War, it was only in the 1980s – seeking to combat the Soviet threat at a time of reduced resources, and working alongside a US Army that had internalised the idea in the aftermath of Vietnam – that Mission Command became institutional doctrine.[34] Even during the Falklands campaign in 1982, the British Army remained caught between the legacy command approach of restrictive control, and the imperative for flexibility that was arising on a more fragmented battlefield, with improved technology and a social climate at odds with the deferential tradition.[35]

It was not until the Gulf War of 1990–91, in which British forces were led by a group of senior commanders who had trained together on the new Higher Command and Staff Course, that Mission Command was more deliberately and thoroughly enacted.[36] Major General Rupert Smith, commander of the 1st Armoured Division that was central to the rapid and successful Allied land offensive in Kuwait, summed up his desire to 'fight the battle not the plan', recognising the need for flexibility in a mission that would see his Division advance almost 300 km in under 72 hours.[37] Directives rather than specific orders were issued at each level of command, which 'lowered the decision-making level, and proved to be instrumental in increasing the tempo of operation'.[38]

In the three decades since, Mission Command has been further codified and entrenched, though not without its challenges. One assessment of the British Army's operations in Iraq in 2003 cited 'missions, and orders generally, that are excessively long, confusing and hard to understand [. . .] inconsistent with the spirit and principles of Mission Command'.[39] Mission Command is an ideal to which the Army aspires in all areas of its work – as much in barracks as on operations – but not one that it always succeeds in achieving. It is a challenging philosophy that demands high levels of trust, tactical awareness and emotional intelligence; an approach that stands and falls on the ability of leaders to create the right conditions for it. As such, an essential requirement of modern Army leadership is to create a conducive environment for Mission Command, one in which trust and respect run deep, common understanding and mutual esteem are rigorously developed through training, and clear and robust communication is encouraged, up and down the chain of command. For Mission Command to work, followers must have the confidence to use their initiative, even if it risks failure, and to challenge or even countermand their commander when the situation calls for it. It is entirely consistent with the philosophy of Mission Command for a subordinate to disobey their superior's order if their awareness of an unfolding situation shows it would be a mistake to follow it. Leaders have an important role in setting a climate in which such behaviour is encouraged when the situation calls for it.

As the following chapters will explore, leaders have multiple roles to play in facilitating the use of Mission Command: from developing leaders around them, to nurturing relationships with their followers and breeding the kind of empowerment that Mission Command relies upon – both instilling in people the skills and confidence to make their own decisions, and the willingness to challenge a superior when they believe them to be mistaken. Leaders also need to use their situational awareness and knowledge of people in how they apply Mission Command. With a highly trained sub-unit familiar with each other and eager for responsibility, it attaches seamlessly to the layers of trust and training that have been built. But with less experienced or confident individuals, and in more dangerous situations, a leader will reasonably choose to scale back the freedoms they release and the responsibilities they delegate. Mission Command is a philosophy that must adapt according to the context, with leaders determining how best to apply its principles in service of both mission and people.

Leaders in business recognise the benefits of this approach.[40] Warren Buffett, the most prominent and successful investor of the last century, preaches a hands-off management style that would not look out of place in a Mission Command handbook. 'To an unusual degree [. . .] we trust our managers to run their operations with a keen sense of stewardship,' he has written of his conglomerate Berkshire

Hathaway, which owns companies across insurance, infrastructure and consumer goods. 'With only occasional exceptions, furthermore, our trust produces better results than would be achieved by streams of directives, endless reviews and layers of bureaucracy.'[41] Yet anyone who has experienced a leadership role will recognise that, to some extent, the desire for visibility and control over situations for which you have ultimate responsibility is human nature. It takes a considerable level of self-discipline to achieve the trust that is necessary to tame this often destructive instinct.

As an approach, Mission Command helps to reconcile this conflict. It asks of a leader not that they relinquish the reins and trust blindly, but that they focus their role on setting an intent, providing the necessary resources and only supporting when further direction is either needed or sought. In this way leaders retain responsibility and accountability, without becoming an overwhelming presence that impedes delivery. They set the direction and set up teams appropriately, then trust in those better placed and informed to drive implementation. And they do this, having invested their time and effort in developing a high-trust ethos that enables the decentralised approach – where all concerned have the necessary training, confidence in each other, and belief that they will not be reprimanded for exercising their freedom to act. On the part of followers, Mission Command provides empowerment with a safety net: knowing they can go back to their commander – or line manager – for clarity and direction if they run into problems. Done well, it offers a symbiotic balance between trust and control that will motivate participants and find the most efficient route to the desired result.

Servant leadership[42]

In developing its leaders, the Army asks officer cadets and aspiring NCOs not just to understand what leadership is and how to do it, but to think about why they want to lead in the first place. The nature of this motivation is paramount. Effective leadership does not arise from the pursuit of rank, status and the perception of power. Those who aspire simply to attain leadership positions – 'because of the need to assuage an unusual power drive or to acquire material possessions' – will never command their people's trust, respect and commitment in any meaningful way. These social bonds, the preconditions of success for any leader, can only arise when leaders embrace the opposite mindset: that they can most effectively lead people by first seeking to serve them.

This paradoxical, counter-intuitive idea was first popularised by the American philosopher Robert K. Greenleaf.[43] In 1970 he wrote that '[a] new moral principle is emerging which holds that the only authority deserving one's allegiance is that which is freely and knowingly granted by the led to the leader'. Accordingly, people 'will freely respond only to individuals who are chosen as leaders because they are proven and trusted as servants'. This chimed with one of the most fundamental ideas behind British Army leadership, the philosophy encapsulated by the motto of Royal Military Academy Sandhurst since its establishment in 1947: Serve to Lead. The anthology of the same name issued to every officer cadet makes clear its importance: ' "Serve to Lead" is, of course, a paradox, but it is a paradox which should be understood by every officer cadet [. . .] If cadets have not understood the meaning of the paradox, they have no business aspiring to be officers in the British Army.'[44]

For most, an innate sense of duty and service is nurtured from the earliest days of an Army career. It quickly becomes self-evident to each leader that they owe a duty not just to the people they are training and fighting alongside, but to the tradition and history of the cap badge they wear, the standing and reputation of the Army as an institution, and to the nation, represented by the Crown, whose interests they serve. An Army career is one of service to these multiple layers of individual and institution. Its leaders must be the most committed servants of all, responsible for meeting the needs and supporting the development of their people, helping them to fulfil their own duty of service. A long-standing principle of Army leadership, this has lost none of its relevance in the modern context.[45] The service mindset of its leaders is the bedrock of the trust, loyalty and integrity that the Army needs in order to function. It inverts the traditional notion that followers exist to meet the needs of their leaders, instead dictating that the primary direction of responsibility must be from leader to led.

As Greenleaf argued, the idea of servant leadership is grounded in a commitment to the care and development of followers. 'The best test, and difficult to administer, is: Do those served grow as persons? Do they, while being served, become healthier, wiser, freer, more autonomous, more likely themselves to become servants?'[46] A servant leader accepts and embraces responsibility for those under their command, committing their own needs, talents, ambitions and time to the service of others.

Not all social scientists and management thinkers have embraced servant leadership as a concept, and it has variously been criticised for encouraging passive leaders, being at odds with the competitive nature of many organisations, and even representing an abdication of some of the primary responsibilities of leadership.[47] But as *Serve to Lead* makes clear, the inherent paradox is deliberate and intended to be challenging to preconceptions about leadership. It would be a mistake to assume that the embrace of service means any surrender of the ability to lead with confidence and clarity. As The Most Reverend Justin Welby, Archbishop of Canterbury, who had a successful business career before his ordination, has described it:[48]

> Servant leadership does not mean servile leadership. It means you're a catalyst, you're a permission-giver, and where you see skills you back them. You're not afraid to have people around you who are cleverer than you are. And you don't feel the need for people to treat you with deference.

The service mindset, he suggested, is increasingly prevalent in leaders across all areas of life: 'I'm very struck by the number of senior leaders I know nowadays who recognise that, if they don't care for their people, they can't ask them to do tough things.'

Service and leadership do not exist in opposition to one another, but as complements. Through the service mindset, a leader gains the credibility and earns the trust to lead by consent. While soldiers may not get to select their leaders, they do ultimately choose how they will follow. Through these silent judgements, authority inevitably ebbs away from those who do not behave as servant leaders. No amount of sophisticated theory or dedicated practice can help a leader who has not first internalised the foundational truth that the ability to lead directly arises from the willingness to serve. That is where every Army leadership career both starts and ends.

Modern British Army leadership is best understood as a synthesis of long traditions and relatively recent developments. Many of the requirements are timeless and would be recognisable to officers and soldiers of any generation, from the centrality of courage and discipline to the importance of delegating authority, something that was emphasised in training manuals written in the aftermath of the Second Anglo-Boer War.[49] As it always has been, leadership remains a human endeavour defined by the ability to inspire and influence people. What has changed is the Army's articulation of leadership and the professional approach now taken to codifying and disseminating its core principles. The leaders of the past may have chafed at the formalised Values and Standards and institutional doctrine that are now regarded as essential to developing leaders and leadership at every level of the Army. By contrast, the modern British Army believes that leadership is too important to be left to chance. Every leader develops as an individual and will hone a personal style, but the collective strength of Army leadership is underpinned by its institutional approach. That begins with the Army's Leadership Framework, which outlines the leader's role, the professional competences they require, and the tasks they must fulfil. The chapters that follow will explore each of these in turn, looking at what Army leaders are, what they know and what they do to achieve success.

4. What British Army Leaders Are

In 2010, the campaign in Afghanistan was at its peak and 518 British soldiers were wounded in action, more than in any other year of the conflict.[1] The most serious casualties were evacuated to Birmingham, to be treated at its critical care facility for military patients. Awaiting their distraught families at the hospital was Warrant Officer Class Two Julie Sessions from the Queen Alexandra's Royal Army Nursing Corps. Her job was clear: to be the constant companion of the families of wounded soldiers, meeting their needs and answering their questions as they waited for the next update. As Duty Critical Care Nurse, the first occupant of a newly created role for which there was no rule book, she served as part comforter, part guardian and part advocate for grief-stricken families. She greeted the families on arrival, chaperoned them through the ward, and stood by them for every doctor's update, taking in every detail that a traumatised parent or sibling might struggle to hear.

WO2 Sessions was 'just the right combination of strength, clear thinking and compassion', according to the military medical historian Dr Emily Mayhew, who observed her at work. Fulfilling a role that demanded empathy and practicality in equal measure, her example epitomises the idea of servant leadership, and also encapsulates the power of the Army's values in action: the selfless commitment to soldiers and their families experiencing the most difficult moments of their lives; the discipline to ensure that no detail was missed, or distressing errors caused; the courage to be a source of comfort and calm, navigating difficult situations as families expressed their pain and grief.

> Sometimes – rarely, but sometimes – she could not read the room. The faces were tear-stained, shocked and hostile. A mum who repeated over and over that her son needed to go home now. A dad whose rage

at his son's wounding exploded from him over her and everyone there, and it took a good two or three days of clear speaking and careful silences before the situation turned.[2]

Her story underlines what British Army leaders are: the individuals who embody its Values and Standards at the times they are most needed. It is the Army's leaders who enable it to function as a values-based organisation, one that draws its strength and cohesion from common, core beliefs and operating principles. They make the values system work by performing multiple roles in service of them: from the straightforward communication and demonstration of those values, to interpreting and applying them in complex situations, intervening when they are at risk of being violated, and judging when they have been breached. While British Army leaders are men and women of different ages, ranks, personalities and styles, they are united in their purpose, which is to lead as exemplars of the Army's Values and Standards: setting the example for others to learn from and follow, using their influence consistently to uphold the standards required, and taking responsibility for those they lead – their safety, their needs and their actions. In that context, this chapter will define and explore three of the fundamental requirements of Army officers and NCOs as values-based servant leaders: to be role models, custodians and parent figures.

Example: The leader as role model

To set an example is both the most obvious function of leadership and one of the most important. This is conscious and unconscious: leaders can set a deliberate example when they know they are being observed; they will also provide one through their actions in moments that may not seem significant, but rarely pass unnoticed. 'The most important thing I learned is that soldiers watch what their leaders do,' said General Colin Powell, who as Chairman of the Joint Chiefs of Staff oversaw military strategy for the coalition in the first Gulf War, and later became US Secretary of State. 'You can give them classes and lecture them forever, but it is your personal example they will follow.'[3] When a leader acts, those under his or her command will be watching and taking note. It means that every visible decision can have a disproportionate impact on culture and behaviour.

Most straightforwardly, a leader sets an example through personal conduct – from their attitude and approach in training to the responsibilities they choose to take on operations. This is true of all ranks, a point illustrated by two leaders from 1st Battalion Welsh Guards during its tour of Helmand Province in 2009: the most senior officer and one of the most junior NCOs. The commanding officer was Lieutenant Colonel Rupert Thorneloe. A widely admired leader, he insisted on being personally involved in some of the tour's most gruelling and dangerous operations. This extended to Operation BARMA, regular patrol drills to search for improvised explosive devices (IEDs) with Vallon metal detectors. During such a patrol on 1 July 2009, an IED detonated under the vehicle in which Lt Col Thorneloe was travelling, killing him and Trooper Joshua Hammond of the 2nd Royal Tank Regiment. The CO had been in the most exposed position – providing top cover (fire support) from the roof of the convoy's lead vehicle – when the blast struck. He was the most senior British Army officer to be killed in action since the Falklands War. As his Adjutant, Captain James Aldridge, said after his death, it was Lt Col Thorneloe's commitment to leading by example that made him an admired and effective leader.

> He demanded the highest standards from those under his command, but justifiably, as he also set the highest standards himself [. . .] He would never have asked anyone to do anything he was not prepared to do himself, and he died doing just that – leading from the front.[4]

Lt Col Thorneloe was not the only member of 1st Battalion to go beyond the call of duty with regard to Op BARMA. The role of 'Vallon Man', tasked with leading foot patrols with the metal detector, sweeping ahead for IEDs, had been designed to be rotated, ensuring that no individual would have to bear not only its physical danger but its significant psychological strain without respite. But not all who were offered relief accepted, as a Welsh Guards company commander recalled.

> Halfway through our tenure in Southern Helmand, I announced at the end of an orders group that the nineteen-year-old Lance Corporal Hill would be rotated out of his role of keeping us safe through exposing himself to untold risk [. . .] There was no surprise. Everyone was happy with that decision.
>
> But when the group split up and returned to their routines of cleaning weapons and smoking endless cigarettes, Lance Corporal Hill waited and then shuffled up to me, and grunted: 'Keep me on it, sir. I'm better than anyone else is ever going to get, and I'll keep us all safer.'
>
> That's what real courage looks like. A scrawny, shirtless teenager, opting in a moment out of the limelight to take more risk for the benefit of others, because it is the right thing to do.[5]

It is leadership by example in this mould that turns the Army's Values from words on a page into tangible realities, enabling them to be understood, followed and embraced by all. Courage is manifested through the decisions of leaders to put themselves in the same situations that they are ordering soldiers into. Selfless commitment is brought to life by decisions like LCpl Hill's, to take great personal risk in the service of others. Loyalty is engendered by leaders like Lt Col Thorneloe, whose care and commitment to their soldiers is absolute: seeing what they see, fighting what they fight and sharing the same risk in equal part.

It is through the tangible example of leaders, at every rank, that the Army's Values and Standards attain their full power and significance. In having these codified, the Army is no different from most businesses and public sector organisations. Faced with constantly changing technology, consumer preferences and market expectations, the most successful companies rely on values to provide grounding, continuity and direction. They also ensure their values are tangible, incorporating them into the design and structure of operations, making them relevant to the everyday work of employees. Values have a paramount role in the Army due to the everyday opportunity, and necessity, for them

to be put into action. The realities of Army life, both on and off operations, make constant demands on people's courage, their discipline,
commitment and loyalty. These Values do not sit in a drawer but are
lived on every exercise and operation, whether they are being fulfilled
or undermined. As role models, it is incumbent on leaders to be the
most active and determined exemplars of the Values and to apply careful judgement in how they are enacted – ensuring that courage does
not slip into recklessness, loyalty does not become blind to context and
circumstances, and discipline is maintained with a light touch.

The leader's responsibility as a role model is not limited to physical
and practical manifestations of Army Values. Leaders must also set an
example of ethical and morally robust behaviour, helping to create a
moral climate that maximises soldiers' ability to make appropriate
decisions in often complex and contentious situations.[6] '[Leaders]
under pressure must keep themselves absolutely clean morally,' wrote
Vice Admiral James Stockdale of the US Navy. 'They must lead by
example, must be able to implant high-mindedness in their followers,
must have competence beyond status, and must have earned their followers' respect by demonstrating integrity.'[7] During the Vietnam War,
Stockdale demonstrated the lengths he was prepared to go to for the
sake of his integrity, when he became the most senior US naval officer
to be captured by the North Vietnamese. For over six years he suffered a relentless routine of torture by his captors, but also inflicted
equally cruel physical punishment on himself, as he maimed his scalp
with a razor and beat his own face so he was not fit to feature in a
propaganda film to be broadcast back to the US.[8]

Moral courage can be manifested in extreme conditions such as
captivity, but it is also needed in the everyday, where it will be tested
in small ways that demonstrate a leader's willingness to put integrity
ahead of expediency.[9] The smallest, seemingly least consequential
situations can be important tests of moral courage. Does a leader correct a subordinate for not saluting them, pick up a soldier for being
inappropriately dressed, intervene when they overhear a comment
that was meant as banter but may have caused offence? This drumbeat of daily interactions sets the tone for a unit of any size, and
moulds its habits. As the entrepreneur Brian Chesky, co-founder and

CEO of the travel company Airbnb, has written, the environment of an organisation is the accumulation of numerous tiny actions and decisions.

> Culture is a thousand things, a thousand times. It's living the core values when you hire; when you write an email; when you are working on a project; when you are walking in the hall. We have the power, by living the values, to build the culture. We also have the power, by breaking the values, to fuck up the culture. Each one of us has this opportunity, this burden.[10]

This responsibility is collective, but leaders should not shirk their duty to set an example. A leader who consistently takes the path of least resistance is encouraging the behaviours that will undermine discipline and cohesion when they are needed most. By contrast, one who is prepared to take the unpopular decision and insist on the inconvenience of high standards is making an essential investment in future success. By extension, they create the permission for others to do similarly, building the collective stock of moral courage through their personal example.

The importance of moral courage is especially acute in the contemporary operating environment,[11] one in which the legitimacy of military operations is constantly questioned, the boundaries between state and non-state forces can be blurred, and soldiers must combine traditional military roles with the work of community and nation building – a challenging and sometimes disorienting combination of situations that require lethal force and others that depend on de facto diplomacy. At a time when the decisions of its people are more subject to public critique and interpretation than ever, British Army leaders must be the embodiment of the morality that is expected in volatile and ambiguous situations. By their own difficult decisions they demonstrate the integrity, respect and moral courage required by all.

When leaders fail to set a moral example, the same values that should serve to uphold the Army's standards of appropriate, lawful and totally professional behaviour can have the opposite effect. In the case of Baha Mousa, an Iraqi hotel worker who died in British Army custody in September 2003, with ninety-three identifiable injuries on his body, it was loyalty that became badly misapplied. The Aitken Report into unlawful killings in Iraq highlighted a 'wall of silence' that surrounded attempts by Service police to investigate Mousa's death, from soldiers and commanders who let feelings of loyalty towards each other override their real obligations. This was a corruption of the Army's Values – actions that, as the report stated, 'are not forms of loyalty, but rather a lack of integrity'. As it concluded: 'Courage includes having the moral courage to challenge unacceptable behaviour whenever it is encountered.'[12] Many serious military failings can be linked back to the departure from fundamental Values and Standards that, in turn, stems from the absence of moral courage and the failure of leaders to demonstrate what this represents.

Accordingly, a counterpart to the leader's role in providing a positive example of Values is a responsibility to prevent their meaning and intent from becoming warped. 'If values are subjective, they can mean whatever an individual or group wants them to mean and therefore can become relative to the needs of a particular group,' Professor Philip McCormack has written. 'This situation is exacerbated when soldiers find themselves in a situation where the normal social reference points are subjected to overwhelming operational pressures.'[13] In certain contexts, the extreme nature of war can be inherently destabilising to combatants' sense of self and normality, and as such can threaten their perception of morality. Leaders must be the first and last line of defence against such moral mission creep, intervening to prohibit what is wrong as much as they proactively demonstrate what is right. The power of a leader's example therefore extends beyond being an affirmative role model. It must also encompass moral example, shaping an environment that prevents the extreme existence of living in a warzone from tainting the behaviour, perceptions and decisions of their followers.

Influence: The leader as custodian

Closely related to the example that leaders provide is the influence they exercise on followers. The ability to influence their people, for better and worse, is something leaders must be acutely aware of. Leaders can affirm the Values and Standards through their example, or they can fatally undermine them through personal lapses, failures to intervene, or ignorance of problems developing under their command. As such, the leader must be not just exemplar but custodian – someone who works to protect and maintain the most important underpinnings of collective culture and behaviour. They must be custodians of the Values and Standards, of the distinctive traditions of their regiment, and of the levels of performance required both in training and on operations.

This custodianship role applies to all the Values and Standards, but is most obviously manifested in the maintenance of discipline. This is something instilled into every soldier and officer from their first day of training. On all operations, combat and non-combat, the Army faces a combination of friction, uncertainty and sometimes chaos. Only discipline can maintain the cohesion needed to overcome these challenges. This explains why unquestioning obedience is demanded in areas including timekeeping, parade ground drill and standards of dress. These stipulations do not exist for the sake of making people's lives difficult, but to protect them. Adherence has direct applicability to mindset and performance on operations. Failure to do up your webbing pouch and you will drop a magazine (ammunition). Failure to do up your trouser pocket and you will lose your map. No map and you are lost in enemy territory. No magazine and you run out of ammunition when you most need it. Lives are put at risk.

Discipline begins with collective adherence to basic regulations, but also goes far beyond it. More often, and most powerfully, it is achieved not by diktat but through the will of the individual soldier, expressing a desire to meet and exceed the standards expected. Self-discipline of this kind is the higher, more potent form: an important contributor to the individual pursuit of excellence and the collective pride of a platoon, company or battalion. 'Discipline does not mean fear of punishment, but the cheerful and willing obedience of commands because the recipients are confident that orders given by their leaders are for the good of the individual and the team,' wrote

Lieutenant Colonel J. G. Shillington, CO of 6th Battalion, King's Own Scottish Borderers during the Second World War. As he suggested, a climate in which self-discipline is habitual perpetuates its own high standards. '[Discipline] goes even further – it entails the desire to find out the right thing to do and to do it and see that others do it so as not to let the team down.'[14] Self-discipline not only engenders high standards but also acts as a critical capability in war, helping soldiers to balance the moments when maximum force is required against an enemy (using precise, disciplined violence to negate threats) with the restraint needed to recognise when those situations have passed, the battle is over, and adversaries must be treated with compassion and humanity.

Self-discipline is what every soldier should aspire to, and the example that every leader must offer. But in the physically and mentally exhausting conditions that accompany a combat tour – on the battlefield, when friends and comrades have been injured or killed, or in the event of captivity – even the highest standards of personal and collective self-discipline can be eroded. The best-trained and most experienced soldiers are still human beings facing the chaos, friction and uncertainty of war. It is in these situations that the influence of leaders as custodians becomes paramount.

This can be illustrated by the story of John Lord, the Regimental Sergeant Major of 3 PARA at its formation in 1941. RSM Lord was captured at Arnhem in September 1944 and sent to the Stalag XI-B PoW camp. 'He arrived [. . .] to find the camp in a terrible state and its occupants in conditions of chaos and misery,' *The Times* reported in 1945. 'They had succumbed to the lethargy that hunger, boredom and squalor easily led to. They lived in decay and wretchedness, and when they died their bodies were taken almost unheeded to their graves on an old cart.' Seven months later, when the camp was liberated, a visiting officer encountered a guard patrol at the gate so pristine that he could not believe it was comprised of PoWs, and assumed another Division had got there first. 'It could have gone on duty at Buckingham Palace,' he marvelled. Despite conditions that saw 400 men sleeping in huts designed for only 150, and with a daily meat ration for 5,000 men that amounted to two buckets of horse meat, RSM Lord instigated daily physical training (PT), turned morning roll calls into full parades, secured from his captors a trumpet that was used to give familiar bugle calls, and gave every prisoner who died a military funeral, Union Jack atop the coffin. Several times, Lord refused to be transferred to a more amenable camp, hiding under the floorboards of a hut for days when the Germans tried to have him moved.

Speaking to officers at Army Staff College in 1963, as the retiring Academy Sergeant Major at Royal Military Academy Sandhurst, Lord emphasised the change wrought by his insistence that the men at Stalag XI-B salute the German officers, as required under the Geneva Convention. '[F]rom that moment on, their shoulders squared back, their heads came erect and the light came in their eyes. And the rehabilitation, the spirit and so on, had started so that eventually we finished by taking over and controlling the camp.'[15] Renowned even in captivity for his immaculate appearance, from the creases of his trousers to the corners of his moustache, the RSM's insistence on re-establishing standards had, in turn, restored self-discipline and rebuilt the group's shattered morale.

In this way, leaders – whether an NCO, private soldier or a senior officer – must be the primary custodians of the Army's Standards, stepping in to correct behaviour that risks undermining them, encouraging a culture of collective pride in the pursuit of high standards, and acting as a galvanising force during moments of crisis. As an organisation employing tens of thousands of people, failures of discipline and breaches of the Values and Standards are an inevitable component of Army life. A minority of soldiers succumb to the temptation of drugs; alcohol-related offences persist; and in rare cases there are incidents of sexual harassment, fraud, bullying and theft. A leader cannot prevent every such case, but through their upholding of standards and use of discipline they can minimise the acceptable space for such behaviour within their environment. By doing so, leaders over time achieve the most important influence, one that has the strength to persist in their absence. Their influence – established by example and reinforced by custodianship of standards – must be powerful enough to have an effect in all places and at all times, helping to guide effective decision making on the battlefield, high standards in training, and appropriate behaviour in and out of barracks.

The leader's role as custodian encompasses the Values and Standards shared by the whole British Army, but is not limited to them. It also pertains to the history, traditions and culture that are part of every individual regiment, company and platoon, something that leaders are acutely aware of, knowing that they walk in the footsteps and wear the cap badge of officers, NCOs and soldiers who forged a proud legacy that is now theirs to safeguard. This applies particularly to NCO leaders, who have grown up and built a sustainable presence in a regiment, where officers can be more transient. Warrant officers and senior NCOs provide the continuity, institutional knowledge and deep appreciation of a regiment's culture and traditions that are fundamental to upholding standards and developing each new generation of leaders and soldiers. Their standing means they act as the primary points of reference for its culture, standards and expectations.

This influence is reinforced by the centrality of the sergeants' and warrant officers' messes – the physical spaces in barracks where senior NCOs come together to eat, socialise and in certain cases live, as do officers in their own messes. As well as being defined spaces, messes are social systems, with their own rules, traditions and governance. As a study conducted for the Army described:

> A Mess, in its essence, is the heart of a military unit. It is the place where new members learn the character, or ethos, of the group to which they now belong and the standards to be upheld – where collective identity is created and constantly reinforced to the point of inculcation and almost instinctive influence of behaviours on and off the battlefield or the equivalent battlespace.[16]

Messes – which in most regiments exist separately for warrant officers and sergeants, officers, and junior NCOs – are a tangible expression of regimental history and how that shapes present culture and expectations. The memorabilia on the walls and the charters and regulations that apply to the spaces themselves tell a story of the standards required. 'It is often said that a good sergeants' mess makes a good unit; it is as important as a good officers' mess, and many would argue even more important,' wrote General Sir Mike Jackson, CGS from 2003 to 2006.[17]

The regimental expectations that are taught and learned in the mess, rooted in history that is intrinsic to collective pride and identity, find full expression on the battlefield. 'In the Falklands we were not bewildered for long in the fight with our enemies, nor did we fear them,' recalled Major General Chip Chapman, then a platoon commander in 2 PARA. 'Every Tom, NCO and officer only feared that he might somehow disappoint those who preceded him, or those around him.' He described how, during the Battle of Goose Green, 2 PARA fell back on its legacy when the fighting was toughest.

> We fought in the footsteps of 6 Platoon at Arnhem. Late in the day on 28th May 1982, B Company were in a spot of bother. We were once again heavily shelled and opened up on, and a fleet of enemy helicopters came in with reinforcements. The casualty figures came on the radio, and they suggested that we'd had seven officers killed.
>
> I went up to [Major] John Crosland and I said, 'What do we do now?'
>
> He said, 'This is Arnhem, Day Three.'
>
> Those in 44's legacy to us was: 'match that'.[18]

Leaders must be the ultimate guardians of these traditions and legacies, ensuring that every member of a regiment knows its history, its greatest achievements, past failings, and the particular standards that are expected. This is an essential role for Army leaders, but one they are helped in by each regiment's strong sense of history and the presence in all of a cohort of long-serving soldiers. Custodianship of culture and tradition is no less important for young organisations, but potentially more difficult in an environment such as a start-up where the employee base grows rapidly and institutional memory is largely vested in the company's founders and their initial team. Whatever the nature and size of an organisation, its leaders must always be custodians of its values, culture and expected standards: both embodying them and working to pass them down to every new generation.

Responsible: The leader as parent figure

After over a month of aerial war, 24 February 1991 was G-Day: the beginning of Operation DESERT STORM's ground offensive, which would in days lead to the retreat of the Iraqi Army and the liberation of Kuwait. Several miles behind the frontline of troops and tanks, battalions including the 1st Royal Scots maintained a rolling supply chain of food and water trucks. In the lead vehicle of its convoy, tasked with navigation, was Lieutenant Wendy Smart of the Women's Royal Army Corps.

'They travelled through the breach in the enemy's defences in their chemical warfare suits and gas masks in the dark and rain, avoiding cluster bombs and anti-personnel mines littering the track, hearing the roar of battle a few miles ahead, watching the flash of explosives ripping across the black sky, feeling the vibrations through the ground. Sometimes the trucks behind would get bogged down in the soft sand and they would have to wait for them to catch up.

'I had a grid point on the map where we were supposed to be and a compass, and if I got the distance and bearing wrong, we could have ended up in enemy lines. So it was on my head.' She had been too anxious to sleep for more than one or two hours as her convoy travelled almost non-stop for four days and nights. 'I worried more about the boys than myself. I felt so responsible.'[19]

This intense feeling of responsibility is intrinsic to Army leadership, where decisions have a direct bearing on the safety and lives of those who must follow them. It underpins the servant leadership principle that applies not only to officers and NCOs, but to every single soldier in the Army: service before self. The responsibility to people's physical well-being, mental health and personal development is the staple of leadership in any field. But it is especially acute in the military environment, one that makes unique demands of its people and, by association, of their families and support networks. People who volunteer to work in often extreme circumstances – committing to undergo physical hardship and danger and to be separated from their families at a moment's notice – deserve an unusual duty of care in return. There is a debt of responsibility that must be repaid.

The responsibility inherent in Serve to Lead means Army leaders must be more than concerned managers helping people to navigate personal or professional difficulties. They are working in an environment where the intensity of the relationships formed, through shared service and sacrifice, has often been described as akin to love. This helps explain why an Army leader's responsibility to those they lead is closer to parenting than managing. It is the same combination of protecting, disciplining, teaching, caring and nurturing that any parent would instinctively recognise: the need to look after people at the same time as preparing them to look after themselves; to know instinctively when it is time to step in, and when to step back. In the view of WO1 Gavin Paton, the Army Sergeant Major, this reflects the people-centric nature of the Army as an institution and fighting force. '[The] Army is about people, not platforms. Our leaders must love and lead our soldiers; they deserve outstanding leadership, they are entitled to it.'[20]

Army leaders are also parent figures in a very literal way, often commanding young men and women, many still in their teens. The sense of duty this creates can act as a burden and source of inspiration in equal measure. It is a huge responsibility to place on leaders who are often young themselves, but it is also what many sign up for: the opportunity to serve and lead, for experiences that will be life-defining, shaping skills and forging relationships that will last a lifetime. Many thrive on the challenge of taking responsibility in circumstances where every decision can make a critical difference. And the best leaders, like good parents, do so while being honest about their shortcomings and owning up to their mistakes – another facet of building trust and respect.

A leader's responsibility and duty of care to individuals – to both their welfare and development – also has a strong bearing on the collective, and is a cornerstone of operational effectiveness. This suffers if soldiers are distracted by issues in their personal lives that detract from their ability to work effectively as part of a team, think rationally, take decisions and manage risk. That their work is abnormal does not

insulate soldiers from everyday realities: there are still marital, financial, personal and familial problems to deal with, sometimes made
more difficult by the peripatetic nature of Army life. The difference
from a normal working environment is in the consequences of someone having a bad day, in circumstances when someone's life can depend
on your next decision.

This entails a wide scope of responsibilities for Army leaders, who
must be a source of support to soldiers and their families, well beyond
the battlefield, both at moments of joy and in times of tragedy. As
well as celebrating personal and professional milestones together,
from weddings to promotions, this means helping people during
some of the most difficult times in their lives. In my personal experience this has included liaising with the families of multiple soldiers
who were killed in combat and one who died by suicide; having to be
the bearer of tragic family news; attending numerous court cases
with soldiers facing charges; helping people who were suffering with
financial difficulties, mental health challenges or alcohol abuse; and
providing job support to soldiers leaving the Army, who faced vulnerable situations if they could not find employment. That is the
reality of leadership when your responsibilities do not, and cannot,
end with the working day: a reality that would equally be recognised
by those working in the NHS and Emergency Services. Because soldiers are committing themselves totally to serve in the Army, the
leader's service to them must be equally unstinting. That means being
a proactive and consistent supporter of people in all their needs –
addressing the whole self and life of the individual, not just their
capability and effectiveness as a soldier.

'You must know every single one of your men,' the US General
and later President Dwight D. Eisenhower told graduating officer
cadets at Sandhurst in 1944, three months before the D-Day landings,
when he was serving as Supreme Commander of the Allied Expeditionary Force. 'You must be their leader, their father, their mentor,
even if you're half their age. You must understand their problems. You must keep them out of trouble; if they get in trouble, you
must be the one who goes to their rescue.'[21]

As parent figures, Army leaders use all the tools at their disposal to encourage development – giving people responsibility, letting them learn from failure, providing a strong example, imposing the right mix of discipline and encouragement. They must also be guided, above all, by compassion, remembering that the sub-units they command represent a surrogate family for soldiers separated from their own. Army leaders function as the heads of their own family units – from the eight-strong section to the battalion of several hundred – that share each other's successes, provide a mutual support network in a work environment that can entail trauma and loss, and recognise that they are carrying forward a proud inherited tradition, one they will pass down to the generation after them.

Separations of time and place do not dissolve the parental responsibilities of Army leaders. In his 1963 speech, RSM John Lord told the story of Corporal Ray Sheriff, who had been under his command across campaigns in North Africa, Sicily, Italy and Arnhem. After three months at Stalag XI-B, he heard that Cpl Sheriff had arrived and that he was badly wounded. Immediately he sought him out.

> I can see this long low gloomy hut now, packed with men of different nationalities. I looked around for Corporal Sheriff and eventually saw him to my far left – sitting on the floor with his head hanging down. He was dressed in some strange uniform which had been provided for him.
>
> I walked over to him and said, 'Hello, Corporal Sheriff, how are you getting on?' and that Corporal – three months after the battle – with no great cause to love me at all, with great dignity stood up to attention, faced me and said, 'Hello, sir, it's good to hear your voice.' And I realised that he was blind.
>
> This was the most harrowing experience, I think, of my whole life. I don't claim, I would not claim, that he was saying this to me personally, but here he was for the first time after all the suffering of the past three months, and he heard a voice from the family. Even in those circumstances he felt that he was back with the family.[22]

Fundamental to servant leadership is that the duty of care continues beyond the duration of a command, in some cases for years. Leaders must do everything in their power to ensure the needs of every soldier are met and that none are ever abandoned, either on the battlefield or in their personal lives. RSM Lord was later asked why, after the liberation of Stalag XI-B, he had declined to take one of the first flights home and chosen instead to stay with his men. His response was a simple encapsulation of what it means to serve as an Army leader.

'I wanted to see them all out.'

5.   What British Army Leaders Know

Addressing officer cadets at Sandhurst in 1952, Field Marshal Viscount Slim outlined his four fundamental qualities of leadership. The fourth of these – after courage, initiative and willpower – was knowledge. 'Know your job and know your men,' he declared. 'Those are the two kinds of knowledge you have got to have.'[1] Within that deceptively simple statement is contained one of the fundamental truths of leadership in any field. Leaders have a profession and they oversee people. A deep, intuitive and constantly refreshed knowledge of both is necessary to earn the trust and respect of followers – showing that a leader is competent and that they care.

It was through his leadership of the Fourteenth Army in Burma that Slim earned his reputation as one of the outstanding British commanders of the Second World War. Arriving in March 1942, he inherited a disastrous situation, with the Burma Corps on the verge of defeat, in the face of a rapid Japanese advance that had seen the Imperial Army occupy swathes of Burma within a few months of its invasion. His first task was to lead a 900-mile retreat to the Indian border, the longest in the history of the British Army. Three years later, the Fourteenth Army took Mandalay and was on the road to Rangoon, whose loss would confirm the Japanese defeat in Burma. Slim's leadership has become synonymous with the extraordinary turnaround and victory of the 'forgotten army': from his training of the 'Burcorps' in jungle warfare, to adroit handling of personalities above, below and alongside him in the chain of command, and his embrace of an operational approach that empowered subordinate commanders. Perhaps most importantly, students of Slim have focused on his role in boosting morale in an Army that had suffered a series of shattering defeats.[2]

As 'Uncle Bill', most famously depicted in jungle fatigues, moustachioed under his wide-brimmed hat, and with binoculars slung around his neck, Slim had a winningly personable approach to leadership, one founded on a deep bond with and knowledge of the people under his command. 'I think it was that sense of being close to us [. . .] that was his greatest gift,' wrote George MacDonald Fraser, who as a teenager served under Slim in Burma, decades before he would make his name as author of the Flashman novels. 'You knew, when he talked of smashing [the enemy], that to him it meant not only arrows on a map but clearing bunkers and going in under shellfire; that he had the head of a general with the heart of a private soldier.'[3]

Slim's success in the Burmese theatre was a testament to the breadth of his insight and understanding as a leader, hard-earned knowledge that spanned strategic priorities, operational tactics, individual personalities, cultural nuances and territorial context. He knew his soldiers, having spent around a third of his time touring the 14th Army to meet them, and share conversations in the eight languages he had command of. Thanks to this legwork he knew the capabilities of his commanders, the state of morale among the ranks, and the terrain they were fighting in: a jungle environment where companies and platoons often had to patrol without visibility or radio communications, making a decentralised command approach necessary. Slim knew the strengths and weaknesses of his enemy, an Imperial Army that, in his later assessment, 'scored highly by determination [but] paid heavily for lack of flexibility'. And he knew when to follow, later reflecting that he had never written a full operational order throughout the entire campaign, because, 'I always had someone who could do that better than I could.'[4]

Slim, who both advocated and demonstrated the essential role of knowledge in Army leadership, highlights the multiple layers of what an effective leader must know and understand. Knowledge begins with the profession, which as previous chapters have explored means doctrine and the specific nature of the profession of arms. It extends to the situation, of which a leader must have sufficient knowledge to make good decisions, without having so much information as to be overwhelmed. And it is most importantly manifested in an understanding of people, human behaviour and relationships.

It has often been said that people are not *in* the Army, they *are* the Army.[5] It is people who gather intelligence, operate equipment, make decisions, issue and interpret orders, undertake tactical actions, and boost or undermine morale. Even as war has become to varying degrees mechanised, airborne, remote and automated, soldiering remains a fundamentally human endeavour. As von Clausewitz characterised it: 'The art of war has to deal with living and with moral forces.'[6] Most of what a leader does, while based on a knowledge of technical and tactical fundamentals, is guided above all by an understanding of these human factors: the capabilities of their soldiers, the personalities of immediate superiors and subordinates, the character and psychology of both enemies and allies.[7] Achieving your intent as a leader requires as much a personal touch as it does military expertise. That entails a need for leaders who understand people, and by association the personal relationships and power structures that bind them together. In this chapter we explore the personal and inter-personal knowledge required of leaders in four areas: knowing yourself, knowing your people, knowing the relationship between leaders and followers, and knowing about power in its various forms.

Know yourself

With a constant need both to focus on the mission and care for those for whom one has responsibility, an ever-present risk is that leaders forget about themselves. A leader who takes himself or herself for granted – assuming that their leadership style, their technical knowledge and their personal well-being do not require constant attention and evolution – is poorly placed to serve. Instead, it needs to be recognised that the duty of care to your people, as outlined in the previous chapter, is indivisible from duty of care to yourself. Knowing yourself – which we define here as a combination of self-awareness, self-improvement and self-care – is a prerequisite of the leader's ability to serve others effectively.

Self-awareness

This begins with self-awareness, a leadership behaviour that can be as difficult to exhibit as it is important. The self-aware leader has many advantages: they understand where their strengths can be put to good use and acknowledge where personal weaknesses need to be compensated for. They develop the empathy to see their leadership as others experience it, helping them to adapt appropriately to different personalities and situations. They are humble and willing to change, where less mindful counterparts are more liable to be dogmatic, convinced their approach is unimpeachable and that it is the job of others to adapt to them. Self-awareness is part of the mindset of any servant leader: the basis of their ability to form relationships and build trust with those around them. The psychologist Daniel Goleman, who coined the idea of 'emotional intelligence',[8] defined self-awareness as one of its five core components, alongside self-regulation, motivation, empathy and social skill.[9]

Yet despite its critical importance, leaders sometimes struggle with self-awareness, believing that introspection entails weakness, failing to assign importance to a human skill whose benefits can be slow-acting and difficult to measure, or so focused on their work that they fail to recognise their effect on the people around them. Nor does self-awareness necessarily sit easily with the self-image of some military leaders. It is a quality that has been conspicuously lacking in some of the British Army's most famous commanders, Field Marshal Montgomery among them. After Allied victory at the Battle of the Bulge was secured in January 1945, he gave a press conference deemed so self-aggrandising and dismissive of his American allies – barely acknowledging the contribution of his fellow senior commanders, General George Patton and Lieutenant General Omar Bradley[10] – that one journalist in attendance even sought out his intelligence officer to ask, 'Why didn't you stop him?'[11] The misjudgement was to have consequences, requiring the Prime Minister to deliver a speech that amounted to an apology in the House of Commons, and leading the Supreme Allied Commander, General Eisenhower, to later reflect that, 'This incident caused me more distress and worry than did any similar one of the war. I doubt if Montgomery ever came to realise how resentful some American commanders were.'[12]

The cost of leaders lacking in self-awareness can be considerable in any professional environment, with the military being no different. When leaders show ego, behave inflexibly and refuse to admit fault, they risk endangering those they are tasked to protect, and undermining the task they are responsible for delivering. By contrast, a self-aware leader will curb tendencies that may be unhelpful to the success of the mission – such as the desire to micro-manage and involve themselves in unnecessary levels of detail, or to impose needless requirements on their people in the name of high standards. They will recognise the areas to which they can contribute most effectively, and others where subordinates are better placed to take on a certain responsibility. They will embrace self-awareness within healthy limits, avoiding introspection that seeps into self-doubt.

Self-improvement

The knowledge gained from self-awareness is essential, but worth little unless combined with the desire from every leader to develop themselves. Self-improvement should be a continuous, holistic process that begins through engaging professionally and proactively with the Army's assessment system. Through both annual and mid-year reports, this gives every officer and soldier a clear baseline analysis of their strengths, weaknesses and priorities for improvement. It is then each individual leader's responsibility to develop themselves, through a combination of practical experience and conceptual knowledge. With a canon of military history, theory and experience that extends back thousands of years, reading is one of the primary self-development tools of any soldier or officer.

'Any commander who claims he is "too busy to read" is going to fill body bags with his troops as he learns the hard way,' wrote former US Marine Corps General James Mattis, who led United States Central Command from 2010 to 2013 and was later Secretary of Defense.[13] He credited much of his command knowledge and competence to his extensive reading habit, with a personal library numbering thousands of books and a new reading list for every campaign and theatre of war. 'Thanks to my reading, I have never been caught flat-footed in any situation, never at a loss for how any problem has been addressed (successfully or unsuccessfully) before,' he wrote to a colleague in 2003. 'Alex the Great would not be in the least perplexed by the enemy that we face right now in Iraq, and our leaders going into this fight do their troops a disservice by not studying (studying, vice just reading) the men who have gone before us.'[14] As Gen Mattis suggested, reading in this context is professional and not recreational: analysing the relevant experiences of past soldiers and commanders to learn their techniques, understand their theories and internalise their lessons from experience. This approach, which starts with the individual but is recognised institutionally through study days, formal training courses and support to study for degrees, underlines that the process of learning and self-improvement must be continuous. A leader who is committed to improving their craft will strive to do so every day, during every deployment, and in light of every important decision.

Self-care

Alongside self-awareness and self-improvement is the importance of self-care. Ultimately, a leader needs to be in a fit state to take command and make decisions with potentially grave consequences. A leader's selfless commitment to those they serve should not entail setting aside or disregarding their own well-being. Effective service can only be rendered to others by leaders who meet their own physical, mental and emotional needs: people who understand their limits, know how to manage themselves through stressful situations, and avoid becoming absorbed in their work to the exclusion of all else. Effective leaders know that expending some of their precious time to take breaks from work and do what they find most relaxing – whether that is a hobby, exercise or socialising – will pay dividends at the moments when urgent, challenging decisions are needed and their resilience and morale will be severely tested. Time away from desk and duty is both personally restorative and an aid to reflecting on difficult problems.

This is true in any profession, but especially so in the context of Army leadership, where the burden of command at moments of crisis can create overwhelming pressure on individuals, who must have a store of personal energy to fall back on. On 24 May 1940, days before the surrender of the Belgian Army and the evacuation of the British Expeditionary Force from Dunkirk, with the Wehrmacht's armoured divisions having cut through Allied defences and reached the French coast, Lieutenant General Alan Brooke observed the toll this rapid deterioration of fortunes had taken on his French counterpart, 1st Army Commander Georges Blanchard. 'He gave me the impression of a man whose brain had ceased to function, he was merely existing and hardly aware of what was going on around him. The blows that had fallen on us in quick succession had left him "punch drunk" and unable to register events.'[15]

Brooke, whose decisive command of the BEF's II Corps was critical to the narrow escape at Dunkirk, would play an even more prominent role in planning the invasion of France four years later. By this point he was a Field Marshal, CIGS* and Chairman of the Chiefs of Staff Committee – the British Army's highest-ranking officer and one of the primary architects of Allied military strategy, working side by side with Churchill. His diaries detail the strain and exhaustion of the continuous round of meetings, summits and negotiations that determined the shape of the war. They also reveal a figure who refused to let his all-encompassing role in an all-encompassing war dominate every aspect of his life.

> I have always held it as essential to cultivate some engrossing interest beside one's profession [. . .] In war the value of such a habit becomes more evident than ever. I sometimes doubt whether I should have retained my sanity [. . .] had I not an interest capable of temporarily

* Chief of the Imperial General Staff, as the head of the British Army was known from 1909 to 1964.

absorbing my thoughts, and of obliterating the war, even if only for short spells when circumstances permitted.[16]

For Brooke, those interests spanned hunting, fishing, ornithology and wildlife photography. As CIGS, he would make time in the middle of his gruelling days to walk around St James's Park and scour the shelves of London bookshops for bird volumes and prints. This deeply held passion provided an essential distraction even at the most pivotal moments of the war. 'We talked of birds and other subjects,' he recorded of a dinner on 1 June 1944, seventy-two hours before the planned commencement of the D-Day landings.[17] Brooke, whom Montgomery considered 'by far the greatest soldier of the war', provides an important reminder that, even when the burden of command seems overwhelming, it does not have to become all-consuming.

Knowing yourself means retaining a strong sense of self, not losing sight of the difference between your job and your life, and maintaining perspective and routine even through the most difficult and stressful times.

Know your people

Knowing yourself as a leader puts you in a position to fulfil the most important duty: to know and serve your people. The servant leadership approach and quasi-parenthood role discussed in previous chapters can only be embodied by leaders who truly know the people under their command: their personalities, capabilities, needs and mindset. This is as true in the Army as in other high-performance environments, including elite sport. The legendary football manager Bill Shankly, who led Liverpool from the Second Division to become the dominant club in European football for two decades, once characterised his job as 'the study of human nature'. He described the level of detail with which he would observe new players to understand them as individuals:

[. . .] every player that comes here, from the day he steps in here, from the minute he steps in here, is being watched, is being scrutinised.

We're reading him like a book. Then, in a month's time, we may know everything about him: all his weaknesses and all his strengths.[18]

As he suggested, leaders need to invest the time and effort to understand their people as individuals, developing a feeling for what motivates them, how they can be inspired and what their most effective role will be. For Army leaders, this is both a pastoral duty and an operational necessity. In training and on the battlefield, a commander can only lead their sub-unit as a collective if they are also leading every individual in it. Effective leadership in these contexts must be highly personal, rooted in a knowledge and understanding of the people who must interpret and implement orders. One commander might respond enthusiastically to having responsibility delegated, consistently trying to push the boundaries, where another will continually refer back to their commanding officer for advice. The first may need a tight rein, while the other requires nurture and encouragement. That the Army runs on shared Values and Standards does not mean its people are expected to be the same, or that they will respond well to being treated as such. Common principles and behaviours provide the platform for individuals to demonstrate their unique capabilities and make a distinctive contribution. Operational effectiveness depends on a leader's ability to draw this out, including from those who have yet to recognise their own potential.

That potential can be realised in varying and sometimes unlikely ways. Sydney Jary, whose account of infantry leadership during the Second World War is standard reading for officer cadets, recounted his experience commanding one individual, Private Charles Raven, who appeared entirely unsuited for war. 'He was no soldier. I doubt if he influenced greatly any of the skirmishes, encounters or battles in which he took part.'[19] Yet Jary looked past these shortcomings to see what Pte Raven could offer the platoon: as a married man, unlike most of the other men, he had life experience that made him a father figure to the new and younger recruits. As a nervous character ('I admit I'm dead windy, sir'), he had the empathy to understand the mindset of inexperienced soldiers, where his fellow platoon veterans preferred to tease new arrivals with their most colourful war stories.

'Fear to him was horribly real and never to be joked about,' Jary reflected. He also described how, despite his abiding terror of the battlefield, Raven found ways to be of service on it.

> Once in Normandy, during a nasty little platoon attack up a sunken lane, 18 Platoon was held up by the inevitable unlocated Spandaus [machine guns]. Straining my eyes through binoculars, I was vainly trying to locate these guns when I was handed a steaming mug of tea. [Raven] should have been observing to his front but, judging the moment right, he had brewed a messtin of tea on a solid fuel stove. By any standards this was an inspired act.

The relationship between the young platoon commander and his unlikely charge underlines the importance of leaders knowing and managing their people as individuals. Instead of berating Raven for his obvious shortcomings, Jary thanked him for his role in stewarding and steadying the younger soldiers. When Raven, his nerve shredded, requested medical leave of absence, it was granted (though not, in the event, taken up). Rather than considering him a liability, Jary ultimately deemed this unsuitable soldier to be essential: 'he was the most complex character amongst my soldiers. That he was an individualist there can be no doubt. He was also a cornerstone of the Platoon.'

Knowing people as individuals is the foundation of effective command and good leadership. To that must be added a keen sense of situation. A truism of war is that it changes people: it can draw out hidden depths of courage and initiative, but over a long duration it also saps even the deepest reserves of courage, morale and resilience. General Sir Peter de la Billière, whose forty-year military career spanned the Korean War to the Gulf War, learned this lesson on his first posting, as a nineteen-year-old second lieutenant with the Durham Light Infantry in Korea. 'I joined a platoon of men who had already spent six months in the war zone and had endured continual exposure to shellfire and the pressure of raids and patrolling,' he recalled. Under his command, there was an incident in which a lance corporal on night patrol 'heard a noise and nervously overreacted, shooting his own companions by mistake'. Two members of the platoon were killed in the friendly fire, for which de la Billière blamed himself, for failing to understand the individual in the context of the situation.

> In this case even though the man had given gallant service, the credit in his bank of courage had run out, and his nerves and fears got the better of him. Through my lack of experience, I had failed to identify his behavioural patterns [. . .] I should have dispatched him to the rear echelons for a rest before he had reached this stage of nervous exhaustion.[20]

Situational knowledge – of terrain, intelligence, available resources and commander's intent – is the foundation of command. Leaders must also be situational in their knowledge of people, understanding when they are best placed to take on responsibility, where they will need support, and the point at which they need to be protected from themselves. To know someone properly is to intuit how they will behave and respond in a wide variety of circumstances, without ever assuming that their actions in one context will necessarily hold true in another. In the extreme circumstances of combat, trusted figures can crumble and unheralded ones emerge in a new light. Accordingly, leaders should be open-minded in understanding their people, acknowledging the potential for character to ebb and flow according to the situation. They must facilitate opportunities for people to shine as well as provide safety nets into which they can fall.

Know the leader–follower relationship

Knowledge of self and others are prerequisites to fulfil the social contract of leadership: the relationship between leader and follower. Followership may be less celebrated and understood than leadership, but it is no less essential to the success of any organisation.[21] As the author and management professor Robert E. Kelley has argued,[22] it is a shortcoming of much leadership discourse that it gives scant consideration to those who are being led, whose skill and participation in that relationship play an equal role in determining its success or

failure. 'Leaders matter greatly. But in searching so zealously for better leaders we tend to lose sight of the people these leaders will lead.'
As he suggested, followership is a concept that leaders must fully
absorb to forge the trusting, productive relationships on which the
fate of their leadership will depend. No amount of insight into individuals will help a leader who cannot grasp the dynamics of the
leader–follower relationship and put them into action.

Leader–follower relationships may exist within a defined hierarchy of rank, but that does not make them binary. A follower in
one context will often be a leader in another, whether by dint of
junior command authority or through showing the innate leadership that does not depend on rank or title. Good leaders do not let
hierarchy restrict their people's ability both to follow proactively
and develop as leaders in their own right. Rather than considering
them as subordinates waiting for orders, they treat them as engaged
followers, individuals who play an important role in interpreting
and implementing their intent, providing feedback and critical
challenge, and quietly averting problems before the leader has
noticed them. In a well-functioning, Mission Command-oriented
environment, a follower is as independent, influential and effective
as their leader. Such followers create clarity and galvanise action,
turning objectives and orders into concrete, achievable tasks for
those around them.

By dint of their position, officers and NCOs will always have followers. The question is: what kind of follower will they be? This
depends to a great extent on the attitude and approach of the leader.
Leaders who know the importance of followership and create a conducive environment for it will benefit from what Kelley defined as
'effective followers', who proactively find ways to turn intent into
action, identify problems the leader may not be aware of, and set the
tone for those around them. By contrast, a leader who treats followers as functional components rather than empowered actors is more
likely to be rewarded with Kelley's 'sheep' ('passive and uncritical,
lacking in initiative and sense of responsibility') or 'yes people' ('a
livelier but equally unenterprising group [. . .] they can be aggres-
sively deferential, even servile'). Just as good leaders foster effective

followers, weak ones nurture sheep and yes people, either through the limitations of their style, or in some cases a deliberate desire to discourage feedback and create a compliant group that they believe will be easier to manage. In these cases, opportunities will be missed, errors encountered that could have been averted, and a sense of alienation from the individual leader, and even the overall mission, can take hold.

Leaders who embrace the core tenets of values-based, servant leadership and a decentralised command approach invariably create the conditions in which followership can flourish. By doing so, they see their leadership augmented by effective followers who provide the supporting, enabling, amplifying function without which no leader – however capable and experienced – can succeed. The changing fortunes of General Headquarters (GHQ) during the First World War, where the British Expeditionary Force's high command was based, bears out the importance of strong followership and leaders who foster it. Under the command of Field Marshal Douglas Haig, GHQ underwent a radical shift in 1917, when his long-serving CGS, Lieutenant General Sir Launcelot Kiggell, was moved aside following illness, to be replaced by Lieutenant General Sir Herbert Lawrence.[23] Kiggell's departure came as part of a wider clear-out of senior GHQ officers, who were felt to have grown distant from the realities of the trenches and the direction of the war.

Lawrence had not been Haig's first choice for the role, though the two were known to each other. When the former resigned his commission in 1903 to start a career in banking, it was to Haig that command of his regiment, the 17th Lancers, had passed. A retired officer recalled to service at the outset of the war, Lawrence brought both business experience and an independent perspective to GHQ, by now a sprawling organisation with a staff fourteen times larger than in 1914. He approached his task as a reformer, insisting that he attend all of Haig's meetings, encouraging him to become a more visible presence to his soldiers, and reinstating the role of liaison officers who restored links between GHQ and the front line. The more professional, connected and informed organisation that GHQ became under his influence has been credited as an important factor in the successful planning and execution of the Hundred Days Offensive of summer 1918, helping bring an end to the war.

As well as being a highly effective leader in his own right, Lawrence epitomised the art of good followership. He identified and cured Haig's blind spots, smoothed over problems – helping to salve the Commander-in-Chief's fractious relationship with the Allied Supreme Commander, Marshal Foch – and ably deputised when he was attending to War Cabinet duties in London. 'Haig and Lawrence never liked each other either before or after 1918, but for the war in 1918 they were a superb combination with the most supreme confidence in each other,' one GHQ contemporary suggested. While in the view of the historian John Terraine, Lawrence corrected a 'distinct weakness of Haig's period of command [. . .] the lack of a forceful and energetic personality at his side.'

Their relationship bears resemblance to a model of leadership put forward by Richard Hytner, former Deputy Chairman of the advertising group Saatchi & Saatchi. He proposes that two kinds of leader and leadership be recognised as equally important: 'A' leaders who are the ultimate decision makers and 'C' leaders, 'the deputies, assistants, and counsellors who support, inform and advise the final decision-makers [. . .] they make, shape, illuminate and enhance the success of the out-and-out A leader and the organisation.'[24] As this suggests, there is an equivalence between leaders and followers that is not captured by traditional hierarchies and the military rank structure. The bond between leader and follower is often founded on the existence of creative tension and divergence in style, experience and personality. Leaders do not benefit from followers who think as they do, draw from similar life experience and share the same interests. The best followers are those who challenge their leaders to think in different ways, to see what they would otherwise not, and when necessary to change their mind and behaviour. By the same token, leaders need the humility and open-mindedness to see how they can benefit from the presence of these critical friends.[25]

In the contemporary Army there should be little place for leaders who fail to appreciate and nurture followership. Today's Army is one in which 'intelligent disobedience', a term coined by the author and executive coach Ira Chaleff, is encouraged through the principles of Mission Command, and the freedom it gives followers to make their own decisions in service of the commander's intent.

> Knowing when and how to disobey is a higher order skill than to just obey [. . .] Intelligent disobedience goes beyond disciplined initiative to address violations of values, asking tough and relevant questions to clarify orders, and looking beyond rationalisations and pressures to engage those giving orders.[26]

When a follower engages their leader in this way, pointing out aspects of a situation they may not understand and proposing an alternative course of action, a leader should consider the feedback carefully – exercising their judgement in whether to defer to them. Those who refuse to do so are not allowing followers to do their job, and failing in their own. By clinging to what Professor Richard Holmes defined as 'leadership diseases' – 'I've made up my mind' 'I can do your job better than you can' – they will, over time, lose the trust of their soldiers and see their authority ebb away. Because they have failed to show leadership, followers will look to alternative figures in the chain of command who can.[27]

Know power

Leader–follower relationships are social interactions but also power exchanges. A leader can harness the power vested in them by their rank, and they can convey it on others better placed to decide and act. Leaders gain trust through judicious use and delegation of power, and they erode it when they rely on the power of authority alone to command. The philosopher Bertrand Russell argued that power is as fundamental a concept to social science as energy is to the study of physics.[28] For leaders, a vague, instinctive and accidental understanding of power is insufficient. It is a subject they need to know both practically and theoretically: understanding the different forms it takes, the opportunities that exist to exercise beneficial influence, and the pitfalls of power abuses.

One of the most useful models for understanding power was set out by the American academics John French and Bertram Raven in 1959.[29] They outlined five 'bases of social power' that govern the relationship between leaders and followers.

- *Reward power*: the ability to give reward, and the expectation of it.
- *Coercive power*: punishment for failure to conform, and its anticipation.
- *Legitimate power*: the right to exercise power via a recognised position of authority.
- *Referent power*: power arising from the desire for affiliation with a group or the individuals in it.
- *Expert power*: power arising from real or perceived expertise and superior knowledge.[30]

In the Army context, as with most organisations, these forms of power all exist in parallel to some degree. Rank conveys legitimate power, providing it is not abused, while the institutional approach to discipline underpins coercive power. Rewards come through the potential for improved pay and promotion, honours and awards for outstanding service, appraisal reports, or even a simple message of thanks from a commanding officer. Expert power arises from the esteem of those who have relevant operational experience or specialist training on which to draw, including reservists who bring distinctive knowledge and expertise from their civilian work. While the ideal of service as a volunteer in the British Army is underpinned by referent power, reinforced by the regimental system and the history and legacy of a cap badge that inspires many to join. A regiment exercises referent power at the collective level, as well as through its most inspiring leaders, whose style and approach followers may seek to emulate.

For leaders, the imperative is to understand these different forms of power, who holds them, and how they can and should be used in combination. An obvious limitation is excessive reliance on coercive and legitimate power: a leader pulling rank to make unreasonable demands on their followers. Speaking of his section commander in Afghanistan in 2009, one private soldier recalled 'a bully who would belittle you if you didn't do what he wanted and threaten you if you didn't come up to scratch'. The damaging influence of such an approach is not just in the obvious effect on morale, but the silent erosion of authority that can follow, even when followers appear to be playing along:

> Whenever we had a break, he would make us sit around him and listen to his stories. We all used to laugh and some even copied the way he dressed just so that he did not single them out [. . .] Those that didn't really know him called him a leader. We knew him and hated him.[31]

Power misapplied will create a negative influence and result in unhappy environments. By contrast, success follows from judicious and subtle management of power dynamics. Sometimes this will involve combining different individuals who draw on complementary bases of power. In my personal experience, this has included situations such as a corporal briefing a US Marine Corps brigadier-general and over fifty of his staff on the air and aviation plan for a large joint UK/US operation in Afghanistan, delivering a seamless brief and answering every question thrown at him. That was a combination of the expert power of a relatively junior individual, given the necessary platform by the legitimate power of their officer commanding. Neither could have had the same effect in isolation. The expert power to convince and persuade, combined with the legitimate power that lent authority to the individual, met the needs of a situation that required both. By contrast, someone with legitimate power who tries to make a case without the expertise to back it up will stumble; just as an expert who has not been given the right platform may lack legitimacy in the eyes of the audience and fail to gain a proper hearing. In the same way, a leader's power to reward may ultimately become hollow if not augmented with the referent power of culture and belonging: the aim should be to create an environment people actively want to be a part of, not one that relies on purely material benefits to provide motivation.

Leaders need to understand the forms of power they possess, the interplay between them, and what a particular situation requires. That power is contextual and must be shaped by circumstance was

one of the lessons of T. E. Lawrence in his work as a British Army
intelligence officer during the Arab Revolt of 1916–18, the uprising
against the rule of the Ottoman Empire in modern Saudi Arabia,
Syria and Jordan (in part encouraged by an ultimately unfulfilled
British promise to support the subsequent creation of a pan Arab
state). Lawrence's initial intelligence report on the outbreak of the
Revolt shaped British support of a campaign that aided their own
against the Turks in Palestine. He went on to play an important role
in influencing the design and success of the Revolt's series of insur-
gencies, which culminated in the capture of Damascus in October
1918 by combined Arab and British forces.

    Lawrence understood the complexity and ambiguity of his pos-
ition as a British officer, who was also acting as adviser to Prince
Faisal, one of the Hashemite leaders, and as a combination of devotee
to the Arab cause and outsider who needed to work hard to build
trust. 'The foreigner and Christian is not a popular person in Arabia,'
he wrote in his *Twenty-Seven Articles*, a summary of his experiences
and advice from the campaign. 'However friendly and informal the
treatment of yourself may be, remember always that your foundations are very sandy ones.'[32]

    His ability to wield power in this context, he believed, was predi-
cated on an immersion in local culture and norms: 'to live in the dress
of Arabs, and to imitate their mental foundation'. This enabled him
to build a role and gain implicit licence to operate. 'If I could not
assume their character, I could at least conceal my own, and pass
among them without evident friction, neither a discord nor a critic
but an unnoticed influence.'[33]

    Lawrence's successes in the Arab Revolt underline how power can
range from the crude – the money and weapons provided by the British Army to the Revolt – to the refined: his personal ability to forge
relationships, balance interests and shape events with a light touch. He
was diligent in his observance of local culture and practice while being
clear-eyed about the purpose of such humility: '[Hide] your own mind
and person. If you succeed, you will have hundreds of miles of country
and thousands of men under your orders, and for this it is worth bar-
tering the outward show.' Above all, he understood that – whatever

your status and the means at your disposal – power can only be wielded by those with a deep knowledge of the situation and people they are dealing with. The final one of his twenty-seven articles of advice was to make an 'unremitting study' of Arab people and culture:

> [Hear] all that passes, search out what is going on beneath the surface, read their characters, discover their tastes and their weaknesses, and keep everything you find out to yourself. Bury yourself in Arab circles, have no interests and no ideas except the work in hand [. . .] Your success will be proportioned to the amount of mental effort you devote to it.

One of the most famous intelligence officers in the history of the British Army, Lawrence provides an enduring reminder of the power of knowledge to inform the practice of leadership.

6. What British Army Leaders Do (and How They Do It)

When Sergeant Ben Wallis's battalion, the 1st Duke of Wellington's Regiment, was ordered into battle on 30 January 1944, the British Army's 1st Division was sixteen hours into an effort to break out of the beachhead it had established at Anzio, eight days after its amphibious landing on the west coast of Italy alongside the US 3rd Division. The planned Allied incursion behind German lines and towards Rome quickly developed into the Battle of Anzio, over four months of bitter and bloody fighting by the sea. At 1500 on the 30th, when the Dukes were sent to join the assault on Campoleone, they had already witnessed the devastation wrought in the preceding hours of battle. As Sgt Wallis recalled:[1]

> I had never been so frightened. We were all frightened [. . .] We'd heard the fighting earlier in the day, seen the dead and dying – now it was our turn. I turned to my mate before the off and we shook hands. The order was given to advance, and we walked into bullets, mortar bombs and shells.

Chaos quickly followed. Beside him, his friend was killed almost immediately by sniper fire. Ahead, the platoon commander also fell and Sgt Wallis stepped forward to take the lead. 'I did what I could to encourage the remainder of the platoon and then spotted two machine guns up ahead almost side by side. Bobbing and weaving our way forward it was about 20 yards out that we just charged, screaming at the top of our voices.' At a heavy cost to the platoon, this desperate assault succeeded, both machine-gun crews surrendering when their positions were overrun. In temporary command of a battered but reinvigorated platoon, the sergeant had to move quickly to control the situation.

It would have been easy for us to follow through and kill them, but I was the leader and shouted to the dozen or so men following me not to do what they really wanted to do. In that moment I knew what needed to be done and what would happen if we slaughtered the enemy in cold blood. Where would it end? We were better than that. We had to keep straight. I got some stick afterwards, of course I did, but I knew it was the right decision and it did not take long for the other blokes to see it as well.

His experience at Anzio illustrates what is often required of Army leaders on operations: to take charge of a chaotic situation, lead soldiers in conditions of extreme duress, and exercise influence in contrasting ways, inspiring action one minute and compelling restraint the next. And it captures the multiple levels at which a leader must operate, delivering the task at hand, leading a team towards that end, and managing the individuals in it. For Sgt Wallis, all three were daunting: his task required a frontal assault on machine guns with murderous capability and intent; his team had been reduced to almost a third of its original strength; and he had just seen many of the key individuals in that team, from his platoon commander to one of his closest friends, killed around him. Despite all of this, he both achieved his objective and showed the composure to keep control of himself and his soldiers in the aftermath. Having admitted how afraid he felt in the moments before the offensive, at the point of contact he showed preternatural calm. After achieving his immediate objective, he did not stop leading his team.

The balance in any situation between task, team and individual is something reinforced by the Army's Action Centred Leadership model. Based on the theory developed by Professor John Adair,[2] who worked at Sandhurst as an academic in the 1960s before going on to become a world-renowned leadership theorist and author, this stipulates that leaders must consistently balance three interdependent needs: to achieve the task, build teams, and develop individuals – all governed by an understanding of the operating context. This is illustrated in Adair's visual model, which demonstrates how the three

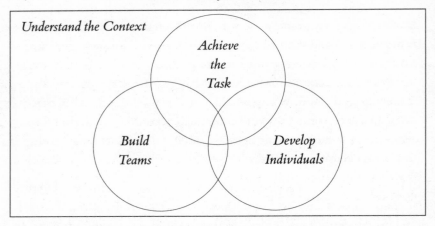

Figure 2: Army leadership model (Army Leadership Doctrine V1, 2016)

priorities interrelate. The Army leadership model builds on this, adding the additional dimension of context. This recognises that leaders cannot just look inward, to their mission and people, but must also develop an appreciation of the operational, political, environmental and cultural context in which they are working, as well as factors that may influence their team and the people in it.

As Army Leadership Doctrine states: 'The circles overlap, suggesting that there will always be some degree of tension between them. The role of the leader is to address this tension, and ensure that the three groups of need remain balanced.'[3] As this suggests, the constant requirement for leaders is to take necessary action while respecting the three components to which they have a duty: task, team and individual. In practice, this means understanding the long- and short-term priorities of your role, and managing the mutual dependencies. There is almost never a perfect equilibrium (consider how small the central intersection of all three circles is) but leaders should be aware of when they may be in 'debt' to any one of the three priorities and need to rebalance accordingly. A leader who is too unrelenting in their everyday work will crush the spirit and stamina of their team, while there will also be situations when the overwhelming need for action calls for task-focus first and foremost. Equally, as Sgt Wallis's experience shows, even when a task has narrowed to the point of a bayonet, the needs of individuals and the relevance of the team are never absent.

Leaders must constantly show an awareness of all three priorities, recognising what to emphasise and when, and managing the constant shifts in focus and energy that are required.

Leadership may be underpinned by theory, but in practice it is an art, to take an understanding of the context, define what needs to be done and determine how that can best be achieved, all without losing awareness of the actual and perceived effects of decisions. Leaders do this while keeping each of their three priorities in balance, recognising that it is not enough to achieve the task at all costs: a mission has not been successful if the team or individuals were broken in the process. Here we will examine each of these elements in turn to explore the reality of Action Centred Leadership and how leaders can achieve success without incurring unacceptable costs or sowing the seeds of future problems.

Achieve the task

The simplicity of the leader's need to take action is belied by the complexity of most deployments. A task that may appear straightforward will, in reality, contain multiple layers and make numerous demands of leaders. First, the purpose of the task needs to be defined and its aims selected. It needs to be planned, often with much less time than any textbook approach would recommend. That plan must be communicated and understood, so that all involved understand the mission and their role in it. And it ultimately needs to be seen through to the finish, with a will and determination to succeed that ensures the mission is not derailed by whatever combination of foreseen or unforeseen difficulties it will inevitably encounter. Leaders must direct all of this while carefully managing the resources at their disposal, including their own skills. They must determine how to use their own time to maximum effect, when and how to delegate, and what support and resources to equip their subordinates with.

To define the purpose and set an aim should be simple enough, in theory, but it is something that many organisations find difficult in practice. Whether struggling to identify their path in the first place, or tempted by apparent necessity or opportunity to change course, losing sight of the mission is a trap that can befall even those with the deepest roots and strongest identities. In the early 2000s, the toymaker LEGO lost its way after being convinced that it needed to move away from its most iconic product. 'We had all these external experts telling us the LEGO brick is going to die,' one employee remembered. 'They said the twenty-first century is not about little square plastic blocks. It's digital.'[4] Only after a string of disastrous product launches and financial troubles, which took it close to bankruptcy, did the company return to its roots, simplify its product line and reclaim its market position. 'The "out of the box" thinking almost put them out of business,' Professor David Robertson, author of a book on the LEGO turnaround, has said. 'What they did after 2003 is they kind of went back in the box. They went back to the brick [. . .] and the other things that not only were what their fans wanted, but were also pretty profitable for them.'[5]

The common-sense idea that missions — whether corporate or military — require a guiding purpose and a focusing objective is much easier to agree on than actually achieve. In the Army, defining this is the first and most important priority in the success of any operation. The entire Mission Command approach falls apart if empowered individuals across the chain of command have not been given sufficient clarity about their commander's intent: the parameters within which they are licensed to operate. Field Marshal Slim may never have written a complete operational order during the Burma campaign, but he did always personally author this crucial element.

> It is usually the shortest of all paragraphs, but it is always the most important, because it states — or it should — just what the commander intends to achieve. It is the one overriding expression of will by which everything in the order and every action by every commander and soldier in the army must be dominated.[6]

From the intent, formulated and concisely stated by the commander, flows a scheme of manoeuvre (when, how and with what resources a force will achieve the intent) and a main effort (the key activity and concentration of forces to drive success). Having selected and formulated the aim, the commander's role then becomes to maintain it. Along with leaders at all ranks, they must continually refer back to the aim, recalibrate resources as circumstances evolve, and ensure the main effort continues to align to the mission. As Land Operations doctrine states: 'Selection and maintenance of the aim is the master Principle of War.'[7]

Clarity of mission is important as a matter of course, but especially so given the complexity of many modern operations, in which Army leaders must pay close attention to the information dimension, the wider context of a deployment, and how their actions will be perceived. This is as true of work in disaster relief and humanitarian support as it is on combat operations. Operation RUMAN, in which the Army deployed as part of a joint forces effort to provide humanitarian relief for British Overseas Territories devastated by Hurricane Irma in September 2017, showed how the practical and the political can fuse. Brigadier (Retd) John Ridge, who commanded the Joint Task Force in the Caribbean, recalled that shortly after his arrival in Barbados, he was directed to make his first priority an appearance alongside the Governor of the British Virgin Islands. 'It quite quickly became clear to me that the most important role I had to play that day was not direct leadership of the Task Force, but to be the person who represented political intent.' Against a backdrop of sentiment that the UK Government had not responded quickly enough to a major disaster affecting its citizens, the first need was to demonstrate a presence. Simply to 'do the job' – distributing supplies, rebuilding infrastructure, setting up temporary shelters and providing medical treatment – would not in itself have been sufficient to achieve the full breadth of the task in its wider context. It took an understanding of that context to ensure the mission would achieve not just specific operational parameters, but its overarching intent.

As Operation RUMAN took shape at rapid speed – from an agenda point in a Monday morning briefing to a decision on the Thursday to deploy the Task Force and initial deployment to the Caribbean the next day – it demonstrated the importance to task success of a clearly defined purpose, robust planning and clear communication. The definition of

the mission, Ridge said, was as much about shaping its intended conclusion as managing its fast-paced beginning.

> We were really keen, from day one, to establish that we were there as
> a stopgap measure. We were the right people to provide support and
> fill the gap while local Governments and agencies rebuilt their cap-
> acity. But from the outset it was about building a narrative that we
> were there temporarily.

Setting end-state parameters in this way is critical to task definition and success: it tells everyone involved both what your purpose
is (in this case to co-ordinate a relief effort that would support British
citizens and their governments through the disaster) and how success
is defined – for RUMAN, the point at which local authorities were
in a position to reassume control of that effort.

As a complex operation with civilian, military and political dimensions, RUMAN needed an operational plan that could meet the
various needs of all its participants. In practice, this entailed placing
military liaisons with the Governors of the three Territories –
Anguilla, British Virgin Islands and Turks & Caicos – to support
communication with the Task Force and reduce friction at the
military–civilian interface; thereby ensuring politicians felt in control of the situation, and Army personnel had the time and space to
do their job. Brig Ridge then focused on communication of the plan,
both externally to the media and internally to those tasked with
delivering it. 'Sometimes we assume you write a set of orders, which
goes out and then gets delivered,' he says. 'I do think it takes more
than that, and you need to show personal engagement.' During
RUMAN, he took the time to tour the Task Force and gather small
groups together to explain how the operation had been structured
and for what reason. 'Doing that face-to-face meant I could look
people in the eye and know they understood the complexity of it,
and what their role was. It also made it credible and helped people to
recognise someone had thought properly about all this.'

Operation RUMAN highlights the many responsibilities a leader
has to ensure the successful delivery of a complex task. They must set

clear parameters around an operation in order to avoid the consequences of mission creep – something that at the extreme can turn an initial engagement into a years-long commitment. They must take on whatever role the operation requires of them, even if it clashes with the job they expect to be doing. In Brig Ridge's case, he spent less time co-ordinating the movement of people and equipment around islands with disaster-ravaged infrastructure, and many more hours engaging with politicians and the media, and communicating the plan to his people. And they must make themselves available to their team, communicating where practical in person. This aids understanding of the plan and helps people to engage with it, including to challenge assumptions and offer suggestions.

In practical terms, a leader's role in delivering tasks and fulfilling the mission can vary endlessly. But the guiding principles are the same, regardless of circumstances. What a leader does is to set the terms of the task, organise their resources and use their own time and authority in the places where it will have greatest influence (much as, in combat, it is often effective to concentrate the forces at your disposal against defined points of enemy vulnerability). A leader cannot physically be in all places at all times, but they must place themselves where they will be most useful, and let a combination of their intent, example and empowered subordinates do the rest. Above all, they must avoid one of the traps of leadership – to fulfil the role that is comfortable and familiar rather than the one required by the situation.

As Alan Brooke wrote of Field Marshal Gort, who had overall command of the BEF during the ill-fated campaign of 1940: 'he just fails to be able to see the big picture and is continually returning to those trivial details which counted a lot when commanding a battalion, but which should not be the main concern of a Commander-in-Chief.'[8] As they focus on what they should be doing, leaders also need to see the other side of the equation, and remember not to get involved with the things that are beyond – or beneath – their purview. What a leader does not do towards achieving the task can be as important as what they do.

Build teams

From the first day of training, every soldier's career happens in the context of the team, and the many layers of teams within teams that make up the Army structure. From the section of up to eight soldiers they may patrol with on operations, to the battlegroup of up to a thousand they are deployed with, and the brigade and division of which that is one component, the entire Army is predicated on numerous, interlocking teams that commit their own distinctive skills and identities in service of the collective. As General Stanley McChrystal, former commander of Joint Special Operations Command and author of *Team of Teams*, has argued, such overlapping groupings represent both a source of strength and a leadership challenge.

> Where org charts are tidy, teams are messy. Connections crisscross all over the place, and there is lots of overlap: team members track and travel through not only their own specialised territory but often the entire playing field [. . .] But this overlap and redundancy – these inefficiencies – are precisely what imbues teams with high-level adaptability and efficacy.[9]

Far more than organisational blocs, these teams are the basis of the Army's culture, identity and ethos. Every soldier, officer and NCO's understanding of what it means to serve is shaped by their regiment and its distinctive legacy and traditions. Soldiers fight and risk dying for the team around them, and to meet the expectations of the cap badge they wear and everything it represents. 'I did it for this,' Lance Corporal Josh Leakey, a sniper in my company, explained of the actions that earned him the Victoria Cross in 2013, pointing to his Parachute Regiment cap badge. 'I couldn't let the Reg down. It's what's expected. It's the Reg.' Even acts of extraordinary personal courage such as LCpl Leakey's occur in the context of and service to the team: the one that surrounds you and the many that have worn the cap badge before you.

These expectations are reinforced both practically and symbolically, down to the colours stitched on to a uniform. As 3rd (UK) Division Command Sergeant Major, WO1 Harley Upham, wrote:

We all know the three Royal Tank Regiment colours: brown, red and green. They mean from the mud, through the blood, to the green fields beyond. When the RTR wear their rank slides on their shoulders, they have brown at the front. It means we are heading towards the mud, and not towards the green fields.[10]

Regimental ethos is the basis of the Army's referent power, creating the desire for membership and association. However, for leaders this can only be the starting point of team building. Legacy, history and tradition help to encourage collective ethos, but it takes a leader to shape all of this into something that is relevant and meaningful for those serving today. Togetherness may be informed by tradition, but it can only be forged by leaders who provide the example, create the climate and engender the sense of empowerment that is needed to build a truly resilient team with deep bonds of commitment and loyalty. However inspired by their history and mission they may be, no team ever built itself.

For Army leaders, team building starts with a deliberate focus on harnessing culture: the invisible chain that connects past to present, individuals to the collective, and symbols to reality. Extensive research has linked the long-term survival and success of institutions with their ability to sustain and renew their culture – something that can resonate through generations when the strategy of previous decades has been discarded and long forgotten. While business practices, tools of the trade and customer preferences may change relentlessly and require an organisation to adapt, culture can provide both the anchor to help it maintain its core strengths and the compass to evolve them. Similarly, the British Army's culture, governed by its Values and Standards, is founded in its history and traditions – a basis from which to tackle contemporary needs and challenges. Educated and trained in this culture, it is the job of leaders to build their teams by teaching them, in turn, to embrace and uphold it. Edgar Schein, the management thinker whose work has been foundational to modern thinking on organisational culture, ascribed an essential role to leaders in determining and shaping culture. 'Organisational cultures are created by leaders, and one of the most decisive functions of leadership may well be the creation, the management, and – if and when that may become necessary – the destruction of culture,' he wrote.[11]

As they build and manage their teams, Army leaders work within the setting of an existing institutional and regimental culture, but they are more than passive stewards of inherited tradition. They must also consciously create the climate of the platoon, company or battalion they lead – the way in which people are expected to work and the standards they are asked to meet. These climates draw on history and tradition, but to a great extent must be the personal creation of the leader. Within the scope of their command, it is the leader's responsibility to set out and uphold the way things will work, the standards that are required, and how success will be recognised. The climate of a specific sub-unit at a particular point in time is created and influenced by its leadership figures, relatively easily forged or damaged. That sits within the deeper layer of company and regimental culture, something which is more ingrained, the product of generations, and a source of ethos on which leaders can draw. For leaders the challenge is to renew and restate these values, principles and standards, adapting them to the context they face and personalising them to meet the needs of the people and team they are working with.

The time to do this is during training. During a deployment, cohesion is something a team must be able to rely upon, not seek to build in flight. On operations, teams will often be brought together that comprise different regiments – and, indeed, Services – but these depend on the solid building blocks of established battalions and companies that can work quickly and flexibly because of the implicit understandings and expectations that exist between them. In situations where teams must constantly work and adapt under extreme pressure, these cultural short cuts are the basis of operational effectiveness.

In order to reach this point, leaders must create the right training environment, one that reinforces everything about the standards they expect and the culture they are trying to build. The Army places heavy emphasis on the idea of 'train hard, fight easy' – insisting on high standards in training to prepare soldiers effectively for the rigours of combat. Such preparation is partly designed to build necessary professional competencies, but most importantly it serves to build cohesion and collective identity. A team that has trained hard together benefits from reference points about how much it can achieve together, and how far it can go under duress. Its people develop an instinctive understanding of each other and how they operate. It is ready both physically and psychologically for the rigours and uncertainty of operations.

A leader's approach to managing training will go a long way to determining their ability to build a cohesive and robust team. Those who are tough but fair generally gain the respect of soldiers, as long as they have been clear about the purpose of the training, justified the intensity they are asking for, and calibrated the effort to the specific needs and abilities of their people. As Lou Rudd, formerly a WO1 in the SAS and now a world-renowned polar explorer, recalled:

> We were our own worst critics. Our leaders, at all levels, would demand the highest standards of professionalism in everything we did and, likewise, the men would tolerate nothing less than the most competent leadership. The strongest leaders were those who brought people along with them; they're the ones we'd follow into the fight.

By contrast, a leader who goes easy in training is not preparing their people, nor likely to win their trust. A lieutenant who served in Northern Ireland in the 1970s reflected:

> We had a company commander who thought he was doing his best for our welfare by ameliorating the hardships of austere training in Kenya. He shortened marches and then arranged for fizzy drinks at the end of them [. . .] But when we got to Northern Ireland I realised that his kindnesses had failed us: we were not properly prepared for the rigours of conflict. The men were soft.[12]

The necessity to 'train hard' does not mean that it must be joyless, however. Competition is an important way in which Army leaders foster the required training environment and build an ethos among their teams – whether pitting units against each other to test professional skills, or through regimental sports, a democratising pursuit in which rank is effectively suspended for the duration of a contest. When I commanded 2 PARA's Machine Gun platoon, we would spend

weeks on training camps, firing tens of thousands of rounds, repeat-
ing drills over and over again. At the heart of this was a fierce but
friendly rivalry between my two corporals, Daz Liney and 'Bootsy'
Lamont, both seasoned and respected veterans, over who could claim
to be leading the better section.

Within the overall scope of military training, there are certain pivotal
exercises whose importance has been established over generations, and
which play an especially important role in team building. For US Army
cavalry troopers, the idea of 'earning your spurs' – demonstrating your
professional competence and fitness to serve – continues today in the
form of the Spur Ride, a two-day patrol exercise designed to test tactical, technical, physical and mental capabilities. Those yet to pass are
known as 'Shave-tails', in reference to the historic practice in which new
cavalry recruits would be given a horse with a shaved tail, marking them
out as a novice.[13] Lieutenant Charlotte Lord-Sallenave of the Blues and
Royals, who has participated in a Spur Ride, observed its importance
not only as a rite of passage for individuals, but as a collective bonding
experience for the team.

> Its ultimate value derives from the neutralised section structure, as
> teams of private soldiers, NCOs and officers are all reduced to the
> role of 'Spur-Candidate'. By levelling the ranks from the start, team
> cohesion developed quickly as officers and NCOs became immedi-
> ately approachable to junior soldiers, and a culture of encouragement
> and camaraderie was established.[14]

The prominent role in the Army of competitive sport, another
environment in which rank is set aside, reinforces the importance of
an egalitarian approach to team building: creating cohesion out of
togetherness and common purpose.

As much as leaders have the power and influence to build a team,
they also have the ability to destroy it. Recognising this, and avoiding
the behaviours that can undermine cohesion and morale, is an ever-
present part of the job. Culture, climate and ethos may begin with
statements of intent, but they are developed slowly through the accumulation of reinforcing actions. Correspondingly, any action by a
leader that cuts across their stated intent for team culture can be

damaging in the extreme. 'It's really hard to build and it goes in an instant if you get it wrong,' Brig Ridge said. 'You see examples where people talk a good game on challenge culture, but then they cut some-one off at the knees and nobody challenges again – ever.' As they focus on team building, leaders must be acutely aware of the power of their example and show self-discipline not to undermine everything good about the ethos and identity that they are trying to instil.

Develop individuals

Alongside task and team – and intrinsic to both – is the individual. A leader's ability to build teams is heavily dependent on their ability to understand the individuals they are working with, help them to develop those capabilities and then put their distinctive skills and personalities to best use on operations. While still defined by the strength of the disciplined collective, today's Army fully recognises the importance of individual spirit, personality and thought. The modern operating environment is no place for robotic leaders or sheep-like followers. Teams are strengthened, not undermined, by the presence of strong individuals: independent thinkers who know and speak their own mind. As the Army becomes a smaller fighting force, it is increasingly reliant on every soldier being able to think for themselves, and leaders who are capable of nurturing their talents.

Leaders should recognise the development of individuals under their command as a key facet of their role in building robust teams. Training people is about more than establishing collective disciplines and techni-cal fundamentals. It should also be about helping every soldier to see and achieve their own potential as an individual. 'Many of our soldiers are blind to their potential, abilities and talent,' WO1 Gavin Paton, the second soldier to serve in the role of Army Sergeant Major, has said. 'It is the job of our leaders to harness that talent, develop confidence and to make our people aware of their ability.'[15] Such personal coaching to support individual, and ultimately team, performance is a pillar of oper-ational effectiveness. But it is also more than a transactional exchange.

Servant leaders, in their role as parent figures, do not seek to improve their people merely so that they will become more capable and effective on operations. They also take pride and satisfaction in providing the opportunity to succeed – helping individuals to achieve what they had never considered possible and to make progress that will be defining in their life and career, in the Army and beyond. Ask any experienced officer or NCO about their proudest achievements, and among them will invariably be small personal stories about soldiers or junior officers under their command who overcame adversity, found hidden depths of talent and character, and went on to provide an inspiration for others around them. These are the essence of the Army's unique family ethos, and the extended duty of care to those who have volunteered and made personal sacrifices to serve.

In this regard, a leader becomes a mentor and coach to individuals in parallel with the team leadership responsibilities that accompany their rank. These are roles that must combine a deep understanding of your people with an instinctive feel for the right balance between challenging and supporting them – helping individuals to grow at the same time as impressing upon them what is required. General Sir Mark Carleton-Smith, who was appointed as CGS in 2018, credits one of his early mentors for having nurtured his development in this way.

> Part of his trick was paying very careful, patrician attention to inculcating the best in us, and exposing us to the full variety of challenges that came across his desk as the company commander. He was very good at giving you your head and your opportunity, but then appearing miraculously, at the critical moment, before you were about to go off the proverbial cliff.

An important part of this training, he emphasised, was the learning and feedback element. 'When one made mistakes, which was the object of the exercise, he was very systematic about going back through how we could have done this better, and what we had learned.' While there are formal assessment and appraisal processes embedded into Army protocol, leaders are mostly encouraged to provide continuous feedback during operations and exercises: a consistent series of small suggestions and interventions, giving an individual the information they need to course-correct and make incremental improvements. In the spirit of Mission Command, the leader's role is to give their people as much responsibility as is reasonable, while creating a safe environment in which they can fail and learn from their mistakes.

Being a coach and mentor to individuals is a challenge that evolves throughout a leader's career. As new generations enter the organisation, leaders must recognise that the expectations of young soldiers and officers may differ markedly from their own and be open to making adjustments in approach, developing people in a very different way from how they were trained. 'The reality is that to the young soldier you are outdated, and the fast pace of modern soldiering will inevitably overtake you at some point,' says WO2 Mike Christian, a company sergeant major in the Royal Military Police. 'The decision-making process and motivations of the next generation of troops will seem like a moral struggle with your own honesty and standards.' As he suggests, the art of leadership in this context is to strike a balance between adapting to changing mores and holding true to enduring lessons of good training and coaching. 'Your job is to navigate that minefield and ensure you maintain operational effectiveness without thinking that the only way is your way.'[16]

A focus on developing individuals must also entail a willingness to handle individualists. Every profession has its conformists and mavericks, with the latter group playing an important role in challenging consensus and providing new ideas. Just as sports teams have their star players, military units will often have individuals most capable of original thought and least willing to work within the boundaries of accepted wisdom. The leadership challenge is to give such individuals the space they need to explore and pursue their ideas, without letting them work in a way that could destabilise the team.

Sir Alex Ferguson, the Manchester United manager famed for his ability to handle volatile talents, was clear that even the most brilliant individual must still serve the needs of the team.

There are occasions when you have to ask yourself whether certain players are affecting the dressing-room atmosphere, the performance of the team, and your control of the players and staff. If they are, you have to cut the cord. There is absolutely no other way. It doesn't matter if the person is the best player in the world. The long-term view of the club is more important than any individual.[17]

Army leaders may not have the same freedom to hire and fire, but the principle of needing to rein in individuals who wish to become bigger than the team holds true. Problems arise when the balance between team and individual becomes skewed in the latter's favour.

As they manage this balance, the Adair model continues to provide a guide. Without ever putting team cohesion at risk, they should embrace individual thinkers of all ranks, letting those with distinctive ideas and experiences make their most effective contribution to the task at hand. This is one of the great challenges of leadership but also something that can deliver handsome rewards – whether in the form of highly motivated and empowered individuals, or innovative ideas that can improve performance or overcome roadblocks. As they juggle their three main priorities, what leaders do is to ensure that the task at hand benefits from the strength of the team and the power of the individual in equal measure.

The Army's Leadership Framework, the combination of what leaders are, what they know and what they do, is one shared across all ranks and roles. A corporal is as much a mentor to soldiers, an exemplar of the Values and Standards, and a builder of teams as a commanding officer. But the two leaders will approach these tasks differently. They have varying types of experience, operating contexts and sources of power. The power of Army leadership lies not just in its fundamental tenets, but the contrasting and complementary ways they are put into action by soldiers and officers of all different ages, ranks and levels of experience. The following chapters will explore this further, illustrating how leadership is done by officers and soldiers respectively, demonstrating both how the two approaches differ and why the combination is so potent.

7. Officer Leadership

On the first Sunday of every Regular Commissioning Course, over 200 officer cadets arrive at Sandhurst and walk up the imposing marble steps of Old College, in the footsteps of generations that have gone before them. They enter carrying their folded-up ironing boards, and will not walk the same steps again until they pass out as commissioned officers, in dress uniform at the Sovereign's Parade. Dating to 1812, Old College is a symbol of the history, traditions and expectations that come with being a British Army officer. 'Passing through the Camberley gate to see beyond the lake and the drooping oaks and willows was like stepping into history,' wrote a Rhodesian officer cadet who attended Sandhurst in 1957. 'The simple off-white majesty of the Old College building, aproned by the crisp gravel parade ground, the sheer beauty and historic significance of the place carried its own momentum towards excellence.' As he reflected, this evocative atmosphere provided its own inspiration. 'It was at once enervating and humbling. This was going to take all I had; and I was going to give it.'[1]

The eleven months that pass between cadets arriving through the doors of Old College and being commissioned in front of it are the induction into what it means to be an officer: the knowledge, standards and behaviour that are required of men and women who accept the sovereign's commission and commit to upholding a centuries-long tradition of British Army leadership. Uniting all elements of this training is the idea of servant leadership. 'I think service is about giving,' General Sir Patrick Sanders, Commander United Kingdom Strategic Command, said at the Sovereign's Parade in December 2020:

> Your colour sergeants and the staff here have spent the last forty-four weeks serving you. They've given their all. It may not have felt like they were serving you, but they put every waking moment into

developing, nurturing and challenging you. They've engendered feelings of love, loyalty and respect in you. That's the role you must now occupy for your new charges.

As he suggested, this willingness to give to people, to know them as individuals, foster their development and serve their needs, defines an officer's ability to lead soldiers:

> You'll earn their loyalty and respect based on how much you give, and how you serve them. Your new pips, and your university degree, and your Sandhurst training, mean little to them. They won't care how much you know, until they know how much you care.

Servant leadership is intrinsic but not unique to the officer's role. Like many aspects of Army leadership, it is a universal requirement for all serving. Equally, officers retain a distinctive role and purpose, one that arises from the commission they hold and the command authority it conveys on them. As the leaders with legal authority to direct soldiers and order the application of violence, they must both exercise the rights and meet the obligations of command. From this flows the responsibility and accountability that define officer leadership at every rank and career level. Officers will rely on their NCOs for much day-to-day management and leadership, but they remain responsible for the outcomes regardless of their involvement in the process. When kit and equipment fails or goes missing, it is the officer who must account for it. When performance flags or standards are eroded, it is the officer who must recognise and correct it. When a soldier experiences crisis in their personal life, it is their officer who must support and help them. And in the most serious situation of all, when a life has been lost, it is the officer who will write to the bereaved family, sit with them at the inquest, and account for the circumstances that led to the death of a soldier under their command.

As they progress up the rank structure, both the nature of an officer's responsibilities and their perception of them will evolve. A young second lieutenant, who has been trained in leadership and drilled in the basics of command, may not actually meet a private soldier until they join their regiment. Few, in their early twenties and with limited life experience, appreciate the full breadth of their role – ensuring the welfare of soldiers under their command as much as overseeing their professional activity – until they have been immersed in it. Into the middle command ranks, as they begin to make decisions affecting the lives of their entire sub-unit or battalion, officers must grapple with the weight of responsibility that comes with commanding hundreds of men and women engaged in the profession of arms, with all the associated duties and risks. While at the organisational and strategic level, senior officers must take decisions that will have a significant bearing on the overall direction of the Army, the careers of those serving in it, and the defence of the nation.

Officers must adapt to their responsibilities as these grow with rank, and find new ways to uphold them. While roles, responsibilities and leadership requirements evolve with seniority, some of the essential tenets remain constant. Officers will be tested with every step up in rank, but they will also lean on their experience from their most junior command roles: the ability to build relationships of mutual trust and respect, the knowledge of when to delegate and when to intervene, the skill to balance the needs of superiors and subordinates, and the recognition that the right to lead must be earned and can never be taken for granted. The responsibility to be a servant leader is also a constant, linking the platoon commander who supports a soldier facing personal difficulties with the four-star general who advocates for the needs of all soldiers at the strategic and political level. This chapter will outline how these capabilities and responsibilities evolve across the key stages of an officer's career, illustrating the leadership challenges they will encounter and the skills they must develop as they progress from selection and initial training to command of a small unit and into progressively senior leadership roles.

Officer selection and training

'You will be called on later to be the brain of an army. So I say to you today: Learn to think.'[2] With these words, Colonel (later Marshal) Ferdinand Foch would begin his lectures to officers at the *École*

Supérieure de Guerre, the French Army's staff college, where he served
as an instructor two decades before he made his reputation as Supreme
Allied Commander in the closing months of the First World War. It
is a timeless message, an unspoken version of which greets every officer cadet arriving at Sandhurst. Above the steps of Old College,
adorning the portico, are the statues of Mars and Minerva, the
Roman deities of war and wisdom. These symbolise the twin purpose of the training that is provided to every officer who enters the
British Army. At Sandhurst they will be taught how to be a soldier,
learning the business of warfighting and the mechanics of command.
In parallel, they will learn what it means to lead, and what a leader
must be, know and do to succeed.

The officers who climb the steps of Old College at the beginning
of every commissioning course will occupy leadership positions in
the Army for years and decades to come. The Army requires of the
same individuals that they develop throughout their careers to excel
equally in command of a platoon of thirty soldiers, as a staff officer,
an indirect leader in command of larger teams, and eventually an
organisational and strategic leader across the Army as a whole. Moving into a new post approximately every two years, they will be
put into contrasting roles that require them to evolve their leadership style as the context changes and, with it, the nature of the
challenge.

This need for versatility puts a premium on the Army's ability to
select individuals with the potential to grow as leaders throughout
their careers, to learn both from the formal training provided and
from experience, and to embody Foch's ideal of an officer who can
bring conceptual and intellectual rigour to their work. When the
Army selects an officer cadet in their early twenties, it is also selecting
its future company commanders and commanding officers, the next
generation of staff leaders, and ultimately those who will occupy its
most senior ranks. For an organisation so dependent on the strength
of its leadership, selection is a process whose influence is both long-
lasting and wide-reaching. Unlike a business that can recruit on the
open market to fill positions and meet needs at all levels, the Army is
largely reliant on those it has developed from the beginning of their

careers, whom it must nurture to fulfil a wide variety of roles throughout their career.

The mechanism for getting this right is the Army Officer Selection Board (AOSB), a two-stage preliminary assessment (Briefing and Main Board) which candidates must pass before being invited to attend the Regular Commissioning Course at RMA Sandhurst. The AOSB is designed to provide a stringent assessment of leadership potential, from the nature of the tests that are undertaken, to the small groups that allow each individual to be closely monitored, and the seniority and experience of those observing and assessing them. During the four days of Main Board, candidates are tested in a variety of classroom and field exercises, spanning planning, command, fitness, current affairs knowledge and presentation.

Command tasks, which require candidates to solve problems such as how to move a 'burden' (heavy object) between two points without it touching the ground, are done variously with designated leaders, and as 'leaderless' exercises that test how individuals work as part of a team, and their willingness to step forward and lead without authority. The command tasks test each candidate both individually and in the context of the group, allowing assessors to understand key elements of leadership potential including the ability to work as part of a team, make decisions under pressure, take appropriate risks, exercise a positive influence on others and demonstrate the humility to follow. The combination of psychometric assessment and observed behaviour in command tasks is designed to tease out those with the greatest suitability for Army leadership. A study of the officer selection process in the 1970s found:

> Successful candidates were more likely to stress 'responsibility for others' while unsuccessful candidates tended to emphasise 'the chance to develop your [own] ability [. . .] The difference in emphasis indicates a greater concern among unsuccessful candidates over what the Army will do for them, rather than what they have to offer the Army.[3]

Candidates are finally judged against four criteria: their personality and practical, physical and intellectual abilities. AOSB is designed to be a stringent process, which some candidates will need to go through more than once to pass. Its robustness and value can be seen in how its pass rate of between 58 and 66 per cent yields a much higher success rate from Sandhurst, which ran at an average of 93 per cent between 2013 and 2016.

Those who arrive at Sandhurst as officer cadets will attend one of the world's most reputed leadership academies, at which multiple heads of state and heads of government have trained, in addition to generations of British Army leaders and, since 1947, over 5,000 future officers from 131 different countries. Sandhurst is where the Army's past and future intersect. The officers of tomorrow learn in buildings many of which date to the nineteenth century, organised into companies that carry the name of past campaigns, studying a curriculum which has a significant military history component. But if much of the environment is historic, the content of the course is forward-looking, incorporating the latest academic expertise in defence and international affairs, communication and behavioural science, and war studies. This combination of past, present and future seeks to impress upon cadets the enduring and historic nature of the profession they are joining, at the same time as equipping them with the broad skillset and knowledge base required of a twenty-first-century leader.

For these cadets, Sandhurst provides a progressive immersion in the fundamentals of soldiering, command and leadership, across three terms in which the complexity of exercises undertaken, the levels of individual responsibility, and standards of expected fitness and performance continue to grow. Whereas in Junior Term the emphasis is primarily on the basics of soldiering skills and military life, through Intermediate and Senior Terms, officer cadets are increasingly exposed to exercises that simulate real operational conditions and test their ability to work as part of a team, develop and implement plans in response to fast-moving situations, and lead and inspire those around them. The course provides a consistent balance between classroom education in the skills and behaviours that are required, and training in the field which tests under pressure whether cadets are capable of implementing what they have been taught. 'The blended learning approach Sandhurst favours means students can have military tactics training followed by two hours of academic education, followed by another two hours of physical training,' Dr An Jacobs, formerly a senior lecturer in Sandhurst's academic faculty, has described. 'The days are long and the programme is famous for being extremely intense.'[4]

Training exercises are designed to put cadets in physically and psychologically stressful situations that will test their abilities, reinforce key lessons, and give individuals insight into their own character, leadership style and areas for improvement. In Junior Term, Exercise LONG REACH, a 70 km navigation through the Black Mountains in Wales, provides a deliberately demanding test not just of navigation, command skills and personal endurance, but the ability to work as part of a team and to lead through adversity. During the exercise's 36-hour duration, cadets must pass through designated checkpoints where they will be tested with command tasks, probing their problem solving and teamwork under the duress of fatigue and often extreme weather conditions. LONG REACH is designed to push cadets to the limit of their personal endurance, showing them what it means to be reliant on those around them and the strength of the team. 'There was one point at which, after falling into water up to neck height [. . .] my life was very much in the hands of my fellow [cadets],' one recent cadet reflected.[5] The exposure to physical exhaustion, personal danger and the pressures of time and inhospitable conditions are designed to crystallise one of the most important lessons of Army leadership: that, however personally challenging a situation, their primary responsibility is always to those around them, to inspire and support them as well as ensuring their welfare. They must be a servant leader in all circumstances, especially the most challenging ones.

The forty-four weeks of the commissioning course (for Reserves, an eight-week course that is broken into some modules completed at weekends, and others undertaken in two-week courses at Sandhurst) mark only the beginning of a young officer's development. Equally, by the end of the course it is expected that newly commissioned second lieutenants have grown as individual leaders through their experiences, developed a deeper understanding of leadership and what the Army expects of them as an officer, and gained both

self-confidence and valuable insight into their personality and character. As Major General (Retd) Paul Nanson, Commandant of Sandhurst from 2015 to 2020, has summarised:

> During forty-four testing weeks, we identify and unlock the poten-
> tial of our officer cadets while breaking the invisible limits cadets have
> previously imposed upon themselves, building upon the raw materi-
> als of their character, heart and integrity by fostering self-discipline
> and emotional awareness, and soldiering and leadership skills.[6]

Newly commissioned officers will soon discover how well, or not,
this experience has prepared them for their first taste of command.

Sub-unit leadership

After receiving their commission and completing the specialist training for the Arm they are joining, a young officer's first command post
will be with a platoon or troop of approximately thirty soldiers, one
of three within their sub-unit. They are stepping into a role for
which they have trained throughout the previous year, and which
many have aspired to and worked towards for much longer. All will
have hopes, fears and expectations about taking up their first command post, which may jar with their initial experiences. Edwin
Campion Vaughan was a junior officer with the Royal Warwickshire
Regiment during the First World War. Commissioned during the
summer of 1916, he sailed to France the following January. He
recorded in his diary the day he travelled to join his unit at the front.

> As I drove down in the rattling, boneshaking old taxi, I tried hard to
> convince myself that the moment I had lived for had arrived and that
> I was now a real Service man. But this was difficult: there was no band
> playing, no regiment bearing the old colours into the fray, only little
> old *me*, sitting behind an unwashed, unshaven driver, finding my way
> alone because I had been told to.[7]

It is as a platoon commander that officers are first exposed to the
realities of their role: managing soldiers, leading through their NCOs,

and meeting the needs of those both above and below them. A platoon commander acquires responsibilities in inverse proportion to their experience. At the outset, they may be the least knowledgeable and capable soldier in a group they have been tasked to lead and set the example for. They have the legitimate power of rank, but must work to earn everything needed to support it: the trust, confidence and respect of soldiers, all of whom know more about their job and what it entails than their newly arrived commander. Junior officers constantly discover requirements for which their training has not prepared them, from the pastoral duties and human side of a role that entails supporting people in all aspects of their life, to the decisions surrounding risk and safety that only a commander can make. At this formative stage of their Army career, a junior officer is having to learn on multiple fronts: not just how to lead soldiers, but how to be a soldier and fulfil the technical requirements of their role.

The Army's approach of giving command authority to newly trained officers over often highly experienced soldiers may appear idiosyncratic, but is rooted in long experience about how the contrasting leadership roles and styles of officers and NCOs can combine to good effect. Whereas soldier leaders gain power through their proximity to those they lead, both as an everyday presence and in terms of the rank they hold, officers benefit from being one step removed, focused upwards on the context and overall intent as much as on what is happening within their team. When appropriately balanced, these contrasting perspectives help to ensure that the leadership of every team in the Army becomes neither insular nor detached from its wider role and ultimate purpose. Good decisions generally emerge when an officer, focused on the context and task at hand, works closely with an NCO who relays ground truth and acts as an advocate for the needs of the soldiers. Throughout its history, the Army has operated on the principle that leadership of a team and leadership of the individuals in it are jobs that, while often overlapping, are distinct and deserving of leaders with a dedicated focus. This model of officers and NCOs as parallel leadership categories is one that is widely used by Armed Forces around the world.

This structure puts a premium on the relationship between officers and NCOs – one which, with experience, becomes a strong working partnership, but begins as one of direct mentorship between a platoon sergeant and their newly arrived platoon commander. As they navigate both practical and psychological challenges, a good junior officer will recognise the extent of their inexperience and their dependence on the platoon's soldiers, especially its NCOs. Lieutenant Bill Bellamy, a twenty-year-old officer taking command of his first combat troop in 1944, recalled that he was quickly put at ease by his troop sergeant, Bill Pritchard. 'It was he who told me that I came to the troop with a good reputation and that, provided I didn't try to be too brave but used my head, then he had no doubt that I would make a good troop leader.'[8]

Officers may be in command, but they rely heavily on their soldiers and must work to build relationships of mutual respect with them, overcoming barriers of age, background and experience. Successful junior officers will be close to their soldiers: knowing their skills, understanding their problems, and committed to helping them develop as both professionals and people. As Sydney Jary quoted one of his corporals from 18 Platoon, Doug Proctor, about what NCOs expect from young officers:

> During my six years army service I knew many Officers – some good, some bad. The most obvious difference between them was not in their tactical awareness as one might expect, but in the relationships they had with their soldiers. No matter how tactically aware an Officer may be, it counts for little unless he can command the trust, loyalty and respect of his men and is able to inspire them.[9]

Platoon commanders will fall back on these relationships when their inexperience inevitably leads them to make mistakes under pressure. Charlie Antelme, who as a Lieutenant Colonel commanded a Welsh Guards battalion in Afghanistan in 2009, recalled one such incident from his days as a junior officer in Northern Ireland. In the immediate pursuit of an IRA sniper who had just shot a police officer, he was proceeding with caution, conscious that a direct route carried the risk of leading his platoon into a secondary ambush. In the dark, surrounded by the thick undergrowth of a river valley, he lost his route to the designated cut-off position.

'Stuck in the middle of the riverbed, getting shouted at down the net [radio], my map was upside down and I was flapping.' He responded by delegating to his section commander, a corporal who calmly stepped in to take over the map reading and lead the patrol to their destination. 'As a platoon we had trained together very hard, we had laughed together, we knew each other, we liked each other. So when I was dropping the ball, help came without judgement.'[10] Whether being helped out of difficult situations, or purposefully deferring to the greater experience of an NCO or soldier in their platoon, junior officers quickly learn the importance of followership. Used deliberately, this is a powerful tool of command and leadership. Letting subordinates with greater experience or situational awareness lead can be one of the most effective ways not just to solve an immediate problem, but for a young officer to inspire confidence in their leadership. It acknowledges that no leader has a monopoly on wisdom or good ideas, it spreads trust through their platoon, and it demonstrates that an officer will not let their ego get in the way of what is best for their team.

As junior officers learn the importance of followership and forging strong bonds with their soldiers, they must also recognise that mutual respect depends on how they exercise their authority. Soldiers are looking for effective and robust leadership, but will also find ways to test whether their green, fresh-faced commander is capable of providing it. They will push boundaries around standards and discipline to see how an officer reacts: a dress code slip here or a verbal challenge there. Edwin Campion Vaughan described his first encounter with senior NCOs on the Western Front:

> Both saluted, and having eyed me up and down, and taken thorough stock of me, proceeded to smoke and lounge about whilst I questioned them. My sense of discipline received a severe shock but I hesitated to choke them off, as they appeared to be behaving in a manner usual to them.[11]

It is as a platoon commander that an officer starts to learn the balance between being close with soldiers and maintaining a professional distance; treating people as friends without losing the ability to exercise authority over them and use discipline when necessary. Being too close to your people, to the point where they no longer respect you as their commander, can be as much a problem as maintaining too great a distance and showing insufficient empathy or care. In parallel, like anyone moving into the first management and leadership job of their career, a platoon commander must discover the balance of when to get involved in the business of their team and when to let people work out the solution for themselves. For many, in the military as in business, this is an instinct that can only be learned through experience. In the 1990s, the Harvard Business School Professor Linda Hill conducted a study of sales representatives stepping into their first management role, following them over twelve months as they adjusted to new responsibilities and a different mindset. As one of her subjects reflected:

> In the first four or five months on the job [. . .] I was intent on gaining credibility with the [sales] reps, having them like me and gaining their trust. When they came in with a problem, I'd grab it and run with it. Now that I have more experience, when they come in with a problem, I sit back and ask them questions and let them find the answers.[12]

After two years in their first command role, an officer will undertake a succession of staff jobs – at either the battalion, brigade or divisional level, or as an instructor at a training centre. In these posts, officers engage properly for the first time with the administrative machinery of personnel, training and operations. Junior officers who have been cocooned in their troop or platoon gain exposure to the wider context of their battalion or brigade, encountering issues from the perspective of a larger formation. They will experience different styles of leadership and observe how officers in much higher ranks operate. As young staff officers, some will find themselves as the resident subject matter expert, required to brief the most senior figures in and around the Army. Major General Charlie Collins, who served as Assistant Chief of Staff at the Permanent Joint Headquarters, recalled one such instance:

[. . .] the person who is my subject matter expert on Ukraine is in fact [a junior] Major. So when Commander Joint Operations or the Secretary of State for Defence wants a brief on Ukraine it is that individual who goes to brief them. And I may or may not go and sit in.[13]

That was my experience of staff work, as a major charged with developing the training programme for the 19,000 Armed Forces personnel who provided venue security at the London 2012 Olympics. With the support of my Director, Brigadier (now Lieutenant General Sir) Ben Bathhurst, I routinely planned and liaised across Government, and briefed superiors up to four-star command, including General Sir Nick Parker, Standing Joint Commander and Commander of Defence's support to the Olympics.

Few officers may have joined the Army with the ambition of doing staff work, but it provides a grounding in the mechanics of the institution that is essential to ensuring they can succeed in higher tactical command roles. Staff roles also put a premium on the ability to absorb, analyse and concisely convey information: skills that will be increasingly important for officers in higher command posts, where they are more exposed to the broad context of a situation and must hone the ability to communicate its salient facts and needs to all concerned.

By the time an officer has reached the next rung of tactical leadership, as a major who is officer commanding (OC) of their sub-unit, they will have a much greater awareness of the context they are operating in, an improved network within their regiment or higher formations, and greater perspective on different leadership approaches and behaviour. This will be between eight and ten years after their commission, having been through multiple staff jobs and often a second posting as a platoon or troop commander, or a company second-in-command. They will also have attended the Intermediate Command and Staff Course (Land) (ICSC(L)), a six-month residential programme covering areas from the skills needed for staff work, to emerging trends in defence policy and warfighting.[14] The benefit of ICSC(L) is partly the opportunity to develop relevant skills and knowledge with expert support, but equally the time and space for an officer to reflect on what they have learned about leadership, and themselves as a leader, from their initial experiences of command. For many, it is the first time they will reflect seriously on their personal approach to leadership, something the course encourages and an important preparation for the more complex roles that lie ahead.

An OC, commanding a squadron or company of up to 120 soldiers, gains their first command position with a material degree of day-to-day independence. Although they have the unit CO above, their focus on the higher-level context and wide range of duties means the OC has a considerable level of freedom and responsibility over their sub-unit. 'As an OC I genuinely feel empowered to run D Company as I deem appropriate, train how I wish within the resources available to meet my CO's intent and the specified tasks set,' Major Al Phillips, a company commander in 4th Battalion The Royal Regiment of Scotland, summarised.[15] This level of empowerment can be daunting, but an OC is still highly focused – retaining the luxury of being able to largely focus downwards, a direct leader who can routinely reach to the soldier level, as well as leading through junior officers and NCOs. A company or squadron commander is both the beneficiary of the Mission Command philosophy – given the independence granted to them – and an officer who must learn how to exercise it effectively through their own downward chain of command.

'The tendency for sub-unit commanders has always been to over-control their people. It is a mistake,' says Major General (Retd) Patrick Marriott, who commanded the Queen's Royal Lancers and the 7th Armoured Brigade and was Commandant of RMA Sandhurst from 2009 to 2012. In the latter role, he would always ask cadets shortlisted for the Sword of Honour accolade four questions, including: 'What have you learnt of leadership?' He recalls that the best answer he ever received was: 'To sacrifice control in order to command.'[16] This represents the ideal command climate, a sub-unit in which every officer and NCO is empowered to deliver the commander's intent, trusted to use their initiative and encouraged to bring forward problems they cannot resolve independently. Junior officers and NCOs may thrive on responsibility, but they cannot grant it to themselves. An OC learns that, while trust needs to flow both ways in a successful organisation, it is the leader's responsibility to take the first step and create the necessary conditions.

With more people under their command, and greater scrutiny on their performance, an OC must recognise the importance of their role in management and administration. The business of managing equipment, supplies and logistics may be the least stimulating part of the job, but failures in this area will erode trust and confidence when mistakes are made. While day-to-day management is the job of NCOs, the overall outcomes are the responsibility of the commander, who must make sufficient checks to satisfy themselves that necessary standards are being maintained and crucial equipment will not be found wanting when it is needed. Successful company commanders learn that the professionalism of their management goes a long way to building confidence in their leadership. They set high standards early, engage with the detail, and show interest in the work people are doing to keep the sub-unit functioning. They recognise that a commander's reputation is not made by writing reports, conducting equipment checks and signing forms, but it can be lost if they show an unwillingness to do these things or an inability to do them to a high professional standard.

As management responsibilities become more complex, so too does the network of relationships that an OC depends upon. This begins with junior officers and NCOs, those the commander leads through, and will be working with, on a daily basis to communicate intent, discuss problems and agree priorities. An OC must recognise their responsibility to coach and develop these people in order to get the best out of them. They rely on their second-in-command (2IC), company sergeant major (CSM), platoon commanders, and NCOs to make the sub-unit run effectively, which means time invested in helping them to do their job better can be time saved from having to solve a problem in the future. This is not just a question of enlightened self-interest, but one of the privileges of command: being in a position of authority that allows them to influence people's careers and lives for the better, giving them well-chosen opportunities to learn and improve, and advice to steer the process.

The work of developing people is essential but often challenging, requiring the best both of the officer and their NCO. Captain Den Starkie, who was my RSM when I was a CO and subsequently 2IC Para Company at the Infantry Training Centre, recalled one experience as a CSM. He had arrived into post alongside a new OC, to be informed by the battalion headquarters that they needed to replace a struggling platoon commander. Their working relationship, he suggested, was forged by the joint decision to challenge that directive and instead commit to helping the junior officer turn around his career. 'We sat him down and said, "Everyone around us is saying that you need to be moved on. And that's not happening." We invested in him, and he became the best platoon commander in the company, in training and on the next tour in Afghanistan.'

An OC has the right combination of rank and experience to make a meaningful difference as a mentor for the first time. As they lead and mentor those below them, OCs must also nurture their upwards and lateral relationships: the CO to whom they report, staff officers at the battalion and brigade level who have expertise and authority they will need to tap into, fellow OCs in the battalion and individuals outside the regiment including the civil servants who play such an important role in the Army, spanning areas from policy, project management and data analysis to recruitment, training, communication and engagement.[17] In this regard, the military is no different from business in the premium it puts on the ability of leaders to network, building relationships with individuals both inside and outside the organisation, people who can provide insight, guidance and intelligence. The nature of Army careers means many of these relationships will be long-standing, offering ample opportunity for individuals to offer help as much as they seek it.

Commanding a sub-unit exposes an OC to the many balancing acts of leadership at the organisational middle: the need to focus both upwards and downwards, to empower a team without losing control of it, and to meet the needs of your superiors at the same time as leaning on their experience and authority. An OC is fully tested for the first time in what it takes to command, at a level where the degree of independence leaves no hiding place. As an OC, commanding in excess of 100 soldiers, you are fully exposed to the demands of meeting these expectations: challenged to become a leader worthy of your followers.

Unit leadership

'The commanding officer of a Battalion is the life and soul of it,' wrote Colonel (later Major General Sir) Matthew Gossett, CO of 1st Battalion the Dorsetshire Regiment for five years in the 1880s. '[He] must have his eye on everything, know everyone's wants, and never imagine, because he has established a good system, that it will keep going without a perpetual greasing of the wheels.'[18]

Taking command of a battalion is the culmination of almost twenty years of experience and development as an officer, and for many who attain the rank it will represent the final and most important command of their military career. The span of a CO's command varies across the Army but is typified in the combat Arms. As the CO of a battalion (or 'regiment' in the cavalry) an officer commands around 650 soldiers as a lieutenant colonel. They lead a unit that is fully deployable and self-sustaining, a command that can extend to over 1,000 soldiers when augmented for operations by additional combat support capabilities including artillery, engineers and logistics. A CO does not have unlimited power, and must work with the team they inherit and within the circumstances of their assignment (whether to a combat unit, a training establishment, a reserve or joint forces unit). But once in their environment, as Colonel Gossett suggested, they are the individual with complete responsibility and accountability for everything that takes place within it. Within their unit, they become the abiding point of reference, often the final judge of difficult decisions and the individual who must take ultimate responsibility for success and failure alike.

'Battalions are much like an organic family. They are held together by intangibles – leadership, comradeship, motivation, morale – that defy quantification or even easy description,' the Canadian military historians Professors Terry Copp and Bill McAndrew described in their study of battle exhaustion during the Second World War.

'Many veterans cite the character and capability of the commanding officer as vital factors in shaping a battalion's collective character.'[19]

To occupy their role effectively, a CO must put into practice all their prior leadership knowledge and experience. They must adapt to a role in which the balance has begun to shift from direct to indirect leadership, and develop a keen appreciation of the power that accompanies their rank: both the authority it conveys to make a positive difference, but also the unintended consequences that can flow from exercising it without due caution. A CO must recognise that, the more responsibilities a leader has amassed, the more carefully the levers at their disposal must be operated. The tightrope of leadership that they began to walk as an OC is now placed much higher, the consequences of errors magnified as authority is elevated. COs must be more discriminating in their exercise of direct leadership, more rigorous in their upholding of standards, and more conscious of the need to shape an effective climate within their unit. The art of leadership – using power with discretion, balancing competing priorities and judging what each situation requires – becomes one of the most pressing considerations.

The ultimate figurehead of their unit, a CO has unmatched power to influence that environment for better or worse. While soldiers will more often take their lead from the platoon or company commander, and some may hardly encounter the CO or even know their name, leaders at this level still have the ability to inspire and encourage. Sergeant Jake Wardrop, who served with the 5th Royal Tank Regiment during the Second World War, recorded in his diary his admiration for a newly arrived CO, Lieutenant Colonel Jim Hutton.

> He was always well up in his tank giving orders on the wireless in a nice pleasant voice, just like the announcer reading the news. The lads would have done anything for him and gone anywhere with him – if he had said we were going to make a frontal attack on the gates of hell, they would have been off like a shot.[20]

The influence of a CO does not have to be benevolent to be appreciated. As Lieutenant Siegfried Sassoon, the war poet, wrote of his CO in the First World War: 'He was the personification of military efficiency. Personal charm was not his strong point, and he made no pretension to it. He was aggressive and blatant, but he knew his job, and for that we respected him and were grateful.'[21]

A CO needs to be aware of the visibility and effect of their actions, and the same is true of their words. While written orders and direct-ives will be carefully listened to and carried out as a matter of course, casual statements can be just as influential. The CO must never forget that they sit at the apex of an organisation of hundreds of people committed to putting their intent into action. In this context, off-the-cuff comments can assume a seriousness far beyond their intention. A passing comment from a CO in the morning can lead to the whole afternoon being spent rewriting a plan, redesigning an exercise or reorganising a mess room, far beyond the scope of the original observation.

By the same token, a CO can use their power deliberately, to make a difference for their people and solve problems in minutes that might otherwise take days or weeks. If a CO hears that someone is in finan-cial difficulties, or cannot obtain appropriate accommodation for their family, they can escalate the issue in a way that will prompt swift action. The impact of such interventions can extend well beyond the person whose problem has been solved. As word spreads, the whole battalion will quickly learn that it has a CO who cares about their people and will intervene on their behalf: a head of the family who will protect all its members. Small actions like this can have an outsize effect in boosting morale and consolidating trust in the CO's leadership. It is another example of the power the CO holds, and the need to be both proactive and discerning in how they exercise it.

Equally, a CO cannot immerse themselves in the lives of 650 people day-to-day, nor should they become excessively involved in matters that are primarily the responsibility of others. Like all leaders they must achieve a balance, managing the unit as a whole without ever losing touch with the individuals in it. This demands the ability to switch between perspectives, being as comfortable with the wider operational context as they are grounded in the reality their people are experiencing. An effective CO should never lose touch with this

ground truth and must find ways to build their own understanding
of it, not simply taking as gospel what they are told by those directly
reporting to them. In this the regimental system, and the career-long
relationships it facilitates, can become a huge asset. A CO will likely
have NCOs in their unit who knew them as a young officer, with
whom they have served and potentially fought alongside. These are
invariably the individuals who can be trusted to communicate honest
ground truth, the strength of an existing relationship lowering the
implicit barriers of the chain of command.

COs also benefit from taking the temperature of those furthest
from them in rank, talking to the soldiers and young lance corporals
who will ultimately be responsible for implementing their orders on
the ground. Here, the distance between ranks can facilitate honesty:
a young private or JNCO has little to lose in sharing their thoughts
with the CO, compared to an OC who knows they are responsible
for everything they report to their commanding officer. Lieutenant
Colonel Graham Seton Hutchinson, a CO with the Machine Gun
Corps during the First World War, made a habit of facilitating conversations with private soldiers under his command. 'I tested them – a
walk here, ten minutes and a cigarette there; the lad by himself, not
in the artificiality of the presence of a corporal, or their comrades.'
As he reflected, such encounters were of mutual benefit. 'I heeded
them to do my will: I needed them to do my will.'[22]

As well as reaching down into their battalion to understand the
ground truth, a CO needs to identify the individuals they can lean
on as their trusted advisers, mentors and supporters. In a two-and-a-
half-year posting that makes relentless demands on the occupant's
time, attention and stamina, every CO needs people they can turn to
when they face difficult decisions or would benefit from a sympa-
thetic ear. Unit leadership is a role that can often feel isolating. A CO
becomes acutely aware that, as the only leader of their rank in the
battalion, they no longer have an immediate peer group with whom
to compare notes and let off steam. They have hundreds of people
addressing them by rank, and none by name. In this context, they
have to work harder to build a support network, from senior staff
officers at the regimental or brigade level who have been in their

shoes; to independent actors such as the battalion's padre who, from a position of neutrality, brings a different perspective; and late-entry officers who, having served in every NCO role, will be among the most experienced soldiers in the unit and have seen numerous COs come and go. The RSM, the unit's senior soldier, will also serve as an essential partner: disabusing a CO of their worst notions and helping them drive their agenda.

Like the leader of any organisation, a CO needs to identify the people who will tell them the truth, help them separate the good ideas from the bad, and improve their thinking about the most pressing issues they face. They need critical friends who are supportive but also willing to debate and challenge. Most importantly, they depend on the emotional support of family and loved ones, who so often make the sacrifices necessary for that individual to fulfil the practical and emotional commitment of an all-encompassing leadership role.

A robust support network is essential at a rank where the responsibilities weigh heavily. CO is the first stage at which an officer has the power – and duty – to make life-changing decisions around discipline. A CO has the authority to reduce someone's rank, move a soldier out of their unit, or set the conditions to dismiss them from the Army altogether. These are decisions that will affect someone's entire life – their income, where their family lives and their children go to school. It falls to the CO to make the judgement of when a serious disciplinary threshold has been crossed, shoulder alone the responsibility of upending someone's life, and have the painful conversation to tell someone that they will no longer hold a rank they worked for years to achieve, or have a place in the regiment they consider home. This duty underlines the extent to which a CO must often lead alone, reaching decisions which only they have the power to make, and for which they will be held solely responsible.

The role represents the pinnacle of direct, tactical leadership in the Army – with all the demands that places on a leader to set a consistent example, strike the right balance between being visible and letting subordinates lead, and to take full responsibility for everything that happens under their command. For many, this is the final role they will occupy in their career as an Army officer. Those who are promoted further attain not just a new rank, but enter a new realm of leadership, at the organisational and strategic levels.

Organisational and strategic leadership[23]

Of all the changes that affect officers promoted beyond lieutenant colonel rank, the most immediate is in their dress. The regimental uniform – with its immediately identifying features of distinctively coloured caps, 'flashes' worn on the upper arms bearing the colours or symbol, and rank slides carrying its name, all worn as a symbol of pride and ethos – is replaced by one that denotes members of the General Staff, the Army's professional body of senior leaders and staff officers. Indeed, General Staff regulations specifically prohibit its members from wearing any item of clothing that highlights their regimental allegiance.[24]

   This symbolic change signifies a structural one in the life and career of an Army officer. Not only has their rank and role changed but, as the new uniform indicates, so must their focus and priorities. In the words of the General Staff handbook: 'officers of the rank of full Colonel and above are ambassadors for and servants of our Army. We serve it as a whole rather than our former Regiments and Corps.' By joining the General Staff, officers move out of the tactical sphere and into new levels of the Army which bring their own leadership requirements.

   As the academics Owen Jacobs and Elliott Jaques outlined, there are three essential layers of leadership in a complex organisation such as an Army: strategic leaders create and apply policy; organisational leaders implement that policy; and tactical leaders translate it to their assigned mission.[25] Organisational leaders manage the Army's largest component parts, from brigades and divisions that span several thousand soldiers, to directorates for key functional areas. While the handful of strategic leaders at the apex of the rank structure set the direction for the entire Army, determine how its current activities should be evaluated, and above all focus on future needs.

Moving to the organisational level can be a disorienting experience, as officers adapt to a role in which much more than their uniform has changed. During the First World War, Lieutenant Colonel Andrew Thorne, CO of the 3rd Grenadier Guards, was promoted to command of 184 Brigade at the strikingly young age of thirty-three. As he admitted in a letter to his wife, the promotion quickly left him pining for his former command. Of the members of 184 Brigade, he wrote of wanting 'to command them as a Battalion Commander instead of as a Brigadier-General. One cannot get at them except through their COs and I feel I could run their show so much better than they could!'[26]

Organisational leaders have responsibility for much larger areas than before – whether in command of a division or brigade, or helping to manage an area of policy that will affect most people in the Army – but their immediate team will be relatively small. Even more than before, they have become indirect leaders who must work through others to exercise influence, enhancing their need to communicate effectively across multiple levels of the organisation, embrace Mission Command to devolve decisions to those with greater knowledge, and juggle the needs and agendas of many different stakeholders both inside and outside the Army. While the observation of the Australian Major General Sir John Gellibrand that 'the Brigadier [in the First World War] had little scope beyond oiling the works and using his eyes' may be an exaggeration,[27] it helps to illustrate the nature of a role in which higher authority entails greater distance from the action, something that only becomes more apparent with further promotions.

In these roles, the job description has changed and with it the style of leadership that is required. The adjustment to a new level of leadership can be challenging. As well as completing the professional education that is provided, with courses that give officers the opportunity to study command, leadership, defence policy and strategic studies at a level pertinent to the work of General Staff officers, leaders must make use of their combined experience and personal network. They will need to lean on mentors, seek advice and reflect on the leaders they have known in these roles, both good and bad. The ability to tap into a career's worth of contacts and experiences will be vital as a leader moves into not just a new role, but an entirely new level of leadership.

The same is true at the highest level of the Army's rank structure, occupied by its strategic leaders. These are the three- and four-star general officers who command its largest formations or have executive-level responsibility for the departments with resources and influence to steer the direction of the entire Army. Strategic leaders have the ultimate stewardship role, looking to the future to set a vision, determine a long-term direction and secure political agreement for their intent. They set the Army's course for both today and tomorrow, a task summarised by General Alan Brooke, one of the British Army's most successful and admired strategic leaders, as 'prevision, preplanning and provision'.[28] Focused as much on the future as the present, the Army's strategic leaders must also look to the Army's place in society, how it is perceived and how it can defend the nation in ways that will continue to command public support and trust.

They must fulfil what the management scholar Peter Drucker defined as the essential role of the CEO: to be 'the link between the Inside, i.e. "the organisation", and the Outside – society, the economy, technology, markets, customers, the media, public opinion.' To perform that bridging function, he argued, a CEO had to achieve two things: first 'to define the meaningful Outside'; and then to gather and present the most relevant information about it to the Inside, galvanising an effective response. 'The definition of the institution's meaningful Outside, and of the information it needs,' he wrote, 'makes it possible to answer the key questions: "What is our business? What should it be? What should it not be?" '[29] Only at the strategic level do leaders have a primary focus that is beyond the organisation, looking primarily towards the trends and threats that will affect it in the future, and working frequently alongside partners spanning Government, UK Armed Forces, industry and international allies.

Strategic roles sharpen the leadership challenges experienced at the organisational level. These leaders have the greatest influence, deal with the greatest complexity, and make decisions that affect the most people, often every single serving soldier. They must navigate the widest range of leadership roles and contexts, from advocating for the needs of the Army in the political sphere to representing it in the public eye and continuing to be a visible leadership presence and example to their own people. '[One] day you are in London in a suit arguing policy, the next day you are in a combat kit and body armour in Basra or Sangin talking to a soldier who has just lost a mate in a firefight or killed his first insurgent,' General The Lord Dannatt reflected of his tenure as CGS.[30] Fulfilling this blend of roles demands leadership development that comes from a combination of new skills acquired and old ones adapted. General George C. Marshall, the most senior American officer of the Second World War, recollected of his promotion to US Army Chief of Staff in 1939:

> It became clear to me that at the age of 58 I would have to learn new tricks that were not taught in the military manuals or on the battle-field. In this position I am a political soldier and will have to put my training in rapping-out orders and making snap decisions on the back burner, and have to learn the arts of persuasion and guile. I must become an expert in a whole new set of skills.[31]

At the same time, strategic leaders will continue to draw on the lessons of their early career experience. The key skills of relationship building, communication, decision making, leading through others and thinking clearly under pressure remain as relevant to the lieuten-ant general as the platoon commander – but must be applied in new ways to the much broader canvas and richer context that a senior officer is confronted with.

Leaders at this level are still learning, supported by the next stage of professional development in the form of the Army Generalship Programme. They must also consider the possibility of needing to unlearn. A paradox of any senior leadership role is that it requires a career's worth of development and experience to attain, while con-fronting its occupant with situations that will sometimes confound and contradict that experience. In the military environment, the consequences of letting past experience become an anchor can be profound, counted in lives lost on the battlefield. Field Marshal The Lord Bramall offered the example of Britain's First World War

Generals, whom he critiqued collectively as slow to adapt to both a changing society and changes in warfare. In a lecture given in 2014, he commented:

> [They] were all products of the late Victorian and Edwardian age in which honour and the defence of the Empire, without counting the cost too much, was all that mattered [. . .] Yet soon they all came to be judged by the very different standards of a very different age in which it was no longer enough to win.

Militarily he characterised them as 'obsessed with mobility', a legacy of the time many had spent as cavalry officers in the Second Anglo-Boer War. This experience, he argued, meant that they 'failed to realise, or only slowly came to the realisation, how much the impeding qualities of barbed wire, massed machine guns and heavy artillery were to demand a completely new technique for the trench warfare that developed'.[32]

The danger of experience clouding judgement and the ability to perceive change is one that can affect senior leaders in any profession. '[An] experienced specialist may be among the last to see what is really happening when events take a new and unexpected turn,' wrote Richards Heuer, the CIA veteran of forty-five years, in his book on the psychology of intelligence analysis. 'When faced with a major paradigm shift, analysts who know the most about a subject have the most to unlearn.'[33] In the same vein, Warren Buffett once cited an observer who said of investment analysts over the age of forty: 'They know too many things that are no longer true.'[34]

The significance and severity of decisions made at the strategic level place a heavy burden on these leaders. Their combination of prominence within the organisation and distance from the tactical level means they feel the full weight of responsibility for errors, problems and tragedies that occur under their watch. The accountability is personal, even when a decision was not theirs, or the event well beyond their control. As Jeff Immelt, CEO of the industrial conglomerate GE for sixteen years, commented in the aftermath of the September 11 terror attacks, which occurred at the very beginning of his tenure: 'My second day as chairman, a plane I lease, flying with engines I built, crashed into a building that I insure, and it was covered [on a television] network I own.'[35]

The combination of elevated responsibility and rank or title can make the most senior jobs in an organisation especially isolating, the so-called 'loneliness of command'. As Manfred Kets de Vries, Professor of Leadership Development at INSEAD Business School has written, 'Hierarchy creates a power distance. The weight of responsibility for others makes it harder to speak to anyone with vulnerability and true honesty.'[36]

To succeed in meeting their responsibilities to others while retaining personal equilibrium, strategic leaders need to further hone characteristics that define successful officers at all stages, from self-awareness to self-discipline, intellectual curiosity and the capacity to form working relationships at multiple levels. A senior general must be the most versatile leader in the Army, as comfortable talking to a private soldier as a prime minister, as convincing in briefing the press as they are when inspiring the troops, as willing to tackle the problems of today as they are to pre-empt those of tomorrow. For these leaders, the habits that have served them through their decades of service as an Army officer can be both blessing and curse. In a role that is most exposed to change, both in and around the Army, strategic leaders must not lose sight of the enduring need to change themselves, furthering their development as a leader even as their career reaches its culmination.

From the moment they graduate from Sandhurst and gain their commission, no two officer careers are the same. Every CO, brigade or divisional commander and general officer has arrived in their post via a different route – a unique combination of regimental context, operational experience and staff knowledge that shapes their approach to leadership. As a collective, the Army's officer leadership is grounded in shared principles and institutional Values and Standards, but it also reflects the broad variety of career paths that the Army offers to its leaders, as well as the wide range of individual personalities it recruits. No two officers will have the same experience of the Army or lead in the same way: a source of strength for an organisation that must forge a wide variety of people, traditions and specialist skillsets together in a common purpose.

While the styles of individuals diverge, and the responsibilities of various ranks differ markedly, there are also essential continuities that connect an officer's role from their first job in the Army to their last. At all stages the job is a balancing act, requiring an intuitive ability to marry expectations from above and below in the chain of command, and an instinct for when to get involved and when to step back and let others lead. The principle of Mission Command, which is as applicable to the everyday management of a unit or sub-unit as it is on the battlefield, is something that many officers will spend their entire career understanding how to deploy effectively, through errors both of intervention and inactivity. To that end, an officer's career, requiring as it does that an individual adapt to roles that are generally held for only two years, represents a continuous education in leadership – new lessons being learned and old skills adapted as an individual attains higher rank, their role changes and the expectations of them grow. Throughout, the constant challenge is to find appropriate and effective ways to uphold the responsibility of command, working within the wide variety of contexts and challenges that an officer's career will present.

8.   Soldier Leadership

'It is said that the non-commissioned officer is the backbone of the army,' Field Marshal Sir William Robertson noted in his memoir. As the only regular soldier in the history of the British Army to have risen from the lowest rank to the highest, few have been better qualified to pronounce on the role and importance of NCOs, the Army's soldier leaders. Robertson joined the 16th (Queen's) Lancers in 1877 as a private soldier, held a succession of NCO roles before accepting a commission in 1888, and ultimately served as CIGS for much of the First World War. This remarkable career equipped him with a unique perspective on the Army's many leadership roles and what it means to hold them. It was the most junior of these positions that he reflected especially fondly on. His time as an NCO and subaltern, he recalled, 'was in some ways the most fascinating and happy of all. For instance, I derived greater satisfaction from being promoted Lance-Corporal in 1878 – the first rung of the ladder – than I did from being created a Baronet forty years later.' But if the Field Marshal was nostalgic about his time as an NCO, he was also clear-eyed about the role. The NCO may be the backbone, 'but it is equally true that he can do much harm unless he is strictly impartial and identifies himself with the interests of his men'.[1]

This underlines the significance of soldier leadership and its power to influence right across the Army. The importance of soldier leaders is grounded in their weight of numbers. Of the British Army's serving regulars, little more than 15 per cent are officers.[2] The vast majority of the Army's fighting strength consists of its soldiers, which means the vast majority of its leadership is undertaken by soldiers, from young privates to experienced non-commissioned officers with decades of service. Most of a soldier's work, whether in barracks, on exercise or on operations, is led and managed by other soldiers, with officers providing direction and oversight. Day-to-day, hour-by-hour, it is NCOs who provide the visible leadership by example from which soldiers take their cue. By doing so, soldiers play an essential and distinctive role in the Army's leadership mix. The NCO rank structure, from lance corporal to warrant officer, runs in parallel with that of commissioned officers: a separate infrastructure and tradition of leadership with its own history, role models and defined stages of development. While there is a degree of movement between the two, with some WOs being commissioned as late-entry officers, these twin leadership tracks mostly exist separately, with distinct styles and intertwining, mutually reinforcing purposes.

The interplay between officer and soldier leadership is one of the Army's characteristic features and, at its best, defining strengths. Where the role of officers is to direct, make decisions and take responsibility for results, soldier leaders are primarily agents of influence and delivery. They convey the commander's intent and ensure it is achieved at the point of contact, whether to engage a hostile adversary, reorganise an equipment store or drive standards in training and PT (physical training). The division of labour between officers and soldiers is one of the cornerstones of the Army, allowing it to benefit from outstanding leaders with complementary skillsets and priorities: NCOs whose focus is 'down and in', focused relentlessly on the performance, needs and welfare of their soldiers; and officers, who must blend an understanding of ground truth with an 'up and out' perspective that takes into account the wider context of an exercise, operation or higher commander's intent.

While these outlooks will frequently combine to achieve best effect, and every leader needs to be aware of what is happening both above and below them, there is a distinctive benefit to having parallel leadership groups with complementary priorities. Done well, officers ensure that activity on the ground aligns with the wider mission and intent, and NCOs that the mission does not become divorced from the people who must ultimately deliver it. The combination is critical to effective use of the Action Centred Leadership model: officers can appreciate and communicate context and frame the task, while NCOs are invariably closer to the team and individuals who must deliver it, and the practical implications of the mission. The productive tension that can result, where ambition meets reality, is often what drives the most effective operational decisions.

While soldier leadership is an important counterpart to that of officers, it also deserves to be understood and appreciated in its own right. NCOs offer leadership in ways, and places, that officers cannot. The more experienced will have spent years or even decades in their regiment, giving them an unmatched institutional standing and credibility to convey its ethos. The rank they hold is achievable for the soldiers they lead, making them relatable and aspirational figures, whose leadership style will often provide the template for those who follow them into the NCO ranks. While their position relative to private soldiers – working, training and fighting side by side – means they epitomise leadership by direct example.

NCOs fulfil a wide variety of roles as leaders: communicating officers' intent to soldiers and ensuring it is carried out, driving standards and performance in training, upholding the traditions of the regiment, delivering the majority of discipline, providing ground truth to officers and acting as a check and balance on their decision making. Their critical leadership role in making units and regiments function has often invited comparisons with the human body: senior NCOs (who are the primary custodians of culture, standards and discipline) as the heart, and junior NCOs (who lead closest to soldiers) as the muscle. The US Army General Frederick Kroesen, whose career began during the Second World War and culminated as commander of US forces in Europe in the early 1980s, developed the analogy further. 'In my view, the NCO corps provides not only a skeleton on which to hang the body but, more important, the nerve system that allows the body to function,' he wrote in 1993.[3] Like the body's nervous system, he suggested, a unit's NCOs provide its first response to external threats, they fire critical messages across the system to where they need to be heard, and they instantly judge how to respond to a dangerous situation. Without effective NCO leadership in this mould, the links between intent and action, context and decision making, would become fatally severed.

Soldier leadership begins with those who hold no rank. Every unit will have senior private soldiers who use their experience to guide their younger peers and provide the Army's first line of leadership. Those who gain rank as non-commissioned officers can then follow a path from junior NCO (lance corporal and corporal) to senior NCO (sergeant and colour sergeant) and ultimately WO (company/squadron sergeant major and regimental sergeant major). This chapter will explore these different levels of soldier leadership in turn, highlighting the progressive roles, leadership skills and capabilities that soldiers fulfil as some of the Army's most experienced and influential leadership figures.

Junior NCOs

A soldier's existence changes the day they are promoted to lance corporal, the first leadership rank in the Army. Overnight they must adjust their outlook and raise their sights, from the obligations of an individual soldier to the duties of a team leader. As a lance corporal they become responsible for the standards, performance and welfare of a team of four soldiers, a fire team, the smallest of the many interlocking teams that make up the Army's units, brigades and divisions. They are charged with ensuring the upkeep and maintenance of equipment which may be worth many hundreds of thousands of pounds and on which lives may depend. And they are responsible for communicating intent and orders from the higher chain of command, then ensuring they are delivered at the point of contact. These are amongst the Army's most junior leaders, but tasked with some of the most acute and important aspects of direct, tactical leadership.

The significance of the lance corporal's role is reflected in the care taken over selection. Each soldier is assessed annually through the SJAR (Servicepersons' Joint Appraisal Report), which grades them in a dozen areas including leadership, adaptability and initiative, problem solving and decision making, provides a written assessment of their current performance and future potential, and suggests their suitability for promotion to both the next rank and the one above that. SJARs are the product of two reporting officers of different seniority, and represent only the first step in a private soldier's potential promotion. A positive report will lead to soldiers attending preliminary cadres at the unit and divisional level, a series of tests and exercises that will allow more assessors to judge their fitness, teamwork and resilience under pressure. Observers are on hand to judge how people respond to adversity, whether they can influence those around them, and if they instinctively work towards individual or team objectives. Both the SJAR and cadre report then go forward to a promotions board at the unit level, usually chaired by the RSM and attended by all WOs, but which in some units will include officers. Reports are marked and sorted into a top, middle and bottom third, with the best being sent forward for the JNCO training required to confirm promotion. The selection process is designed to be thorough, with each candidate assessed by multiple experienced judges, including those who know them closely and others with a more independent perspective. And it is slanted towards identifying potential: individuals with the character to lead and the appetite to develop the technical knowledge and management skills they will need.

For those who gain promotion, the approximately ten years spent as a JNCO – typically around four to five each as a lance corporal and then full corporal – are the proving ground for the leadership skills that will be required in all subsequent ranks. Junior commanders learn about the importance of the relationships that bind a unit and sub-unit together, and the need to manage both their team and every individual in it. They learn how to convert an order into action, galvanising their people to deliver a commander's intent in challenging circumstances. They learn how to behave and conduct themselves as a leader, recognising the influence that their actions have and their responsibility to be a role model. They learn the importance of trust, and how their role depends on being trusted in equal part by the commanders giving orders, and the soldiers who must deliver them. And they learn about themselves, developing a style of leadership that embodies their own personality as much as the values, standards and requirements of their regiment and Army as a whole. Crucially, JNCO leaders are given the opportunity to learn these skills in the familiar environment of the troop or platoon, one in which they are among friends and can make mistakes they will learn from.

In that small unit environment, JNCOs represent the most prevalent voice and symbol of leadership. For every platoon's commander and sergeant, there will be three corporals and six lance corporals ensuring their intent is understood and their orders are carried out. These JNCOs are the most visible, proximate sources of leadership for soldiers. Whether in barracks, during training exercises or on operations, their voices will be heard most often and their personal example most consistently observed. While during the crisis situations that can arise in combat, everything can depend on their ability to independently assess a situation and make a rapid decision, in circumstances where there is neither time nor means for recourse to those above them in the chain of command. The JNCO ranks, therefore, serve at once as the most important proving ground for soldier leadership and the driving force of the direct, on-the-ground leadership that keeps the Army moving. They are simultaneously the roles where soldier leadership is learned and where it is practised at the sharp end. WO1 Gavin Paton, the Army's senior soldier, has summarised their importance.

> [JNCOs] are the people who deliver victory on the battlefield for our commanders at the point of contact. They're the soldier that executes every order. They're the people who make soldiers leave the Army and the people who make soldiers stay in the Army. They are our vital ground.[4]

A soldier's development as a JNCO will both challenge them to develop their leadership under pressure, as well as providing the support to help them learn. This learning curve is especially steep as a lance corporal, often described as the hardest rank in the Army to gain and the easiest to lose. For any private soldier stepping up to lance corporal, one of the most difficult adjustments is to recognise that not only has their rank changed, but with it their status in the group and relationships with their peers. The friends they grew up with in the sub-unit are now the soldiers they are responsible for and who must follow their commands. Soldiers are now subject to the JNCO's orders, their standards and their interpretation of discipline.

Like anyone graduating into their first managerial role, lance corporals must come to terms with the requirements of a promotion that demands a change in mindset to fulfil a shift in role. They are no longer just part of the team, but accountable for its standards and performance; no longer able to share in every gripe and complaint, but responsible for either resolving issues or telling people to move past them. To fulfil this role, lance corporals must learn how to simultaneously stand apart while being a fully engaged part of the team, using their authority lightly but firmly, and not fighting shy of disciplining their friends. Colour Sergeant Aaron Kerin has summed up the tensions inherent in the role.

> Throughout your time as a leader you have to make decisions that some won't like. The hardest time to do this is when you lead as a Lance Corporal. 'The unpopular man': You are the first to pass on the jobs, the front-line disher-out of 'crap jobs' but also one of the lads. It's a very thin line that almost every Lance Corporal struggles to get right.[5]

By learning to court unpopularity, insisting that the work gets done to a high standard without being heavy-handed, and getting the balance right between delegating and doing, lance corporals are immersed in some of the defining requirements of Army leadership: continuous relationship building, honest communication, and judicious exercise of authority. They also develop one of the most important leadership muscles: to use the mixture of persuasion, example and coercion that will get people to do things they don't want to do, or don't believe themselves capable of doing. In doing so, JNCOs must hone their ability to communicate with soldiers whose personalities and life circumstances may vary widely, and who need to be handled accordingly. This can be especially true in the Army Reserve, as Huw Davies, a troop corporal with the Reserve Light Cavalry, has suggested.

> I command a section that includes police officers, high ranking civil servants, students, bankers and small business owners. Each of these individuals brings their own life experience, and each soldier's background is vastly different to the soldier to their left and right.

This demands of junior leaders that they truly get to know their people and how to motivate them.

> Some are more 'high touch' than others. Those with issues in their civilian life – be they work or family related, will require more attention. It is impossible to fake this understanding, so in order to get the best out of your soldiers you need to know them both in a professional (Army and civilian job) and personal (family) context.[6]

As well as learning from mentors and through experience, NCOs are prepared for their responsibilities through the Army Leadership Development Programme (ALDP), a series of courses starting at the lance corporal level that is designed to equip them with all the technical skills required to do their job, to enhance their communication and decision making, and to expose them to the leadership requirements of commanding a section of eight soldiers. Alongside training in tactics, use of equipment and the section commander's role, JNCOs are trained in the Army's seven leadership behaviours (Figure 3), a conceptual handrail both for understanding their role and developing their individual leadership style. The courses are important as much for encouraging individuals to reflect on their own development as a leader, and their own approach to leadership, as in training them to develop specific technical skills and leadership behaviours. 'It's a very personal journey,' says Corporal Natasha Theodossiadis of her experience as a reservist NCO in the Royal Army Medical Corps. 'One thing you do learn is that you don't want to be like everybody else, and the best way is for you to be you.'

Lead by example
Encourage thinking
Apply reward and discipline
Demand high performance
Encourage confidence in the team
Recognise individual strengths and weaknesses
Strive for team goals

Figure 3: The Army's seven leadership behaviours

The behaviours are underpinned by three guiding concepts:

- **Vision:** Leaders must provide a clear and unifying purpose, generating a sense of team cohesion and direction.
- **Support:** By being fair, consistent and showing confidence in others, leaders provide a platform for their people to excel.
- **Challenge:** Leaders must not only test themselves, but challenge their people.

The leadership requirements of a JNCO continue to grow for those who progress to corporal, a rank at which both responsibilities and the ability to influence increase. Corporals, who provide the main body of instructors at the Army's training centres for new recruits, are the most prominent role models for private soldiers, especially those who have recently joined the Army. During the fourteen weeks of Phase 1 training, it is corporals who do most to impress on new recruits what it means and takes to be a soldier, succinctly expressed by Staff Sergeant Lee Waite.

> The corporal is the first person you meet as a civilian, the scariest person you've ever met in your life. After the first few weeks of training, you start to think I want to be that person: I want to look like that, I want to be able to march like that, I want my kit to be like that. That's what a corporal is.

The same is true in the regimental environment. The standards of a corporal become those of their section, from diligence in dress to care of equipment, performance in PT and general attitude and enthusiasm.

Working as an instructor is a revealing process that, for many, plays an important part in their leadership development. 'I have a section of twelve junior soldiers, and initially I didn't realise how different those individuals' needs were,' says Corporal Henry Bignell, an instructor at the Army Foundation College, which trains junior soldiers aged sixteen to eighteen. 'What I recognised is that, more than someone to teach them skills and drills, they needed a role model to guide them and help them grow as a person, not just in uniform.' Fulfilling that role, he believes, has prompted useful self-reflection about his approach to leadership.

If you are constantly trying to help others, you inadvertently help to develop yourself as a leader as well. It was something that happened naturally from having to deal with different welfare cases with the junior soldiers, or helping them to develop on certain tasks and realising my approach wasn't working.

The experience of training also reinforces to instructors the importance of knowing and treating people as individuals. 'Some of the junior soldiers respond well to being put under pressure and will operate brilliantly the harder you push them. But there are others who would crumble, and with that approach you will get nothing out of them,' Cpl Bignell suggests.

This dual benefit of training, and its ability to benefit the instructor as much as those being instructed, is a timeless feature of the Army experience. 'There is only one known method of creating leaders of men and commanders whom men will follow,' said Lieutenant General Sir Ivor Maxse, Inspector General of Training during the First World War. 'It consists in giving the leader his own men to train.'[7] In the modern Army, more effort than ever goes into ensuring that instructors are prepared to deliver training to the highest possible standard. The establishment of the ARITC Staff Leadership School★ in 2007 marked a shift in approach, with NCOs being trained in a transformational leadership approach to instructing that focuses on 'providing an inspirational vision of what training will lead to, helping trainees to understand the challenges that must be overcome, and providing individualised support to help them overcome those challenges'.[8] The emphasis on coaching skills and a transformational leadership approach in training was the product of extensive academic research into the Army's training methods, and the factors that were found to have the most bearing on recruit performance and mental health.

If the role of JNCOs is paramount in barracks and training environments, it can be magnified still further during operations. On the

---

★ When this school was set up, it was called the ARTD (Army Recruitment and Training Division) Staff Leadership School. Now it is the ARITC (Army Recruiting and Initial Training Command) Staff Leadership School.

battlefield, corporals are the first level of command responsibility, working with their platoon or troop commander to provide intelligence from the section level and to negotiate the direction of the battle. Where the platoon sergeant, its senior NCO, will typically be at the rear dealing with ammunition and casualties, corporals lead from the front, standing alongside their soldiers and trusted by their officers to give advice and shape decisions as well as to execute orders. For example, it may fall to a corporal to tell an OC that a critical part of the operation must wait until problems with the equipment have been fixed. Or to step in and prevent their officer from making what they believe to be a mistake, even if that involves cutting across the chain of command.

Officers may be in command, but they are heavily dependent on their JNCOs to achieve success on the battlefield, the leaders who not only carry the tip of the spear, but help to aim it. As Lieutenant Colonel, later General Sir, Hew Pike reflected on a critical moment during the Falklands War, when he was CO of 3 PARA: 'You are struck, as never before, by how profoundly reliant you are upon the cohesion of each fire team of four, each section of eight, and especially upon their leaders – tough, determined, confident, youthful corporals.'[9] This heightened level of responsibility during combat often puts corporals in situations where they must make delicate and critical judgement calls independently. It is section commanders who will be faced with split-second decisions about how to handle an unknown actor on patrol, whether and how to use force in situations of escalating unrest, and how to balance the need to achieve their objective with the obligation to protect their people.

These challenges have become more acute in the operating environment of the last half-century, in conflict zones from Northern Ireland to Afghanistan that have seen small units working in urban settings at close quarters with civilians, enemy combatants and those whose role and allegiance is unclear. Operation BANNER, the long-running British Army deployment to Northern Ireland that began in 1969, was one in which the burden of critical decisions frequently fell to section commanders. Patrolling streets, often at night, where insurgents blended among civilians and ambushes were an occupational hazard, JNCOs consistently had to make snap tactical judgement calls with potentially huge consequences. Recalling a night patrol through a South Armagh village in 1972, one soldier from the Argyll and Sutherland Highlanders described how his section was suddenly faced with an unknown force alongside them, a patrol that might have been friendly or could have been the IRA. The section commander's response was calm.

> Moose [. . .] went up and spoke to the guy. They went back that way and we went our way. It was later Moose says, 'Aye, you were lucky tonight boys.' And that was when we found out that it was one of their [IRA] patrols. He more or less said that, 'If we all start shooting, then most of us will get killed here because we were so close [to each other].'[10]

As General Charles Krulak's concept of the 'strategic corporal' has illustrated, modern combat operations increasingly require platoons and their sections to operate in isolation, with section commanders exposed to challenging circumstances that put a premium on their judgement, situational awareness and moral courage.[11] A young corporal's decision can avert needless violence and loss of life, or it can turn a dangerous situation into a deadly one. Their example can provide the necessary check-and-balance on soldiers' actions, or it can abet serious transgressions of the Army's Values and Standards. JNCOs have their chain of command, but they are also the leaders nearest to the soldiers who must close on hostile situations, and they are empowered by the Mission Command philosophy to use their initiative. Their decisions during the stress and chaos of combat operations will often make the difference between success and failure. As the Israeli general Yigal Allon, his country's Deputy Prime Minister from 1968 to 1977, summarised:

> The most brilliant plan devised by the most capable general depends for its tactical execution on the section-leaders [. . .] This is for one simple reason: the section-leader is the sole level of command that maintains constant and direct contact with the men who bear the brunt of the actual fighting.[12]

For all of these reasons, the rank of corporal is one of the most challenging in the Army, but also widely regarded as the most enjoyable. For many, the chance to lead soldiers in combat is why they volunteered. Many JNCOs, selected for their leadership potential, thrive on the high level of responsibility and relative independence that defines the role. Whereas more senior NCO ranks are increasingly required to focus on administration and the management of larger teams, corporals can be relentlessly focused on the development and performance of their section of eight soldiers. While being fully aware of the intent and expectations of their chain of command, they primarily look downwards, towards the needs, problems and development of the soldiers they know best. They are the leader to whom soldiers look first for advice and inspiration, and to whom more senior figures turn to assign essential tasks and critical responsibilities. Typically in their early-to-middle twenties, they are experienced professionals in their physical prime. For many soldiers, the rank of corporal will be the pinnacle of their career, whether or not they achieve higher rank. That reflects the premium placed by the Army on its junior leaders, whose minor rank belies the significant responsibilities that are required of them and the high esteem in which they are held by the entire chain of command.

Senior NCOs and warrant officers

Soldiers who are promoted from corporal to the rank of sergeant have served on average for ten to twelve years, as a private and then JNCO. They are highly experienced soldiers, long-serving members of their regiment, and NCOs who have absorbed the lessons of countless examples of good and bad leadership during their career. These are the seasoned soldiers in their regiment, who have proven their professional competence and leadership capabilities on numerous occasions, often in the most challenging environments. They are every unit's most visible sources of legitimate, expert and referent power: soldiers with significant experience, professional knowledge and regimental standing.

For those who attain them, the senior non-commissioned ranks represent both a substantial career achievement and a new set of challenges, requiring existing leadership skills to be honed and additional ones developed. They require sergeants, and later colour/staff sergeants and WOs, to become the ultimate exemplars of standards, no longer observed by a handful of soldiers but by dozens or hundreds; to be mentors not only to their soldiers but to the junior officers who must lead while learning their trade; and to use their experience to steer the decisions of their officers, both conveying honest ground truth upwards and driving the imperative for action downwards. Everything that has been learned as a JNCO is tested in new ways: the relationships are more numerous and complex, the canvas they operate on is bigger, and the power of their rank greater.

The focus of a SNCO and WO must also change, away from the tunnel vision of direct tactical leadership towards logistical and administrative needs, the climate of their platoon or company, and its contribution to the wider regiment. As a member of the Warrant Officers' and Sergeants' Mess, they are exposed to new levels of administrative machinery, new obligations as a senior member of the regiment, and a stronger sense of its history and traditions. An understanding of these ranks can help illustrate universal leadership requirements for those stepping into middle or senior management: the need to adjust to the challenge of overseeing larger teams, to use experience to steer those both above and below without being overbearing, and to embrace – as WOs must – the power of indirect leadership.

This transition begins with the role of platoon or troop sergeant, in which a SNCO becomes the most experienced soldier in their immediate environment, the natural focal point for soldiers and officers alike. For soldiers, sergeants represent the most accessible source of professional knowledge and experience. More worldly-wise than corporals and more relatable than officers, they are often uniquely trusted and respected figures within the small unit. Sergeant Arthur Human of the 2nd Leicesters recalled how, on the Western Front in 1915, a dying corporal turned to him with his last words and effects.

I knew he could not live but still tried to buck him up by telling him the old yarn of him being in England in a couple of days [. . .] But he knew he was for the next world. He gave me instructions [of] what to do in case of his death and his wife's address. Just to show you how my men trusted me: he gave me his pay book and money and all his personal belongings to send to his wife. When I tried to hand them to [Lieutenant] Pegg he would have none of it, but said, 'Sergeant, take it. I know my wife will get it then.'[13]

At the same time as they have a platoon of soldiers looking to them, a newly promoted sergeant must also develop a new kind of relationship with their officer counterpart. As a section commander they had a direct chain of command to their platoon commander, but as their sergeant they occupy a different and more ambiguous role. As the platoon's second-in-command, they are paired with a young officer who may be taking on his or her first leadership role. Although the officer is in command, at the outset they may have almost no experience as a soldier, compared to the dozen or more years of service their SNCO can call upon. The platoon sergeant therefore becomes a mentor to someone who is senior to them in the chain of command, and must carefully manage the power balance of this unusual relationship. Their challenge is to give that officer the benefit of their experience, and help them to develop as a leader, at the same time as respecting their rank and command authority, says Warrant Officer Class One Chris Nicol of the Household Cavalry regiment.

As a platoon sergeant you've got a young officer, fresh out of the factory from Sandhurst, who is very inexperienced but has the command. You need to manage that relationship between you, mentoring them, influencing them and helping them understand the climate of the unit they are in. That relationship can make or break a platoon, and the sergeant is the core of it because he or she has direct influence over the section commanders and 2ICs who will amplify their message to the soldiers.

For inexperienced junior officers, anxious to impress their chain of command, and trying to reconcile orders from above with the reality of resources below, a SNCO acts as a vital guide and sounding board, someone who can speak from experience about what is possible and which course of action is advisable. In my first posting as a platoon commander, joining my battalion halfway through a tour to Northern Ireland in 2000, I was heavily dependent on my platoon sergeant, Sergeant Mick Southall. Having served in the Falklands War as a seventeen-year-old soldier, he knew better than most the realities of being thrown into your first operational theatre, and regularly gave me the benefit of his experience and opinions while being staunchly supportive of my command. As the best SNCOs recognise, there are limits to the role. A sergeant can report and advise, but never decide for an officer or contradict their final decision. A good SNCO brings to bear the full weight of their knowledge, without ever over-stepping their authority or forgetting who commands and who is ultimately responsible.

When a junior officer and SNCO work well together, it spreads confidence through the ranks and boosts cohesion. By being a good follower – critical but loyal – a SNCO both supports their officer and provides an essential example to their JNCOs and soldiers of what effective followership looks like. By contrast, an overbearing sergeant who does not respect and show loyalty to their platoon commander sets a pernicious example to those below them, undermining the climate of the group and making it harder to maintain discipline. As the most experienced soldier in their immediate environment, it is the SNCO's responsibility to help their officer succeed, giving them the ground intelligence and voice of experience that enables them to make the best available decision. Nurturing this relationship is not just important to achieve immediate objectives. A young officer's platoon sergeant may become their sergeant major as a company commander and the RSM to their CO. The relationships that are forged in the platoon environment can persist to the top of the regimental hierarchy, where the push-and-pull between officer and soldier continues to play an essential role. They are friendships and working relationships that define careers and determine the climate of a regiment.

While sergeants may be closely involved in steering tactical decisions, ultimately this is the domain of the platoon commander, leading through their JNCOs. The platoon sergeant's defined role as second-in-command (2IC) is to manage logistics and administration. The sergeant's logistical role extends to the battlefield, where they are responsible for distributing equipment and ammunition, managing casualties, co-ordinating medical assistance and ensuring continuity of supply lines. Ultimately, whatever is practically required for a platoon to function and maintain its fighting power is the sergeant's responsibility to manage. Their job epitomises servant leadership: a commitment to ensuring that everyone around them has the tools, the training, the professional example and the moral support to succeed. In fulfilling this role, sergeants act as the natural parent figure of any small unit: responsible as much for well-being as discipline; as committed to the safety of all involved as they are to the upholding of professional standards. Throughout British Army history, it has been sergeants who have been the most consistent guardians of the interests and welfare of their soldiers, as an example from the Crimean War demonstrates. During a long march a young lieutenant – on horseback, with the men on foot – instructed Sergeant Timothy Gowing, of the 7th Royal Fusiliers, to imprison a 'slacking' soldier. As Gowing later recalled:

> The unfortunate man was doing his best to keep up and he gave our young officer such a contemptuous look as I shall not forget as long as I live [. . .] The poor fellow was made a prisoner at once, for insubordination. But when I explained the case to our Colonel he took quite a different view of the matter, forgave the man, and presented him with a pair of good warm socks and a pair of new boots; for the poor fellow had nothing but uppers and no soles for his old ones.[14]

As they adjust to new responsibilities, SNCOs must accustom themselves to a fundamental change in role: from leading side by side with soldiers to stepping back and taking the wider view – ensuring that soldiers and their tactical commanders are equipped with everything they need to fight and win. In turn, they must accept one of the challenges of leadership in any field: as you rise up the ranks and acquire new responsibilities, none of the old ones go away. A sergeant still needs to lead by example, to set high standards in PT and to be visible during exercises. Even as their administrative burden increases, they cannot allow themselves to be confined to their desk. And even as they step away from tactical command, they cannot become distant from the decisions that their officer and JNCOs are making. Like all leaders getting used to the challenge of a more senior role, they must find ways to juggle new responsibilities with existing obligations.

They also benefit from the next stage of the Army Leadership Development Programme, which focuses increasingly on the conceptual understanding of leadership. 'Sergeant and above is really the beginning of your leadership knowledge,' says Captain Andy Stephen, a late-entry officer who served in all NCO ranks up to Regimental Sergeant Major with the Royal Corps of Signals.

> Up until then you've been a doer, a leadership practitioner. You didn't necessarily need that much theory or understanding. At this point the study of leadership becomes important: you look more in depth into different models, how to assess each subordinate as an individual and how to adapt your leadership style.

The Army Leadership Code provides the theory to support this work, outlining six leadership styles (Figure 4) on a spectrum from transactional leadership (control, process and incentive oriented) to transformational leadership (encouraging and inspiring people to achieve the desired ends). The purpose of this model is not to prescribe how individuals should lead, but to illustrate that leadership exists on a spectrum, with different approaches that will need to be used independently or in parallel, the combination determined by context. 'As a corporal you can get away with your natural style, but when you move into the platoon sergeant role, you come unstuck if you don't understand the different approaches you have to use,' Capt Stephen suggests. 'That's where on senior ALDP you dive deeper into those leadership styles.'

As a SNCO or WO, soldiers must fulfil multiple roles in parallel: indirect leaders through their subordinates, mentors both to their soldiers and to inexperienced junior officers, and leaders who must work in tandem with the officer who has command authority in their immediate environment (a platoon sergeant working alongside a

- **_The Directive Style_**: *well understood and most effective when a leader requires a rapid, unquestioning action*
- **_The Participative Style_**: *the leader asks for and values input from the team*
- **_The Pacesetting Style_**: *the leader provides challenge, demands high standards and leads by example*
- **_The Coaching Style_**: *the leader encourages dialogue and focuses on the future*
- **_The Affiliative Style_**: *the leader focuses on the needs of both individuals and teams, building bonds and creating rapport*
- **_The Visionary Style_**: *the leader explains the 'why' but not the 'how', encouraging imagination and initiative*

Figure 4: Leadership styles

platoon commander, company sergeant major alongside a company commander, and regimental sergeant major alongside a battalion's commanding officer). These contrasting roles require leaders whose understanding of leadership and ability to lead according to the needs of the situation must become more sophisticated.

Those who progress to the warrant officer ranks move further into the realm of indirect leadership. A WO2, usually the company sergeant major (CSM), takes responsibility for the logistical needs of the entire sub-unit, comprising three platoons totalling around 100 soldiers. A CSM works alongside the OC to lead their sub-unit, providing a pivotal influence on its climate, standards and discipline. With so many soldiers looking to them as a leadership exemplar, they must ensure their personal standards and behaviour are unimpeachable. WO1 Nicol, quoted earlier in this chapter, summed it up.

> As a Squadron Corporal Major [CSM equivalent] I was responsible for one hundred and twelve soldiers. You become more aware of yourself because you are the standard that's set. It's not a case of 'do as I say, not as I do'. It's about displaying the behaviour you want to see in others, setting the example.

WO2s are also learning the art of indirect leadership, leading through the platoon sergeants and JNCOs, using their rank and experience to convey their intent and inspire others to deliver it. Although a visible example and prominent voice, they must also find ways to lead from a distance: a quiet word to set a platoon sergeant right, or a raised eyebrow that encourages an officer to reconsider. They must be fully aware of what is happening at all levels of the sub-unit, but limit their interventions and work through the rank structure, acting as mentors to their NCOs and supporting their leadership development. Ernest Powdrill, a WO2 with the Royal Horse Artillery during the Second World War, emphasised how success in the role depends on the ability to lead through others and harness the multi-faceted power of the rank.

> [A WO2] is by no means a drill sergeant. That he is responsible [. . .] for the discipline of the men means that he did it mostly by his personality and expressed military knowledge. He had to earn respect, particularly from his nine troop sergeants. Not to do so made for an uncomfortable situation.[15]

A CSM is the fulcrum of their sub-unit, the guardian of its heritage and ethos and the individual best placed to understand both the ground truth of what soldiers are experiencing, and the wider context of what officers require. Their balancing act is to be loyal and attentive to both these perspectives without becoming the prisoner of either. A CSM must be the voice of their soldiers without echoing every gripe and grumble from the ranks. And they must be the agent and follower of their OC, ensuring their intent is carried through, without becoming their sycophant. A good CSM will challenge the company commander's thinking, point out what they may have missed, and emphasise when and why they are in disagreement. But these debates will happen in private, with both officer and WO presenting a united front to the sub-unit. As Lieutenant Colonel Anthony Birch of the Australian Army suggests, 'Sergeant Majors need to be fearless and honest in their private advice to commanders and then staunchly aligned to command direction once decisions have been made.'[16]

The pinnacle of soldier leadership at the regimental level, and a figure of legendary standing within the British Army, is the regimental sergeant major (RSM), a warrant officer class one (WO1). This is a rank achieved by only the most exceptional soldier leaders, who have proven themselves through long service careers encompassing all NCO ranks. The RSM is a walking, talking role model: the ultimate embodiment of their regiment and its referent power, the figurehead for its soldiers and the right-hand to the CO. Their prior experience, which typically includes service in key administrative roles such as regimental quartermaster sergeant, helping to oversee supplies and provisioning, gives them an innate understanding of the workings of their regiment, and an appreciation of the full range of challenges faced by the soldiers and leaders below them. RSMs are figures whose physical presence and immaculate dress – characteristically maintained even in the muddiest fields and the sandiest deserts – cements their status as figures of surpassing authority, as much to the Army's most senior officers as to its youngest soldiers. General Sir Mike Jackson wryly recalled the implicit but unmistakable reprimand he received from the Garrison Sergeant Major of HQ London District after his late arrival to the Queen Mother's funeral in 2002, where he was representing CGS.

> He looked at his watch ostentatiously and sniffed. He sniffed again as I dragged on my frock coat and buckled my ceremonial sword. 'Very good to see you, Commander in Chief,' he said in a voice radiating disapproval [. . .] Only in the British Army could a four-star general be rebuked in such a way by a warrant officer.[17]

Their unique status and reputation confers huge referent power on the RSM, who can use this to their advantage but must also acknowledge its limits. The RSM is a symbol, but must also be a practical and involved leader, available for subordinates to bring problems to them. An RSM cannot simply sit atop the hierarchy but must use it to hone their sense of the regiment's mood, its people, and any issues that may give cause for concern. Like any senior figure, they must be dextrous in the art of leadership and its many balancing acts: visible enough to set an example without impeding the work of others; professionally distant while remaining approachable; and equipped with a keen sense of when and how to use the full weight of their authority.

When the RSM does intervene, their words carry the power to

galvanise an entire regiment. Their intent cascades through the rank
structure to leave no soldier in any doubt as to what is expected.
Doug Beattie was RSM of 1st Battalion The Royal Irish Regiment at
the outset of the Iraq War in 2003, and subsequently commissioned
as a late-entry officer. His CO, Lieutenant Colonel Tim Collins,
became famous for the speech he gave on the eve of the invasion,
outlining the gravity of the task and the risks that lay ahead. His
words were admiringly reported around the world, but less appreciated on the ground by his RSM. He later wrote:

> I knew I had a problem . . . [The CO] had told the men they would
> not all be coming back, and now it seemed the majority of them were
> asking if they would be amongst the fallen. They had to be snapped
> out of it.

RSM Beattie followed the oratory of Lt Col Collins with a speech of
his own, delivering a tirade to the same audience, minus officers, about
the state of the regiment's dress, its shoddy equipment, poor timekeeping, failure to salute officers, and the lax leadership of its NCOs.

> I accused the warrant officers of running slack companies. I blamed
> the sergeants for not properly advising the young second lieutenants
> and captains who depended on them. Finally, I embarrassed the sec-
> tion commanders for their lack of control over their men.

He then summoned his five WO2s for a private pep talk, before
stepping back to observe the effect of his work.

> I watched as the CSMs returned to their men and continued where I
> had left off [. . .] Within ten minutes of my initial merry hell I saw
> men furiously cleaning weapons, emptying and re-packing rucksacks,
> checking their kit.[18]

With a few stern and timely words, and by leaning on the rank
structure, RSM Beattie had achieved his objective: to turn an atmosphere of apprehension into one of collective readiness.

For most of the British Army's history, RSM was the most senior
position in the NCO hierarchy. That changed in 2015 with the advent
of the command sergeant majors, a network of former RSMs who

act as advisers to two-, three- and four-star generals, providing the same soldier perspective that officers benefit from at the unit level, and ensuring that the soldier's voice is heard at the most senior levels of the Army – not unlike the employee representatives that sit on some company boards, to represent the view from the shop floor. At the apex of this network is the Army Sergeant Major, who as the senior soldier provides direct advice to CGS. They act as a thermometer, a translator and a courier: taking the temperature of soldiers across the Army to understand emerging problems, ensuring that key priorities are understood at the soldier level, and acting as a two-way messenger between the highest and lowest levels of the rank structure.

These new NCO positions have brought soldier leaders, previously concentrated at the regimental level and in the tactical sphere, into the organisational and strategic layers of the Army, where they may have less direct experience, but their innate understanding of soldiers is no less important. They are one reflection of how soldier leadership has grown in importance and esteem in the modern British Army. NCOs have always played a vital leadership role, but in the distant past that would typically have been thought of in terms of maintaining fighting spirit, instilling discipline and teaching young officers about the inner workings of the Army. The modern soldier leader must do all these things, but at the same time is expected to be a critical friend to their officer, an independent decision maker, and a champion for leadership within their environment. Soldier leadership has never been more important to the Army, a fact acknowledged by the growing emphasis on leadership training and development for soldiers, closing the historic gap between what is provided to soldiers and officers.

These developments underline the full importance of soldier leadership within the Army: not just a force to galvanise action, but a means to connect the disparate elements of a complex, multi-layered organisation, 'the glue that holds an army together', as Lieutenant Colonel Bernd Horn of the Canadian Army has written.[19] While as General Kroesen defined it, the collective body of NCOs constitutes the nervous system that acts both as an early-warning mechanism and as a rapid communications network: the best guarantee that intent in one place will be understood and swiftly implemented where it matters. From a teenage LCpl to an RSM with decades of experience, it is the Army's soldier leaders who are trusted with the business end of the profession of arms: putting orders into action, delivering harsh truths to individuals both above and below, upholding the Army's standards and traditions, and binding its many layers into an effective fighting force.

Across all ranks, the Army's officer and soldier leaders will work together in the many different, overlapping ways needed to develop teams, build morale, drive standards and hone operational effectiveness. These different leaders also work in many different circumstances, whether doing the critical work of preparation for deployment or delivering an operation at home or overseas. The role they play and the challenges they face are ultimately determined by these changing contexts: the chapters that follow will explore the differences between leading in times of peace and during war.

9. Leadership in Peace

'Man's fate in battle is worked out before the war begins,' wrote Dr
Charles Wilson (Lord Moran), over two decades before he became
a public figure as Winston Churchill's doctor. In his book *The Anatomy of Courage*, which remains a reference text for Army leaders, he
emphasises that individual and collective behaviour on the battlefield
is conditioned by the prior development of character during times of
peace.

> Character as Aristotle taught is a habit, the daily choice of right instead
> of wrong; it is a moral quality which grows to maturity in peace and
> is not suddenly developed on the outbreak of war [. . .] acts in war are
> dictated not by courage, nor by fear, but by conscience, of which war
> is the final test.[1]

This captures an enduring truth for the Army: what is delivered
on operations is the product of what has been practised during
peacetime, in barracks and on training exercises. Everything that the
success of a military operation depends upon stems from a well-
trained, well-prepared, cohesive team of soldiers with the individual
resilience, collective knowledge and mutual trust to overcome
adversity. The skills and behaviours that make the difference under
duress can only be developed gradually, through consistent rehearsal
when the stakes are low and there is scope to learn from mistakes.
The critical moral component of fighting power – its human
aspects – must be carefully and consistently nurtured to be relied
upon at key moments.

This imperative means that peacetime is precious for every Army
leader. It is their window of opportunity to establish the critical
foundations of success: learning about their people, developing
their teams, and forging a collective climate and ethos. The months
spent in barracks are the time to invest in everything that a team will

need when deployed. Yet this imperative clashes with the reality of having to lead soldiers in camp, without the galvanising sense of purpose that is ever present on operations. While the challenges of an operation are sharper and more obvious, those posed by long periods spent in barracks can be harder to overcome. Boredom, lethargy and frustration can easily set in, actively undermining the cohesion, discipline and standards that a leader is trying to engender. 'I learned most about leadership on operations, but found it much harder to lead in barracks,' says Capt Andy Stephen. 'You've not got that captive audience, you've not got that shared purpose, and people have got lives to get back to at the end of the day.' Peacetime, therefore, represents not just the vital ground for a leader who is trying to mould a successful team, but also a distinctively challenging leadership environment. In peace, leaders are seeking to develop readiness and build operational capability, preparing their teams to be resilient and effective in fast-moving, unfamiliar operational circumstances.

Whatever the ultimate circumstances of an operation, military teams will rely on collective discipline, trust, morale and ethos to be effective. These elements of cohesion arise from a range of contributing factors. 'What makes soldiers work well together in combat?' the Army officer turned anthropologist Dr Charles Kirke asked a focus group of infantry soldiers, while researching the social structures of the British Army in the 1990s. '[I] received the following answers, to which all agreed: group friendships; training so that doing the job comes naturally; receipt of orders; maintaining or enhancing the battalion's reputation.'[2] As this suggests, critical elements of cohesion include the strength of personal relationships, the pride that comes from being part of a successful unit, and the confidence that arises from effective training. These are the foundations that leaders must build in peacetime: creating a collective identity and building both individual and group resilience. This chapter will examine what this work entails in barracks and on training exercises, and how the benefits can be witnessed during the crisis situations in which the Army often works on homeland operations that respond to peacetime emergencies.

In barracks

'At formation level on operations you are working to three horizons: you've got the current battle, you're planning the next one, and you're looking at contingency work,' says Lieutenant General (Retd) James Bashall, who served in senior command roles including as General Officer Commanding (GOC) 1st (UK) Division and Commander Home Command. This captures a central challenge for leaders in barracks, who must prepare their teams for a wide spectrum of possible future operations. The next planned deployment could be over twelve months away, but equally there could be a last-minute request for personnel to be diverted to support an exercise or homeland operation. The next operation could be one that closely resembles the last, or it could see a unit play a different role in another part of the world. The plans that leaders have for the next week and month are always under threat of being thrown into disarray by an emerging priority that arises without warning. As Gen Bashall suggested, this means leaders in barracks must constantly be thinking in three modes: 'What now, what next, what if?'

When the nature of the next operation is by definition unclear, the focus must be on preparing teams and the people in them to perform, whatever the circumstances. Leaders may sometimes be training their people for a specific requirement, and there is a consistent need to hone the technical skills relevant to each Arm, but an equally important priority is to develop a general set of capabilities that will equip teams for all operational weathers: the ability to adapt to unfamiliar conditions, quickly establish a plan of action, and work confidently under many different kinds of pressure and duress. The work to do this happens during peacetime, and much of it stems from the climate that leaders create in the barracks environment.

The climate of a unit builds upon the culture, Values and Standards of the Army as a whole, but will also be specific to it: shaped if not entirely created by the officer and NCO leaders in every platoon, company and battalion. This climate conditions what is accepted, encouraged, upheld and ultimately achieved. It sets the frame for everyone working within it, facilitating either the best or the worst kind of military behaviour. While culture is deep-rooted, climate is something that leaders can quickly shape through their actions and example. 'In his eighteen months with the Battalion, the Colonel had transformed it into his personal instrument,' Major Geoffrey (later Colonel) Powell, of 156th Parachute Battalion, wrote of his commanding officer during the Second World War.

> The Colonel's eyes were still, but he never missed anything: the unfastened pouch from which a grenade or Bren magazine could slip; the slack chin-strap which would fail to hold a running man's steel helmet in place [. . .] All of them knew his ways, and by now they had learned that his fads mattered.[3]

Climate sets expectations and can also condition behaviour. When soldiers and subordinate commanders feel able to use their initiative and challenge questionable orders from above, it is because they are working in a climate which supports this, providing the confidence that they will not be explicitly or implicitly punished for doing so. By the same token, when discipline frays and standards slip, it is invariably because the climate has permitted this through lax inspections and the failure of leaders to set an appropriate example. The climate of a unit is contagious: high standards are self-perpetuating, setting a competitively high bar for others to clear, just as slack ones provide the permission for others to follow suit. It can also be long-lasting, with the behaviour of the current generation of leaders exercising significant influence on how the next one develops. As Serjeant Ben Hayden of The Rifles has written, a climate in which micromanagement is the norm risks breeding a generation of micro-managers in its wake. If NCOs over-control their people, '[it] leaves us with a group of soldiers who are scared to make small decisions. It may not seem like much, but a soldier who is stopped from thinking for him or herself can turn into a "flapper" later in their career.'[4]

To shape the climate they want to see, leaders must express clear intent about the standards they expect and how they plan to operate. While specific details about direction, from training focus to personnel management, may take time to develop, a leader should arrive in their post with a clear sense of the climate they want to shape and be willing to express their intent from the outset. Equally, while they outline these expectations, leaders – whether a section commander, platoon sergeant or commanding officer – must also be conscious that they are not working with a blank page. Many of the soldiers will have seen multiple individuals occupy the same position, each with their own ideas and biases. There is a natural cynicism and caution about what the new broom will bring with it, and what exactly it intends to sweep away. In this context, a collaborative approach to defining the climate can be important, with commanders shaping rather than prescribing the process.

Lieutenant Colonel Will Meddings, CO of 2 Royal Anglian and previously a founding member of the Centre for Army Leadership, worked with his entire command team (comprising company commanders, senior staff officers and RSM) to establish the parameters of its climate. Together they defined a mission statement ('we exist to serve the British people'), an ethos ('humble excellence'), and three principles for action: making the team tighter, making it better on operations, improving and safeguarding its reputation. Every formal meeting in the unit begins with a reminder of these ideas: a reason for being, an ethos to aspire to, and handrails for making decisions and judging appropriate behaviour. The important thing, he suggests, is not just to set principles that define a climate, but to work hard at ensuring they can be widely understood. As he explained, 'It's about crafting your intent in a way that's easy to communicate, and a format that's designed to be communicated.' By doing so, the boundaries of what is expected and accepted are clear for all, encouraging initiative and independence within them:

> I've said repeatedly to SNCOs and soldiers that if you make a mistake but were trying to make us better on operations, make our team tighter together or were thinking about our reputation, then I will absolutely have your back. And as a leader, armed with those principles, I've been comfortable to let my team get on with business.

Leadership in barracks may begin with statements of intent, but these must be consistently reinforced to be of value. Leaders cannot simply set an aspiration and sit back. They must monitor how people respond, and intervene when required, an active custodian for the climate they are trying to create. Discipline and reward are powers that must be used with discrimination but also decisively. There can be no room for even small breaches of required standards. As General Patton observed: 'You cannot be disciplined in great things and undisciplined in small things.'[5] The behaviours that are established and tolerated in barracks will, without exception, be replicated and magnified on operations. Either the right habits are encouraged and when necessary enforced, or the wrong ones will take root and grow in their place. An effective command climate, clearly communicated and consistently upheld, is an important means of getting on the right side of this equation. When dealing with disciplinary cases as a CO, as well as asking people to consider if and how they had breached the Values and Standards and Service Test, I would hold them to account against the four principles of the battalion under my command: success on operations, one team, protect the brand, and leadership at all times, at all levels.

Equally, leaders are more than watchdogs and should always look for opportunities to reward and champion the best of their people's work. A letter of thanks from the CO, or a verbal recognition or handshake from a warrant officer, can all go a long way to ensuring people feel appreciated and positively reinforcing the intended climate. These tokens of recognition can also have a wider audience. When she was CEO of PepsiCo, leading an organisation with over 200,000 employees, Indra Nooyi would write hundreds of letters a year to the parents of people on her team, a practice she found to be especially meaningful for all involved.

> I tell the parents what a great job their son or daughter is doing. That recognition is worth more than money, stock runs, hugs, tickets – anything – because at the end of the day, when your parents say to you, 'I'm so proud of you; your boss just wrote to me saying you're awesome,' the look on their face is worth more than one million dollars.[6]

At the same time, leaders must remember that their power to influence with minor actions cuts both ways, and must take care not to cause unintended damage as much as they seek opportunities to forge goodwill. 'An ill-timed scowl at a JNCO or a flippant remark to a young officer will be taken quite seriously and unnecessarily damage a relationship,' one RSM cautions.[7]

Leaders may reinforce the command climate through appropriate use of reward and discipline, but they can only truly sustain it by developing their people. A unit is only ever as effective as the quality of leadership at every rank. As an organisation with limited scope for lateral entry, the Army is entirely dependent on the ability of its leaders to grow others around them, maximising the potential of every individual. Developing a deep bench of leaders is a priority of time spent in barracks, and should be the work of the entire rank structure. Every rank holder in the British Army has the responsibility for developing the leadership of the people below them, from lance corporals encouraging their handful of soldiers, to sergeants mentoring their JNCOs and junior officers, COs encouraging the independence of their OCs, and so on. They must build relationships, delegate to the point of discomfort and allow them to fail in ways from which they will learn. In a well-functioning command climate, where every leader has a clear sense of their role and the associated freedom to act, this will happen as a matter of course, in the spirit of Mission Command.

In other circumstances, an individual leader may need to step in, make adjustments and reset expectations. One former CO[8] recalled how, upon assuming a new command, he quickly recognised that he had inherited a unit with problems:

> I took over a battalion that was pretty bruised, run into the ground and where some pretty unpleasant cultures had been allowed to develop. In the first couple of months it took some drastic action and a lot of effort to transform from the bottom up, to make things good and reset the culture.

Among the issues, he observed that the unit was failing those being promoted into their first leadership role as JNCOs:

You need lance corporals to understand what it means to have a bit of authority and to be separate from their peers, and that was not being trained into people. Newly promoted JNCOs weren't being afforded responsibility, given freedom to train and develop people, or having trust given to them. They weren't understanding the fundamental requirement that you can't walk past standards you know are unacceptable.

His response was to reinvigorate the corporals' mess, giving newly promoted LCpls a sense of identity and distinction from their former peers, to enhance leadership training and education at the lowest level, and to emphasise to his subordinate leaders that they must delegate more:

Something that really made the difference was prevailing on OCs and platoon commanders to give their people more responsibility and really make them feel like they were somebody with rank, and the freedoms and responsibilities that a JNCO should have.

Also key to the success of the turnaround, he suggests, was an approach that encompassed the entire unit:

I chose to work from a starting point that it was about everybody, not a particular company having a problem, but making the whole entity right systematically from the start. It was about attacking the cause, not the symptom: the deficit of leadership education and training at the lowest level.

Developing people as leaders also relies on the time and effort invested to understand them as individuals. The time in camp represents a leader's best opportunity to spend time with their people and learn about their personalities, career ambitions, family circumstances, strengths and weaknesses. Effective use of Mission Command can be facilitated by such detailed knowledge of individuals: a task that may be the making of one subordinate could crush another at a different stage of development, and it is the leader's job to know the difference. To some extent the nature of Army life encourages this, with people living and socialising together and being pushed to the limits of physical and mental endurance on exercise or operations. But Army leaders also need to go further, making every effort to understand the individual and what motivates them, not simply relying on assumptions about what people will or should think. 'You need to find out people's aggravations and motivations by listening to them,' says Brigadier (Retd) Nicky Moffat, the most senior female officer in the Army when she left in 2012.[9] This is particularly important, she suggests, in the context of change and uncertainty that so often surrounds the Army's work. Leaders 'have to make sure that we are listening to what our people are saying, we're trying to decipher what they're thinking, and, really importantly, we're getting a sense of what they're feeling.'[10]

As they strive to foster a climate and develop their people, leaders must come to terms with a paradox of leadership in peacetime: in a lower-stakes environment where there should be greater freedom to delegate and implement the Mission Command philosophy, it is often less consistently applied. 'In barracks everything is scrutinised and you don't have the same freedom of movement as on operations,' one former RSM suggests. Peacetime should be the testing ground for Mission Command, with leaders delegating freedoms to accustom their teams to the discipline of making independent decisions within the bounds of a commander's intent. Too often, however, the barracks environment leads to the opposite. A lower risk threshold, lack of consistency in personnel (with people being moved around according to need), and limitations on resources all represent constraints facing leaders during peacetime. In this context, the mindset to seek out opportunities to delegate authority and challenge people becomes important. Leaders cannot alter the context they are working in, but they must still be proactive about finding ways to achieve their intent.

In parallel with seeking to instil the habits and mindset that will be needed on operations, leaders must guard against the kind of negative behaviour that can undermine the entire climate of a unit, and which takes root most readily in the barracks environment. The question of 'toxic leadership' has become widely debated in military circles over recent years.[11] Lieutenant Colonel John Dagless, who has researched the subject on behalf of the Army, suggests that this is characterised by leaders primarily motivated by self-interest, who then create a 'poisonous relationship' with their subordinates, exploiting their rank and relying on intimidation and autocratic measures to achieve their short-term goals.[12] Such a harmful approach, one that inverts the principle of servant leadership, can occur in any organisation, but is a risk to which the military is arguably more susceptible, given the prevalence of the rank structure, the emphasis on loyalty to the regiment, and the need to drive people hard as a matter of course.

It is the responsibility of leaders to ensure that the work needed to achieve high standards does not cross the line whereby discipline becomes punitive, competition tips into peer pressure and people's loyalty to their peers and their regiment is manipulated. Guarding that line and stamping down on the first indications of toxic leadership is an essential role for the leaders of every team. The risk of not doing so is both that individuals will suffer, and that the overall climate will be undermined by dominant figures whose leadership example is the opposite of what is required, spawning a problem that becomes difficult to uproot.

The work done by leaders in barracks is only the beginning of building the climate and cohesion that their people will rely upon during operations. The habits that are encouraged and exemplified daily in this environment create a baseline of behaviour within every unit and its constituent teams. It is through training – another core discipline of leadership in peacetime – that these behaviours are built upon and sharpened into the crucial components of fighting power.

On exercise

'If you look at real conflict, it's not your weapons that win the war, it's not your equipment, it's your mental ability to sustain yourself under stress,' Major Chris Keeble recalled of his service in the Falklands War, in which he assumed the command of his battalion after its CO, Lieutenant Colonel H. Jones, was killed in combat. 'The whole point of war, really, is to apply violence to break the enemy's will, not destroy his weapons or his cities, but undermine his will to fight for what he believes in. Now, how do you reinforce that in a body of people who've never been to war?'

This is one of the most pertinent challenges of leadership in peace: the need to prepare soldiers for the rigours of operations they may never experience, but for which they must be permanently ready. Such training has multiple objectives, which only begin with the need to enshrine technical skills and tactical awareness. Equally important is its role in developing the moral component of fighting power: the morale and fighting spirit of a team of people, their trust in each other and identity with the unit in which they serve. Through rigorous training in extreme conditions, teams gain reference points for their ability to overcome adversity and achieve collective goals. While individuals gain experience of leading in situations that resemble those they may encounter on operations, through exercises that confront them with the requirements to make decisions and be responsible for the well-being of those around them.

In the experience of Maj Keeble: 'We had spent our practice training fusing the individuals together. The fire of war merely tempered that process.'[13] When training is done well, the results can be measured in a team's cohesion and self-confidence. As the sociologist Randall Collins has written, training 'is not simply a matter of learning; it is above all establishing identity with the group who carry out their skills collectively.'[14]

The scope and scale of training can vary widely, from the sub-unit level to large-scale exercises which involve entire formations for weeks at a time. But the purpose is common: to develop and maintain key competencies, build trust and relationships within teams, and give individuals the opportunity to practise assuming responsibility, both of the rank they hold and those one or two levels above that they may be required to assume in an emergency. Everything that needs to function smoothly in the operational environment, from mission planning and tactical deployment to management of casualties, must be honed on exercise if it is to be relied upon during operations. The same is true of the intangible factors essential to success: relationships between leaders and followers, the self-confidence of commanders, implicit trust, and understanding between team members. Training must develop a team's psychological as well as physical and tactical muscles. Although this luxury has not always been available to the British Army, notably during the mass mobilisations of the twentieth century that limited the scope for professional training, its importance has long been understood in the context of the Regular Army. As *Infantry Training*, an Army manual published in 1902, made clear:

> [. . .] no good results are to be expected [in war] unless the subordinate leaders have been trained to use their wits, and unless they have been given ample opportunities of acting on their own judgement in attack and defence, and have constantly, in peace practices, been called upon to consider the necessity of departing from their original orders.[15]

As well as getting teams and individuals ready to fulfil the roles they are assigned to perform on operations, exercises must prepare them to encounter the unexpected and to respond when plans go awry. Here it is not the geography of an operating environment that must be simulated, but the experience. Exercises deliberately put leaders of all ranks into situations that help to teach them the responsibilities of their role, under the duress of fatigue and the stress of plans being disrupted. Corporal Oscar Searle, a reservist with The Royal Yeomanry, recalls a formative moment on Exercise CAMBRIAN PATROL, the Army's largest annual patrolling event, after a setback had caused a breakdown in discipline among his section.

> The Captain turned to me and said, 'I don't know what to do. You're the NCO here, what do you think?' I had to really sit and think for a second: my back hurt, my feet hurt, we were halfway through a sixty-kilometre patrol through the Welsh mountains and had been told we were no longer going to be able to complete the course. It was the moment as an NCO I saw how I could have an effect on the team. Eventually I turned around to everyone and said, 'Get your bergens on, we're going.' And we managed to get a certificate of achievement for completing the course.

That sticks in my head as the moment I felt I grew most as a leader. No one said that's what I was going to achieve when I went away that weekend. It was very much the environment, the competition, the way it was orchestrated that constrained everything towards that outcome.

The benefits of robust training are immeasurable, but require determined and creative leadership to achieve. The leaders who design training need to make exercises both interesting enough to engage people's full attention and effort, and challenging enough to stretch teams to the point where they learn the most valuable lessons. 'The expert trainer of troops is the one who, despite the protestations of the Jeremiahs, can select an objective which, although it appears unobtainable, is in fact just within the capabilities of his soldiers,' suggested then Lieutenant Colonel Edwin Bramall in a leadership guide he wrote in the 1960s as CO of the 2nd Royal Green Jackets. 'Then having won through, his men will feel that they have done the impossible and their sense of achievement and morale will be correspondingly great.'[16]

As the sports psychologists Wade Gilbert and Jean Côté have contended, a good coach focuses on building multiple capabilities in their charges. Their 'Four Cs' model of coaching effectiveness points to the related outcomes of competence, confidence, connection and character as the signifiers of coaching effectiveness – a framework that could equally well apply to the military as to high performance sport.[17]

To achieve these outcomes, leaders who deliver the training, usually NCOs, must strike a balance between pushing people hard and recognising their limitations. Training should serve to raise the level both of a team collectively and of every individual in it, a requirement that demands a light touch from instructors to balance both needs against that of the task at hand. Sergeant Mark Davey of 2 Signal Regiment recalled one such example of careful handling during training for the regiment's Lanyard Trophy, a forty-mile endurance competition that has been held annually since 1979. 'It was thirty miles into the event over the North Yorkshire Moors [. . .] having had an episode of cramp and slowly feeling that my feet were disintegrating, I hit a psychological barrier and stopped.' His team leader stepped in.

Despite being neck and neck with our nearest rival, he ordered the team to stop and allow the precious minutes for me to check my boots. He then asked me to head the team of eight and navigate and set the pace to the next checkpoint. A deliberate act of leadership that brought me back from almost giving up.[18]

As well as setting the bar intimidatingly high and husbanding individuals through challenging exercises, leaders must ensure the buy-in of their teams by communicating clearly about the purpose. Hard training without reasonable context is as likely to breed discontent as it is to mould cohesion. 'I had to train 1,400 soldiers to go to the Gulf War, taking them through Battle PT,' remembers Major (Retd) Glyn Sheppard, who served in a range of training and instructor roles with the Royal Army Physical Training Corps, at Sandhurst, and as a late-entry officer. 'It was a hiding to nothing unless you could develop their spirit and get them to understand why they were doing it. So we worked on the mind – we educated them on why they had to do this.'

Alongside military training and tactical exercises, sport and adventurous training (AT) also play a role in developing individuals and teams. AT, which has a long tradition in the Army, has been part of formal training since the establishment of Army Outward Bound Schools in Wales and Norway in the aftermath of the Second World War. Soldiers and officers of all ranks have periodic opportunities to participate in activities including mountaineering, sailing, paragliding, caving and kayaking. In very different environments from standard military training, these expeditions teach many fundamental leadership lessons: how to assess risk and make decisions under pressure, how to work as a team in situations that cannot be overcome individually, how to face the unfamiliar and solve unforeseen problems. AT can be an important way of building cohesion within teams, as well as stretching and developing individual leaders, especially those who undergo the specialist training to lead expeditions. 'We do it to expose our leaders to challenging situations, in risky environments, with challenges they wouldn't normally expect to find in the barracks,' says Glyn Sheppard, who designed much of the Army's policy around AT leadership training.

The influence of AT can be significant not just on new recruits and young leaders, but on those with considerable experience of working in extreme conditions, putting people in situations that test their resilience, adaptability and decision making in unfamiliar settings. Major Al Seaton, OC of the Joint Service Mountain Training Wing, wrote:

> [Speaking] with an AT instructor who jumps out of planes for a living, it was surprising to learn that he found himself up against a complete psychological block when trying to abseil down a rock face [. . .] His view of fear, failure and emotional dissonance had been completely altered by attempting a new task in a new environment. He said that he had been forced to rethink his normal coping strategies for something that had become routine in his work life.[19]

These are the lessons that matter for people who will encounter the unexpected, the unfamiliar and the adverse as a matter of course while doing their job. In a chaotic operational environment, even those with ample skills and experience can find themselves stretched to the limit. At the sharp end of an operation, soldiers will rely on their training, and their leaders will be judged on how effectively they designed and delivered it. The Army's recent experience on homeland operations – from helping to deliver the London 2012 Olympics to contributing to multiple flood relief efforts and the national response to the Covid-19 pandemic – illustrates just how important that preparation is in circumstances where military teams find themselves thrown into unusual circumstances, working alongside unfamiliar partners, required to adapt rapidly in situations of national importance and emergency.

On homeland operations

When Brigadier Lizzie Faithfull-Davies took command of 102 Logistic Brigade in March 2020, a combat service support formation in 1st (UK) Division, she had barely arrived at her headquarters before immediately having to deploy with a staff team into a fast-unfolding crisis. With the first wave of the Covid-19 pandemic reaching a critical point, 102 Logistic Brigade was asked to provide support to the

Department of Health and Social Care (DHSC) as it developed a national Covid testing programme under extreme time pressure. 'I didn't know any of my team at that time,' she remembers. 'I'd just arrived in the brigade headquarters, so my chief of staff picked a group of people that were deployable, able to move to London and who we thought covered the right mix of skills.' That core staff of ten would remain in place over the months that followed, co-ordinating military support and resources as testing sites were established across the country, new laboratories were built or scaled up to process results, and national supply chains were established.

Just one part of Operation RESCRIPT, the integrated Armed Forces response to the pandemic, the work of 102 Logistic Brigade illustrates the immediacy and unpredictability of homeland operations. The Army may go through long periods where it is not deployed on combat operations, but peacetime does not mean operational inactivity. Extreme weather, health emergencies, public service strikes and terrorist attacks can all require military support and expertise. These homeland operations have a distinct character and pose particular leadership challenges, from the speed at which they can arise, to the nature of working in integrated military and civilian teams, and the intensity of work that is invariably undertaken in crisis situations. 'It was such a fast-paced environment,' says Brig Faithfull-Davies of the initial period of Operation RESCRIPT. 'Of all the military deployments I've done in my career, I'd not operated at the pace we were working at in those first thirty days in the DHSC. I'd never seen anything grow at the pace of what we had to deliver to get to 100,000 daily tests within a month.'

Homeland operations require the Army's leaders to move at speed, amid uncertainty and often into the unfamiliar territory of leading without authority. Often the Army will play a support role alongside other Government departments, agencies and the emergency services, requiring its leaders to work in a different way than they would commanding a team of soldiers.

In February 2014, when heavy rainfall led to flooding in the Thames Valley, the Army participated in Operation PITCHPOLE, the joint

services flood relief response. Major Ben Acton, then a staff officer
with 16 Air Assault Brigade, was dispatched with a small team to support the emergency services command headquarters in Surrey. With so
many different stakeholders involved, he recalls that 'unity of effort
was the struggle initially. You had the police, the fire service, the Environment Agency, local authorities and the Army – all of whom speak a
different language operationally.' This context determined both the
role that 16 Brigade would fulfil, and the style of leadership that was
required. 'Our biggest role was to bring some coherence, battle rhythm
and to provide a framework that everyone could work within. We provided a structure and a planning process.' This had to be achieved
through building consensus about a common mode of operating. 'It
was persuasion. In terms of command we didn't have primacy, so having the soft skills to communicate, to suggest rather than tell, was
fundamental. It was about offering an option and a solution rather than
just saying, "This is the way we do it." ' As this suggests, the need to
move quickly in chaotic circumstances does not mean that the work of
team building can be ignored. Effective navigation of a crisis situation
requires tact and diplomacy as much as it does decisive action – the one
enabling the other in circumstances where there are many different
participants, all with specialist skills to contribute, who need to be
brought together within a common framework.

Operation PITCHPOLE underlines how much operational success depends on team building, and the ability of leaders to forge
cohesive teams from people and organisations who will often be meeting each other for the first time. The team for a homeland operation
will be a one-off assembly of different cap badges, joint service partners and civilian organisations – brought together for a specific task
that has neither been rehearsed nor is likely to be repeated. On that
team, leaders will typically have a mixture of people they know well
as individuals, unfamiliar colleagues with whom they nevertheless
share common military culture and operating principles, and third
parties with whom there is the least amount of common ground,
albeit a strong sense of shared purpose. Without the benefit of a pre-
existing relationship with each team member, they must be able to
make a quick assessment of those they are temporarily commanding

and working alongside. For Brig Faithfull-Davies, this meant being clear about the capabilities each individual could offer.

> I looked at the people we worked with in that programme and in my mind I broke them down into five different groups. There were the thinkers, who come up with policies and ideas. The doers, who take those ideas and turn them into something practical. The co-ordinators: structured, logical brains that come up with a clear and decisive plan with deliverables in a certain timeframe. The coherers, with the emotional, soft skills that smooth the path, build the relationships and make the programme work seamlessly. And the disruptors, who bring an important challenge function to your programme.

Having defined individual skills in this way, she says, the key was to assign people to an area where they could find and define a role that suited their skillset and personality. 'A lesson I will take away is how quickly you can empower your people. If you trust them, you empower them. They will find the niche where they can add value and make a difference, and they will do that really quickly.'

Once a team has been brought together and appropriate roles assigned, authority must be delegated to enable speed of action and decision making at the level of operational necessity. On Operation RESCRIPT, the importance of this was demonstrated by the work of a small team of NCO leaders who did much to shape the development of the entire Army's testing capability. Lt Col Will Meddings relates:

> A group of corporals from 2 Royal Anglian were tasked with learning how to deliver Covid tests, in the early days before the Army was formally involved in testing. They then came back and were told you're the only people we have trained to do this, so we need you to design a course to train others. Over the next week, they designed from scratch a short course on how to deliver COVID tests, covering everything from how to lay down parking lanes to create infection-free zones, to how to administer the test itself. This was a group of people in their mid-twenties, whose only relevant experience was teaching infantry courses, running a programme that ultimately produced in the region

of 30 per cent of the UK's testing capability, by training the trainers for almost every one of those testing teams.

This example of Mission Command in action, with NCOs acting both as leaders and followers – picking up a commander's intent, being given significant freedoms and demonstrating initiative and professionalism to deliver outstandingly against their objective – underlines the importance of work done prior to deployment. 'It was about the pre-condition of having eight people who were the right ones to do the job when we needed to call on them,' Lt Col Meddings suggests. 'That's about successive commanding officers and RSMs before me who worked really hard to select and promote the right people and develop them.' In turn, those people relied on a command climate that gave their immediate superior – a junior staff officer – and others in the chain of command the confidence to let them lead and take responsibility for a matter of critical importance.

Homeland operations throw the Army's people into situations they have not directly trained for, in a supporting role they may not be familiar with. They are operational circumstances characterised by their immediacy and organisational complexity – a distinct leadership challenge for people often accustomed to working in the military environment with its familiar handrails of hierarchy and command authority. These operations are stretching environments for the Army's leaders, but also circumstances that can bring out the best of their leadership experience and capabilities. Every successful leader is at heart a team builder, and must learn to be as adept bringing together a disparate group in a matter of hours or days as they are in building a cohesive unit over months and years. They are comfortable communicating intent and providing the right balance of direction and freedom to allow followers to make their own decisions. In the rapidly unfolding context of a homeland operation, this balancing act is the foundation of a team's ability to move at the speed of events. These operations test whether the preparation undertaken in barracks and on exercise has nurtured both the collective climate and the individual confidence to put that philosophy into action.

★

For the modern British Army, which retains its global footprint and role in the context of a shrinking headcount, peacetime can be close to a misnomer. The occurrence of 'white space' in which units are not training to assume a directed state of readiness, planned deployment or being diverted on to a new operation, is increasingly rare. This constant need for preparedness underlines the importance of leadership in barracks and on exercise, as soldiers face being deployed on a widening range of operations with different requirements. Army leaders have responsibility for teams that could be cleaning and maintaining equipment on a Monday and deployed into an operational theatre on the Friday. They must be creative, persuasive and unerring in their efforts to ensure that their people are ready for whatever the next week, month or year may bring.

They must use the time they have in barracks and during training to instil in teams the qualities they will rely upon in challenging operational conditions: the cohesion that stems from people's trust in those around them, their pride in the platoon, company and battalion of which they are a part, and their confidence that they are capable of almost anything that their commander may ask of them. Leaders may be most recognised, visible and directly accountable on operations, but they are rarely more important than in the largely unseen business of preparing their people for the challenges ahead of them. Often, their greatest contribution to operational success has been made before the first boot is on the ground.

10. Leadership in War

By the fourth day of Operation MARKET GARDEN, 20 September 1944, the audacious plan to propel the Allies over the Lower Rhine was facing severe disruption. An assault predicated on the ability of airborne soldiers to capture and hold multiple bridge crossings was in peril, as the soldiers of the 2nd Parachute Battalion hung on grimly to their position at the northern end of the bridge at Arnhem, cut off from all support. Repeated attempts to reinforce them had foundered against a rapidly organised German perimeter around Arnhem, forcing the remainder of 1st Airborne Division to retreat into a defensive position of its own, in the suburb of Oosterbeek. Having incurred heavy casualties over successive days of intense fighting, Major General Roy Urquhart, General Officer Commanding (GOC) of 1st Airborne, lamented that, 'with the weak force now left, I could no more hope to reinforce [2nd Battalion CO John] Frost than reach Berlin.'[1]

With enemy soldiers combing the woodlands and lanes of the Dutch countryside, even the retreat to Oosterbeek had become a perilous exercise. Scattered units had to fight their way back to the perimeter in an atmosphere of confusion. 'No one seemed quite certain where they were going or what was happening,' recalled Major Geoffrey Powell, a company commander in 156th Parachute Battalion, whose fighting strength by this point numbered just 120 fit soldiers, from an original strength of 603. 'It was all so hopeless. Out here in the woods, we hardly stood a chance.'[2] When his brigade commander, Brigadier (later General) 'Shan' Hackett, ordered Powell to lead an assault on a hollow occupied by German soldiers, he believed it was a suicide mission, but nevertheless complied.

> It was absurd. The men were finished. Only a few minutes ago I had realised that they were past defending themselves. Now we were being told to assault that Boche position [. . .] With my back to a broad

tree which hid me from the enemy in front, I looked down at the upturned faces [. . .] My naturally loud voice carrying down the line of men above the sounds of the battle, I bawled at them to follow me, adding the comment that it was better to be killed going for the bastards than lying in that bloody ditch.

What followed was one of the more notable actions of a legendary operation. As Maj Powell led the hopeless assault – 'We did not stand a chance, but this was the right way to go. This was the proper way to finish it all' – he brought his Sten gun to his hip and felt the mechanism jam as he fired it. Even more remarkable was the picture that greeted him as the hollow neared, of German soldiers sprinting through the trees, fleeing the assault of a company that only moments earlier had felt itself defeated. 'The sight of the savage, screaming parachutists streaming towards them had been too much for the Germans, even though they had to do no more than keep their heads and shoot straight.' What became known as 'Hackett's Hollow' would be held for several more hours, under repeated German assault, until the brigadier personally led a charge out of the clearing: 'yelling, screaming men, filthy and blood-stained, weapons in their hands, bayonets dull and menacing, a fearful sight to anyone in our path'. Against improbable odds, the remains of a shattered brigade made it back to the Oosterbeek perimeter, to fight on.

The events at Hackett's Hollow capture the essence of leadership in war, across the endless variety of contexts and circumstances in which the Army has fought throughout its history. While combat at the tip of the spear and the barrel of the gun is something soldiers can go an entire career without experiencing, it remains the fundamental reason for the Army to exist – to fight wars and defend the nation against its enemies. In service of that, soldiers may be asked, as Maj Powell was, and so many others like him have been, to go themselves and lead others into the face of mortal danger. It is this requirement that makes the profession of arms different, and it is what sets leadership in war apart. Never is the human element of leadership more visceral, nor the need for it more urgent. Morale and cohesion are required at all times, but in war they become the defining factors separating victory from defeat, and it is the animating purpose of leaders in war to sustain fighting spirit on their own side while destroying that of their enemies. As 156 PARA discovered in the woods outside Oosterbeek, it is leadership that can turn a defeated group into a successful one. Powell wrote of his company after they had seized the hollow:

> Everyone was elated by the success, slight though it was [. . .] at last we had struck back and seen the enemy run. We were ourselves again, ready to fight, different altogether from the dispirited wretches who half an hour ago had crouched for shelter in that ditch.

It was leadership, most notably Hackett's, that had revived them and would sustain the subsequent break-out. 'For the second time that day the Brigadier was ordering us to do what seemed to be impossible. But our trust in the Brigadier's judgement was now implicit.'

The leadership required in war, and in any combat situation, builds on everything that has been practised, taught and learned through an Army career. Yet war is also different, a set of circumstances that can paradoxically make leadership easier even as it presents leaders with their ultimate test. The management challenges of leading soldiers in peacetime – when boredom, frustration and distraction can set in – fade in the face of combat situations when the objective is clear and every individual is dependent on the focus and discipline of those around them: doing the job they signed up to do. War presents the Army's leaders with unique practical and psychological difficulties, but equally at no other time will they command people so intently focused on the job at hand. Operational conditions are galvanising, an opportunity for leaders to demonstrate their worth and exercise meaningful influence as much as they represent a daunting responsibility.

Equally, they are also sources of chaos and confusion that stretch leaders to the limits of their abilities. On the ground, leaders of every rank must contend with faltering equipment, unforeseen problems, plans that go awry and the response of an enemy that may – as was the case at Arnhem – prove much stronger than expected. They must adapt, reformulate plans on the go and constantly assess how, and from where, they can best command. They must find ways to boost the morale and maintain the discipline of their people, confronted with an enemy that is trying to deplete exactly those things. And they must do all this in the context of combat: under fire, with the psychological burden of lives at threat and being lost, and often exhausted from lack of sleep and food. The leadership challenges are equally pressing at the strategic level (where operations are envisioned) and the operational one (where they are planned in detail). This requires the ability to select and maintain a viable aim, judge the appropriate balance of risk and reward, manage the inevitable trade-offs between the perfect plan and the available resources, win the necessary support for an operation to proceed, and ultimately determine when the time has come to withdraw, either in victory or defeat.

Focusing primarily on three contrasting conflicts spanning the second half of the twentieth century – the Malayan Emergency, Korean War and Persian Gulf War – this chapter will explore the various levels and requirements of leadership in war, from the job of planning and preparation to the business of combat and the enduring obligation that leaders have to their people in both the immediate and long-term aftermath of battle.

Planning and preparation

'By the spring of 1950, though we had survived two dangerous years, we were undoubtedly losing the war.' That was the assessment of Richard Clutterbuck, a Royal Engineers officer and later academic, of the British position almost two years into the Malayan Emergency, the long-running confrontation with the armed insurgent wing of the Malayan Communist Party, a conflict that bridged the final period of the British Empire and the early years of the Cold War. 'There was a growing danger that the police and the civilian population would lose confidence in the government and conclude that the guerrillas in the end must win.'[3]

This was the situation that Sir Harold Briggs encountered when sent to Malaya as Director of Operations in April 1950. He entered a theatre in which over 30,000 British soldiers were deployed, and 124 major insurgent incidents had been recorded the previous month, but where he would operate as a civilian, directing a conflict that could not be designated as a war, to protect the commercial interests of British rubber planters.[4] Briggs, who had retired the previous year as a Lieutenant General and Commander-in-Chief of Burma Command, was duly tasked not to command forces but 'to plan, to co-ordinate, and direct the anti-bandit operations of the police and fighting forces'.[5] His difficulties were numerous: a military strategy which had failed to adapt to jungle conditions or consistently to source reliable intelligence; the requirement both to overhaul the Army's work and to harmonise it with that of the police force and civilian administrators; and the task not just to neutralise the Communist insurgency of the Malayan National Liberation Army (MNLA), but to erode the civilian backing on which it depended – the *Min Yuen* (People's Movement) of civilians who provided critical support, intelligence and supplies to the MNLA.

The circumstances in which Briggs began his work are indicative of the complexities of operational planning during war. While the idea of military planning suggests a world of neat boundaries, tight timetables and clear dividing lines, combat operations invariably present situations characterised by ambiguity, from the extent of military force that is appropriate, to the role the Army and its leaders should play alongside both military and civilian partners. Leaders have to work and plan within the context of shifting and competing political opinion, differing views about how to proceed, and in some cases the legacy they have inherited from their predecessor. These challenges of planning are considerable, whether the campaign is long or short, and across different kinds of warfare, from counter-insurgency to regular conflict. Each presents the leadership challenges of defining an achievable aim, securing the resources necessary to achieve it, and building the team to deliver it, all while facing the threat of an armed and motivated adversary whose next move is uncertain.

Selection of the aim, a defining principle of any operation, can be

as testing a requirement as it is essential – a cornerstone that is nevertheless subject to change. During a conflict that would prove much
longer and more complex than its early leaders had anticipated, the
Army ultimately planned and implemented several different kinds of
war. In the 'counter-terror' phase of the Emergency in 1948–9, the
emphasis was on large-scale 'jungle bashing' operations to seek out
and combat MNLA insurgents.[6] The arrival of Briggs in 1950 con-
firmed a shift in approach, with a focus on separating the MNLA
from its civilian supporters and enablers, a plan primarily implemented through the relocation of around half a million of Malaya's
Chinese population into 'New Villages', guarded by the Army and
largely governed by their inhabitants. When his successor, Lieutenant General Sir Gerald Templer, took over in 1952, the focus had
evolved again. In the joint role of Director of Operations and High
Commissioner, Templer's directive from the British Government
was to facilitate Malaya's development as 'a fully self-governing
nation'.[7] This gave rise to his observation that: 'the shooting side of
the business is only 25 per cent of the trouble and the other 75 per
cent lies in getting the people of this country behind us.'[8] Templer's
efforts to build such support – coining what would become the familiar counterinsurgency language of 'hearts and minds' – included
work to improve security and autonomy in the New Villages, begin
the work of building a future Malaysian Army, and introduce a policy by which restrictions including curfews and rationing were lifted
in areas of the country deemed free of insurgent activity.[9]

Although the Emergency would formally continue for another six
years, it was during Templer's tenure of 1952–4 that 'the backbone of
the insurgency was effectively broken'.[10] In the course of the Emergency's first six years, therefore, the planning and conduct of the
campaign shifted from a period of largely ineffective jungle warfare
to a counterinsurgency effort focused on population control, and a
nation-building operation with the stated aim of facilitating Malaya's
independence.

In a variety of guises – Briggs working as a civilian, Templer in a
joint role with military standing – the Army's leaders in Malaya were
required to evolve their approach to the conflict multiple times, based

on a combination of lessons from experience and changing political intent. Wars are not static entities, and in the long-running, irregular conflicts in which the British Army has frequently been engaged since 1945, leaders face the challenge of continuously iterating their plans to adjust to changes both on the ground and in their wider political environment. There is rarely, if ever, the luxury of a single plan that can be executed as it was first intended. As in business, there may also be the need periodically for new leadership to refocus a failing plan and re-energise the people responsible for delivering it.

'Transformations often begin, and begin well, when an organisation has a new head who is a good leader, and who sees the need for a major change,' John Kotter, Professor Emeritus of Leadership at Harvard Business School, has argued. '[A] renewal process typically goes nowhere until real leaders are promoted or hired into senior-level jobs.'[11] Such vigorous, galvanising leadership was palpably on display during Templer's two years in Malaya, as a civil servant working for him observed. '[Word] spread fast. There was this vigorous General with the critical eye and the caustic tongue popping up unexpectedly all over the place, dissecting everything that he was shown and a great deal that he wasn't meant to see, encouraging, threatening, rebuking, helping.' The impact of such interventions was measured in terms of overall progress. 'The Emergency was transfigured. A new, exhilarating spirit was born in the land. Firm, clear directives on the conduct of all aspects of the Emergency appeared.'[12]

While the energetic approach will often be important, leaders must also recognise the need in certain situations to tread lightly. The private advice given to Templer on his appointment by the recently returned Prime Minister Winston Churchill – 'Ask for power, go on asking for it, and then – never use it' – underlines the careful balancing act that was being required of him: to drive events without overreaching his designated or implicit authority.[13] In turn, it reflects the nuanced role Army leaders must typically play as they plan and direct combat operations in countries other than their own. In limited wars – those seeking an aim short of an enemy's unconditional defeat and surrender – their perennial challenge is to bring military focus and methods to bear without losing sight of the cultural and political context they are operating in, and the explicit and implicit permission they require to fulfil their mission.

Arriving in Saudi Arabia at the beginning of the Persian Gulf War, General Norman Schwarzkopf, the American Commander-in-Chief of coalition forces, quickly acknowledged that his role would be as much diplomat as commander.[14]

> I had to mask my sense of urgency in my dealings with the Saudis. To my consternation, their most pressing concern was neither the threat from Saddam nor the enormous joint military enterprise on which we were embarked. What loomed largest for them was the cultural crisis triggered by the sudden flood of Americans into their kingdom.

Even in the fraught circumstances of preparing for war against Saddam Hussein's Iraqi Army, he did not underestimate the importance of committing time to this diplomatic effort, or his personal responsibility for it.

> I kept reminding myself that I had a lot of guys who could do the military planning, but I was the only one who could assure the Saudis that the Dallas Cowgirls were not going to come over and corrupt the kingdom that was the guardian of Islam's holiest cities, Mecca and Medina.

At the organisational and strategic level, leaders must identify and commit time to the jobs that only they have the standing or experience to do, delegating those which are no less important, but which can equally effectively be achieved by others. As Gen Schwarzkopf suggested, the most senior leaders will often find their irreplaceable role is to communicate and win permission for a plan that has largely been devised by those below them.

In retrospect, the Gulf War can be seen as a model campaign: one that decisively achieved its aims within the course of half a year, culminating in a ground war of just five days' duration. But the planning challenges were no less great for it being a short war, nor should the ultimate success of the operation disguise the lack of clarity with which commanders had to grapple in its early stages. The scale of a campaign that mustered close to a million soldiers from a thirty-five-nation coalition was also uncharted leadership territory for even its most seasoned commanders. Gen Schwarzkopf reflected of the initial mobilisation in August 1990:

> I'd never dealt with anything so complex, nor had to make so many key decisions so quickly, in my life. Problems were coming at us from Washington, from Riyadh, from units and bases across the United States [. . .] I was accustomed to conferring with my staff on matters of importance but there was no time for that now. I just gave orders, one after another.

General Sir Peter de la Billière, Commander-in-Chief of British forces, faced a similar realisation when arriving in Riyadh two months later to lead the British deployment.[15]

> I was in the extraordinary position of suddenly becoming the managing director of a business with several thousand employees but absolutely no structure or facilities. Troops were pouring into the airport at Jubail, on the coast, and their heavy equipment was beginning to arrive by sea at the port nearby, but the men had no accommodation or communications beyond what they brought with them. Everything had to be created from scratch.

Logistical work represented only the beginning of the planning challenges of an operation whose initial focus was fluid, encompassing multiple possible roles for the forces that had been assembled. The Iraqi invasion of Kuwait at the beginning of August had prompted an immediate response, with the US dispatching troops to defend its ally Saudi Arabia and beginning the process of building UN support for a multinational operation. Yet as coalition forces mobilised in Saudi Arabia over the course of the autumn, it was unclear to senior commanders exactly what kind of war they would be fighting – a defensive one to repel a potential Iraqi invasion that could have come at any moment, or an offensive campaign to expel the Iraqi Army from Kuwait, where their presence had been declared illegal by the UN. 'The future is no clearer than when I left,' de la Billière wrote in a letter home on 15 October. 'It seems as if an alarm clock is ticking away to something – but what? When?' Such uncertainty, he suggested, reflected the lack of a single political opinion of how best to proceed.

> The Arabs are pushing for us to go in and get it over with before Christmas and Ramadan [. . .] The Americans are currently playing it long – two years, said [US Chairman of the Joint Chiefs of Staff] Colin Powell, the other day. [British Prime Minister Margaret] Thatcher has been playing it short, for results and action, so it is a most confused picture.

This captures the context in which Army leaders must work during war, with those at the strategic level facing the greatest responsibility to act as a bridge between the sometimes competing demands of political decision makers and the desire among their own subordinates for knowledge and information. Uncertainty in the political sphere will echo down to the tactical level of the Army: a disagreement among leaders in Government over the duration of a war, for example, ultimately means a question for soldiers and their immediate leaders about how long their tour will be. As de la Billière related, the uncertainty over the war's duration 'caused ripples of concern all through my time in the Gulf. Whenever I addressed groups of servicemen, I was inevitably asked when they would be going home and, as their commander, I felt obliged to try to give them some guidance.' Senior leaders have to be a source of clarity and confidence in the uncertain environment of war, without making promises they do not have the power to keep. They must be chameleon figures, as adept at advocating in the political sphere as they are when communicating at the soldier level.

Equally pressing is the work of team and coalition building. The challenges of integration were felt both at the national level, in terms of bringing together the efforts of the joint force, and in terms of multinational coalition building. Building a cohesive force from numerous armies with their own capabilities, operational procedures and domestic audiences was both a military and political task. 'Every country involved in the Gulf was sovereign and wanted assurances as to how its forces would be used,' General Colin Powell, the US

Chairman of the Joint Chiefs of Staff, later reflected. 'Very possibly, Norm Schwarzkopf's greatest single achievement was [. . .] to weld this babel of armies into one fighting force, without offending dozens of heads of state.'[16] Achieving this required tact and compromise on all sides.

As planning for the Kuwaiti offensive took shape in November, the British requested that its main force, 1st (Armoured) Division, be deployed not in support of the US Marines who would lead a diversionary attack, but as part of the primary assault by the VII (US) Corps – a position that its commander believed would allow it 'to be fully stretched and employed', in tactical conditions that would suit its capabilities and afford its work due prominence.[17] As Schwarzkopf later recalled:

> I didn't see how we could refuse that kind of request from a close ally, even if it was purely political and not military in intent. So we made the change – over the strenuous objection of [Marine Corps commander Walt] Boomer, who was impressed with the Desert Rats and wanted the combat power of their tanks.[18]

The land forces, which would overwhelm their adversary in a matter of days following the beginning of the ground war on 24 February 1991, came in the wake of a six-week air campaign that had done much to create the conditions for this rapid victory. By the time the ground war began, around half of the original Iraqi force in Kuwait is estimated to have deserted in the face of the aerial bombardment, and its armour and artillery strength had been reduced to two-thirds of its original capacity.[19] The ultimate success of a joint operation across air, land and sea emerged from considerable effort that went into integrating the three services. 'Most of the senior officers in the Gulf had never met each other, let alone worked together, and most had never been members of a tri-service organisation,' de la Billière recalled.[20] 'Somehow I had to convince the sailors and airmen, many of whom had powerful personalities and definite views on how things should be done, that they now needed to work as a corporate, tri-services group.' While ensuring that each service head was responsible for their own domain, he also sought to establish that they 'would not get the right answers by bypassing the system or going back up the single-service chain of command'.

The success of integration in the Gulf was not just the product of high-level bargaining and inter-services diplomacy. It also rested on personal relationships and symbolic adjustments that helped to forge common understanding. Colonel Tim Sullivan, who provided the British presence on the US staff team planning the invasion, took to wearing an American uniform to break down barriers with allies accustomed to operating as a closed circle, with important documents classified as 'NOFORN' (no foreign nationals – information not to be passed to anyone who is not a US citizen). He also continued to wear his colonel's rank after being promoted to brigadier, to ensure parity with his US team leader.

In the Gulf, coalition forces were on the ground for six months, and ultimately engaged in offensive combat on land for only a few days. While that may be an extreme example, it points to an important truth: if war is a rarity for the Army, combat in war is rarer still. The vast majority of any leader's time on operations is spent on planning, preparation and management. For many leaders, especially at the sub-unit level and above, the most testing decisions will be about how to organise and commit forces towards achieving the designated objective – where possible, through measures that fall short of armed confrontation. As I discovered in Afghanistan in 2013, one of the most demanding responsibilities is to balance the resulting equation between risk and reward, often when faced with contrasting perspectives from above and below. Commanding a company, I was often required to reconcile the hunger of my soldiers and NCOs to push the boundaries of risk with the overall directive to achieve our aims while minimising casualties. As the commander it was my responsibility, and mine alone, to make those difficult decisions. And it was my job to communicate to people why those decisions had been taken and the context they arose from – ensuring people understood the rationale, even if they did not always agree with the outcome.

This work must be done in unfamiliar situations, in which leaders are dealing with problems that extend well beyond the military sphere, discovering first-hand the wisdom of Clausewitz's famous remark that war is the continuation of politics by other means.[21] Yet while planning is paramount, and combat is a rarity for the Army, there comes a time during war when it becomes necessary to commit troops into harm's way on the battlefield. Combat remains the job the Army and its people are uniquely equipped and trained to fulfil. It is combat that every Army leader has been preparing for since their first day of training, and which presents them with situations, decisions and leadership challenges they might never otherwise encounter.

Combat

As the Korean War's first spring arrived in April 1951, UN forces were entrenched in a defensive position north of Seoul, the South Korean capital they had recaptured the previous month. The Chinese People's Army was about to begin a concerted offensive that would mobilise over 300,000 troops, but on the ground there were few indications of the fierce fighting to come. 'There had been no movement along the entire Battalion front for days,' recorded Captain (later General) Anthony Farrar-Hockley, Adjutant of the Gloucestershire Regiment, already a decade into a decorated military career that would continue for a further thirty years.[22] 'No movement along the northern bank of the winding Imjin River, now lazy, slow, and somnolent in the dry April.' Patrols that had ventured miles to the north following the establishment of the position on 5 April had revealed little or no enemy presence, and no indications of imminent action. Early in the afternoon of 22 April, Farrar-Hockley sought out the battalion's intelligence officer, only to be told he was elsewhere, with the CO. 'They're all down at the river. There's some sort of flap on.' Small patrol groups of Chinese soldiers had been sighted moving south, and at the river bank he found a group of his fellow officers directing mortar fire towards them.

Within hours the Gloucestershire Regiment, and the 29th Infantry Brigade of which it was part, would be engulfed in a battle on the hills overlooking the Imjin River, three days of intense combat against an enemy with vastly superior numerical strength, which saw almost the entirety of the Glosters killed or captured. Yet the small handful of soldiers that provided the first glimpse of the assault to come could have indicated multiple possibilities. As Farrar-Hockley wondered, 'Was it a deliberate blunder, only a deception; or was it the real thing done by parties of rather badly trained soldiers?' His CO, Lieutenant Colonel James Carne, was more confident but by no means certain. 'This looks like the real thing,' he told his Adjutant. 'It may only be a feint – we've had all these other reports about patrol action to the east; but I don't think that it is.'

This ambiguous beginning to a momentous battle demonstrates the uncertainty that surrounds the vast majority of combat in which the Army engages during operations. Even when setting the agenda in a carefully planned offensive, no leader can control every variable or prepare for every eventuality. More often, as at Imjin River, they are required to react to a rapidly unfolding situation in which there is little time between the first indications of combat being required, and the battle itself beginning. As Farrar-Hockley reflected, that brief period of realisation is when the theoretical prospect of combat becomes soberingly real for those who must decide where troops will be committed, what risks should be taken, and how much can be asked of those who will be putting their lives in danger.

> Before a battle, there must come a time when every commander reviews his strength, his dispositions, and – his prospects. And, regardless of past successes, each ensuing combat must raise for most at least a momentary doubt, a second's fear, as to its outcome.

The Battle of Imjin River, a hugely costly defeat which ultimately fulfilled a strategic purpose, helping to stem what would prove to be the last major Chinese offensive of the war, illustrates numerous elements of leadership during combat. Across its three days there were frequent examples of inspiring courage and leadership by example, of the challenge of managing risk when both lives and the mission are at stake, the question of who should make decisions in constantly changing situations with strained lines of communications, and the dilemma of when to finally accept that the need to surrender has overtaken the urge to fight on. Above all, Imjin River demonstrates the timeless nature of combat as a contest of wills, in which the most important job of leaders is to sustain their own side's will to fight, while finding ways to break that of the enemy.

As the Chinese offensive began in earnest on the evening of 22 April, a few thousand soldiers of 29th Brigade were strung across more than seven miles of the defensive line, four battalions – three British and one Belgian – with gaps of up to two miles between them.[23] On the left flank, where the fighting would rage fiercest and longest, just 773 of the Gloucestershire Regiment and its Royal Artillery support were stationed.[24] Outnumbered by a Chinese force comprising around a tenth of the strength it had mustered for the Spring Offensive, this threadbare defensive line, concentrated on a handful of hillsides there had not been time to fully fortify, was quickly broken through and its units encircled. The battle soon became a confusion of retreats, counter-attacks and attempts to reinforce 29th Brigade's diminishing line in the face of the seemingly innumerable Chinese attackers. 'I had never seen so many soldiers in my life,' recalled Private John Dwyer of the Royal Ulster Rifles, a national serviceman like many who served in Korea. 'The hillside was literally covered in them. If you've ever seen on a film when lemmings go over a cliff, it was just like that.'[25]

One of the most notable of these counter-attacks came after the Glosters were driven off the highest point of their defensive line. The OC of A Company, Major Pat Angier, ordered the commander of its 1st Platoon to retake the position.[26] 'Phil, at the present rate of casualties we can't hold on unless we get the Castle Site back [. . .] We shall never stop their advance until we hold that ground again.' The response of that officer, Lieutenant Philip Curtis, demonstrates the extraordinary courage often shown by individuals who are faced with situations of perilous necessity on the battlefield. 'Everyone knows it is vital; everyone knows it is appallingly dangerous,' as one eyewitness observed of the task Curtis had been given. Leading the assault, he was quickly wounded by machine-gun fire and dragged back to cover by members of his platoon. Then, with the same soldiers trying to restrain him until a medic could be found, he struggled back to his feet to resume the

attack. Watching on, Farrar-Hockley observed the timeless power of
leadership by example:

> And suddenly it seems as if, for a few breathless moments, the whole
> of the remainder of that field of battle is still and silent, watching
> amazed, the lone figure that runs so painfully forward to the bunker
> holding the approach to the Castle Site: one tiny figure, throwing
> grenades, firing a pistol, set to take Castle Hill.

Lt Curtis's death in this action came as he struck a telling blow of his
own, one of his grenades taking out the Chinese machine-gun crew
whose bullets felled him in the same moment. The citation for his
posthumous VC recorded the significance of his bravery: 'such furious
reaction [ensured] that [the enemy] made no further effort to exploit
their success in this immediate area: had they done so, the eventual
withdrawal of the Company might well have proved impossible.'[27]

Displays of personal courage could not disguise the parlous situation in which 29th Brigade found itself, one that brought to the
surface the difficulty of mediating information and decisions across
multiple layers of command, between individuals with different
perspectives and positions on the battlefield. As the extent of 29th
Brigade's predicament became apparent, its commander Brigadier
Tom Brodie twice requested permission from his chain of command –
the US-led I Corps – to withdraw. Some in his headquarters believed
that their commander had failed to make the case forcefully enough,
or to communicate the situation in terms that an American General
would understand. 'When Tom told Corps that his position was "a
bit sticky", they simply did not grasp that in British Army parlance,
that meant "critical",' one staff officer suggested.[28]

Differences in emphasis and language – a challenge of leadership
in multinational coalitions – were not the only source of difficulty.
In increasingly parlous circumstances, decisions were needed about
whether to prioritise reinforcement or withdrawal; where to draw
the line between the imperative of the present mission and the need
to limit casualties and preserve future fighting strength. By the
afternoon of 24 April, with the Glosters reduced to fewer than 400,
low on ammunition and with many weapons 'damaged or smashed

completely beyond repair', Lieutenant Colonel Carne relayed the situation to his Brigadier. 'What I must make clear to you is the fact that my command is no longer an effective fighting force. If it is required that we shall stay here, in spite of this, we shall continue to hold. But I wish to make clear the nature of my position.' The response was apologetic but firm: '[Brodie] said he realised how things stood with us, but the job had to be done; and we were the only one who could do it.'[29] While the other battalions of 29th Brigade were able to retreat, the surrounded Glosters, the batteries of their wireless radios running dry and their ammunition depleted, faced destruction. After the battle, just 169 of its 850 members were present for the next roll-call. Over half, 459 men, were taken prisoner.[30]

The fate of the Glosters at Imjin River underlines the fragile link between information and decisions that is present on any battlefield. To a lesser or greater extent, commanders are constrained by the decisions of those above them, decisions shaped by a perspective that can both benefit from being removed from the heat of battle and be limited by a failure to fully recognise ground truth. A fortnight after the battle, General Matthew Ridgway, recently appointed to overall command of UN forces in Korea, privately expressed his belief that the Glosters had fallen victim to a failure of leadership, notably at the senior level. In a letter written a fortnight after the battle, he confessed 'a certain disquiet that down through the channel of command the full responsibility for realising the danger to which this unit was exposed, then for extricating it when the danger became grave, was not recognised nor implemented.' As he reflected, one of the perennial challenges of leadership during combat is for those with the greatest responsibility to determine when the moment has come to overrule others who may be closest to the consequences of a tactical decision, or believe themselves best placed to make it. 'There are times [. . .] when it is not sufficient to accept the judgement of a subordinate commander that a threatened unit can care for itself or that a threatened situation can be handled locally.'[31]

Yet if the Glosters were placed in a desperate situation by the decisions of their commanders and the extent of their enemy, the manner of their famous rearguard action is a testament to the importance of morale, regimental identity and fighting spirit on the battlefield. 'We wore on our heads the common or garden dark blue beret as issued, with our Glosters' badges gleaming proudly,' wrote Private Donald 'Lofty' Large, later a Squadron Sergeant Major in the SAS. 'The back badge is worn as a battle honour from a war long ago, when the regiment had to stand back to back (surrounded as usual) in order to win the day. Looking at the history of the Glosters, one could get the impression that some situations are habit forming.' As he recalled, this heritage proved a source of both inspiration and humour during the worst of the battle:

> 'B' Company was being slaughtered, but not in spirit. An obviously officer's voice shouted: 'Stand fast the Glosters – remember the Back Badge!' and an obviously trog's [private's] voice immediately shouted back: 'F— the Back Badge – I want out' [. . .] I was amazed to find myself laughing and heard the laughter of others through the clatter and roar of the battle.[32]

Even as the inevitability of their fate closed in, morale was not broken. 'This looks like a holiday in Peking for some of us,' the battalion's padre, Sam Davies, was overheard remarking on the morning of 25 April. As the historian Sir Max Hastings noted in his account of the battle,[33] the importance of this collective spirit was widely recognised by those who fought at Imjin River.

> The quality about the Gloucesters' stand upon which all the survivors focused in their later accounts was the confidence: the serene conviction of most officers and men that they could cope, even as their casualties mounted, their perimeter shrank, and their ammunition dwindled.

Such fighting spirit and collective confidence is both the product of good leadership – forged by individuals who have trained their units effectively and nurtured common knowledge of regimental tradition – and also one of the most important aids to leaders when they face situations that only the battlefield presents.

If Imjin River helps to illustrate the character and leadership requirements of a defensive battle, the land component of the Gulf War, Operation DESERT SABRE, highlights the challenges posed by an offensive action. In the Gulf, these began with the question of whether such an assault would even be necessary to achieve the objective of expelling the Iraqi Army from Kuwait. 'We all hoped that there wouldn't be a ground war,' suggested Major General (Retd) Patrick Cordingley, who commanded 7th Armoured Brigade in the Gulf as a brigadier, on the twenty-fifth anniversary of the conflict.[34] '[At the time] we couldn't see how Saddam Hussein, when he saw how effective the air campaign was [. . .] wouldn't pull out of Kuwait.' Accepting the requirement to commit troops in the field, to face an enemy whose true strength is never easy to quantify, is a sobering reality for any commander. 'We were all concerned,' he remembered. 'The Iraqi Army was 400,000 men strong, and although it clearly wasn't well led and its equipment turned out to be not very good, we didn't know that at the time.'

Once the necessity for a ground campaign has been accepted, leaders must also recognise the importance of preparing their people for the realities of using offensive force. Maj Gen Cordingley recalled:

> Very few of us had been in the Falklands War. A lot of us had been in Northern Ireland, but there you were reacting to people firing at you. Here we were saying to the soldiers, 'It's perfectly alright to kill people, we're going to fire first.' And that is a jump in the mindset of what you're trying to do. You're trying to get everybody absolutely aware of what it was that was legal to do, what we were expecting people to do [. . .] It was a huge mindset change for them.

To that end, Cordingley's fellow brigade commander, Brigadier Chris Hammerbeck, issued the following instruction to his soldiers on the eve of the offensive, providing the moral leadership that is so important in battle: 'Be firm with those who resist, and humane and caring for those who surrender and are injured. Respect human life for what it is and do not allow yourself to sink, no matter what we may see in the days ahead.'[35]

Alongside the work to prepare individuals were the questions of how to manage command, communications and logistics in an assault that would cover 180 miles in under 72 hours. Major General Rupert Smith, commander of 1st Armoured Division, determined a plan 'to fight lots of little fights quickly, over a period, rather than a few big ones over the same period.' This conditioned a battle rhythm whereby one of the two brigades would be committed in combat, with its counterpart dropping into a support and logistics function, 'speeding up the process of re-organisation and replenishment'.[36] It was a plan characterised by his Commander-in-Chief in pugilistic terms: '[Smith's] plan, in brief, was to fight his two brigades as if he were a boxer, punching first with one, then, while that brigade replenished, punching with the other.'[37]

This approach relied on a willingness to devolve decision making down the chain of command, reflecting the philosophy of Mission Command that had recently been enshrined in British Army doctrine. 'As a matter of principle I set out to lower decision levels, thus reducing the need for information to flow upwards and speeding action,' Maj Gen Smith suggested. With communications struggling to keep up with the rapidly advancing battle, he came to appreciate this commitment to agility. 'The Divisional nets [radio channels], let alone those available to the Corps, became fragmented with all the movement [. . .] The devolution of decision and the groupings to allow for this, paid off in these circumstances.' The repeated switching of his two brigades was designed to achieve what Smith characterised as tempo, 'which in these circumstances I define as the rate at which one is ready for and starting the next fight'.

Lecturing in 2018,[38] he expanded on the importance of this in offensive warfare:

> It is the intensity that kills and shocks your adversary into defeat. There must be tempo: a combination of speed, organisation, supply and maintenance, so as to do it again and again, faster than your opponent can react. This, among other things, will lead you to achieving tactical surprise on the battlefield.

The success of this approach, he further suggested, rests on the quality of leadership throughout the chain of command, not simply delegating responsibility but ensuring that leaders at all levels have been trained and empowered to act in a way that allows them to seize fleeting opportunities as they arise, and make decisions accordingly. 'You need morale: bold leaders, crisis-proof leaders who will take the most aggressive course of action, who [. . .] enjoy causing havoc [and] accept uncertainty.'

Whether combat is short or sustained, offensive or defensive, the same fundamental principle applies. Almost regardless of context, the objective of combat is always to break the will of the enemy, something that may be depleted long before their equipment is broken and their supplies exhausted and their positions overrun. Gen Sir Peter de la Billière wrote:[39]

> In the event, it soon became apparent that the Iraqis' will to fight had been severely eroded by the air war. Weeks of bombardment, lack of sleep and proper food had reduced their efficiency so much that their morale was at rock bottom even before the Coalition launched its ground offensive. Then, under the speed and ferocity of the Allied assault, they collapsed, unit by unit.

The breaking of the enemy's will may mark the end of combat, but until a truce has been declared or peace terms agreed, a state of war persists. Regardless of the political dimension, there are the very practical dangers of a large Army still operating in a theatre of war, one whose guard may be down. As de la Billière noted about the aftermath of DESERT SABRE:

> Now that the tension had been suddenly reduced, there was an inevitable tendency for everyone to relax and lose vigilance [. . .] People who had survived the war could kill themselves needlessly by wandering into minefields, entering buildings which had not been cleared, falling asleep while driving or simply by collecting unstable souvenirs.

As this suggests, the need for leadership in war does not expire the moment that the fighting stops. The work that leaders do in the aftermath of a major combat engagement can be as important as the role they played on the battlefield.

Aftermath

The work of leadership does not end when the battle, or even the entire war, is over. Whether returning home, facing captivity or preparing to continue their operational tour, the duties of being a soldier and the responsibility to lead continue. The importance of fighting spirit does not diminish once the battle has ended, as the story of Fusilier Derek Kinne, who fought with the Royal Northumberland Fusiliers at Imjin River, demonstrates. As a prisoner of war, he suffered appalling treatment at the hands of his Chinese and North Korean captors, including regular beatings, solitary confinement in rat-infested conditions, and torture whereby he was made to stand on tip-toe with his head in a noose. Yet he continued to resist, attempting further escapes, refusing political indoctrination, and even facing punishment for fashioning a rosette in June 1953 to celebrate Queen Elizabeth's coronation. Finally released as part of the last group of Korean War PoWs to be repatriated, his George Cross citation recorded the influence of his leadership by example: 'His powers of resistance and his determination to oppose and fight the enemy to the maximum were beyond praise. His example was an inspiration to all ranks who came into contact with him.'[40]

In the wake of momentous battles that can amount to a collective experience of trauma, the need for morale to be boosted and common purpose restated is paramount. In these moments, individual leaders may serve to lift the spirits of their people, as Lofty Large observed of his CO when their paths crossed in captivity.

> I saw Colonel Joe Carne. He was standing apart from his column, greeting all the men in my column as they passed. As I approached him I was very surprised when he said, 'Well done, Large. Chin up, we'll be OK soon.'
>
> What a man, how could he even remember the names and faces of nearly all his battalion, even to new arrivals like myself – who certainly had not looked like this the last time he had seen us.[41]

Equally, the same effect can be experienced in reverse: a commander being buoyed by the spirit of their soldiers. As Major Gerald Rickord, acting CO of the Royal Ulster Rifles – the third of 29th Brigade's British battalions at Imjin River – recalled:

> I believed that we had lost the battle, had suffered a disaster. But I was afterwards reassured that it was by no means a disaster. The morning after we came out, the soldiers were singing Irish songs, playing a banjo [. . .] forty-eight hours later, they were fit to fight again, which was a wonderful feeling. I think they felt very proud of the fight they had put up.[42]

Leaders have a responsibility to boost their people and rebuild their teams, but must also come to terms with their own emotions in the aftermath of battle, when the tendency to relive events and agonise over decisions can be difficult to resist. Maj Gen Roy Urquhart, following his command of 1st Airborne Division at Arnhem, found himself unable to eat at a dinner that was held to mark his shattered formation's return. 'The food nauseated me. The battle still raged in my head.' For some time after the battle, he found his ability to work as normal impaired. 'I shared with other survivors of the division an incredible lassitude that was to persist for weeks so that it required a conscious effort to attend to routine matters which normally I would have taken in my stride.'[43]

For those who return after months or years in captivity, the adjustment to a world that has moved on without them can be especially jarring. 'I could not help twinges of jealousy at seeing someone else commanding that which for so long had been mine,' Lieutenant Colonel John Frost, who had commanded 2nd Parachute Battalion in its desperate struggle at the Arnhem Bridge, reflected on his return to England in 1945. 'I soon realised that no one was going to be able to form a welcoming party for the rather battered prisoners arriving in dribs and drabs.'[44]

The job of leaders in the aftermath of war is long-term as well as immediate; operational as well as personal. Leaders must provide the continuity and institutional knowledge that allow the lessons of past wars to be retained and integrated into training and future planning, a model for conflicts that lie ahead without becoming a millstone that restricts the ability to adapt and evolve. The failure to do this can be keenly felt, as it was during the initial period of the Malayan Emergency, when recent experience of jungle warfare in the Burma campaign of the Second World War did not prevent the Army from reverting to unsuited tactics, 'thrashing about' in conditions that negated conventional force and instead rewarded the precision work of small units with strong junior leadership and effective intelligence networks.[45] Even as this lesson was gradually learned, there continued to be frustration at the inability to learn from experience and share best practice widely.

In one of his 'red minutes', missives which could lead to the recipient's dismissal if a swift response was not forthcoming, General Templer made his feelings clear:

> I am not entirely happy in my mind as to whether the best jungle tactics are practised both by army units and by the Police [. . .] whether there is any system of sucking the brains of Commanding Officers of units who have had more experience and better success than others, such as 1st Suffolks, I do not know.[46]

It is the job of leaders to promote institutional learning both during long campaigns and in their aftermath, but also to recognise the limitations of what can be learned from experience. Strategic leaders in particular must recognise that the next war may be nothing like the last one they experienced, or the one they have anticipated. 'We had been planning for this kind of war on a grand scale for years at NATO,' Gen Colin Powell wrote of the build-up to the Gulf War. 'But we had assumed it would be fought amid hills and forests against a Soviet enemy, not across sand dunes against an Arab foe.'[47] As he later reflected during his political career, the demise of the Soviet Union and the end of the Cold War had been a jarring experience for a soldier who had only known an operating environment in which both loomed large.

> I spent so much of my career ready to fight this enemy and, suddenly, it was gone. We watched the Iron Curtain come down; we watched as Germany unified itself almost overnight; we watched as all those Eastern European nations were told pursue your own destinies; and

we watched as the Soviet Union ended. The world we knew just fundamentally went away at that point, and became a mosaic with changing bits and pieces every day – almost a kaleidoscope.[48]

The lessons and legacies of past campaigns are personal as much as institutional. In Army careers that can span decades and operations spanning a wide variety of circumstances and conditions, every leader is inescapably shaped by their experiences. It is in the aftermath of a campaign, facing the human costs of an operation, that leaders confront the true meaning of their responsibility: what it means to make decisions that, by necessity, may place the lives of your people at risk. Like many Army leaders, I have sat in a hospital ward with the family of a badly wounded soldier, who faced the silent agony of not knowing if he would live or die. The experience stays with you: though this soldier had not been under my command, and thankfully recovered, it is a stark reminder of how the worst can happen to the people you are ordering into harm's way. Such experiences go beyond the personal. They can also have operational consequences, conditioning the attitudes of leaders to risk in future campaigns. As Gen Sir Peter de la Billière suggested, old wars and past failings had a significant influence in shaping the direction of the Gulf War on all sides, and the approach to fighting the land campaign. 'The thing that was of paramount importance to Schwarzkopf and me was the need to avoid casualties [. . .] in my mind this came from Korea, where there were heavy casualties, and to his mind, from his experience in Vietnam.'[49]

Battles live with those who fought them throughout their military careers, as sources of inspiration and cautionary tales, and also for the rest of their life outside the Army. The experience of death and destruction, of having to kill and see others killed around you, is one people carry with them, whether subconsciously or openly acknowledged. In this regard, those who serve in the Army share much with those across Armed Forces and emergency services who encounter death and destruction in the course of their work, experiences that can have long-term effects on mental health and well-being. 'Once in the pub the faces of nearly every dead person I'd ever dealt with flashed across the front of my eyes and I burst into tears,' recalled Roger Moore, a fire fighter for thirty years, in 2017.[50]

The experiences of those who had to watch on while others fought and died can be equally affecting. '[A] veteran who, through no fault of his own, did not fight in the battle, broke down fifty-seven years later during a telephone conversation with me,' the author Andrew Salmon wrote in his account of the Battle of Imjin River. '[He] was still devastated that he had been unable to take part, with his friends, in the battle.'[51]

People leave the Army, but their experiences in it never entirely leave them, which means the responsibility of their leaders is life-long. The duty of care continues, and in many cases both individual relationships and regimental bonds will endure for years and decades. Both are essential to helping soldiers who have left the Army and may be struggling with the often difficult transition to civilian life, removed from the environment of camaraderie, clear expectations and common identity that the Army represents. 'In the Army there's a lot of purpose. You're all working together as a team towards a sin-gular aim or task or whatever you're doing and there's immense pride in it,' says Chris Dodd, who served for eleven years in the Princess of Wales's Royal Regiment and now works for the Royal British Legion. By contrast, he suggests, 'civilian life is about as polar opposite as you can get to serving in the Armed Forces. There is definitely that feel-ing of "square peg round hole" at times, you don't really know where you fit and what you're supposed to do or what your purpose is.'[52]

Helping soldiers adapt to civilian life is both an institutional respon-sibility of the Army and a lifelong commitment of individual leaders. Official help is facilitated by a range of support services and charities, from Veterans UK within the MOD, which assists with pensions, wel-fare and the transition to civilian life, to charities such as the Royal British Legion and ABF The Soldiers' Charity. Regimental associa-tions, which maintain active networks of veterans and serving personnel, are another vital source of support and a manifestation of the enduring regimental family and its role throughout the lives of service people. For many, they are the most meaningful connection with their former service, and a first port of call when problems arise. In parallel, support will often be unofficial and between individuals. The bonds forged through years of shared service are lifelong, and a leader's sense of responsibility to their team and its people will endure for years and decades after their command ends. These obligations are unspoken but strongly felt: personal experience suggests there are few leaders who do not continue to provide active support to many individuals they once served alongside and to whom they feel an ongoing sense of responsibility – whether attending family events, championing charitable causes, or helping both individuals and their families with specific personal or professional problems.

The Army's strong tradition of memorial plays an important role in lifelong support, from the annual Remembrance Sunday events to those that commemorate individual conflicts and battles, such as the annual pilgrimage to Arnhem, which was attended by over 100,000 on the seventy-fifth anniversary of the battle, in 2019. As General Hackett reflected, such memorials acknowledge the cost of war while also reinforcing its meaning and legacy.

> This was a battle but its significance as an event in human experience transcends the military [. . .] those of us who fought through this battle have become aware that what remains with us can best be described as a spiritual experience. To see Dutch children who were not born when all this happened; most of whose parents were not born either, laying their flowers year after year on the quiet graves in the Airborne cemetery at Oosterbeek teaches a lesson not easily forgotten.[53]

As this suggests, the aftermath of war is ultimately generational and long-term. The need to support those who have survived, and keep alive the memory of those who did not, remains as important years and decades after the event as it was in the immediate aftermath. Much as no war is ever finally over in the minds of those who fought it, nor are the responsibilities of its leaders extinguished while they, and those they fought alongside, remain to remember and relive it.

Leadership in war may be a rare experience for the Army's leaders, but often it will be a defining one. Actions in war shape careers, define reputations, and leave individuals with the memories of decisions made and unmade that they will continue to reflect on for the rest of their lives. For those who rise to positions of senior command, experiences of war early in their careers will often prove formative, conditioning their priorities, their attitude to risk and the questions they spend most time pondering.

This balance between past and present is a constant consideration for the Army's leaders in war, and when preparing for future conflicts. Every war is different, but there is much about warfare that does not change, as an enduring contest of wills in which the maintenance and destruction of fighting spirit lie at the heart of success and failure. It is for this reason that the kind of historical examples explored in this chapter remain a central part of the Army's leadership training.

Equally, the context and character of war is constantly changing, as the Army's operating environment evolves and the national threat landscape shifts. Army leaders must be as capable of assessing the future as they are of drawing lessons from the past and meeting their immediate challenges. The final chapter will explore this question of the future, looking at how the Army can meet its perennial need to fight the next war and not refight the last, as the character, tools and context of warfare undergo rapid and dramatic change.

11. The Future

In 2009, at the height of the Taliban insurgency in Helmand Province, British troops sought advice from Afghan leaders about where to situ-ate a new Forward Operating Base (FOB) in the district of Nad-e-Ali. They were quickly pointed to an obvious site – one the British Army had used before. FOB Shawqat was duly established amid the ruins of a mud-brick fortification that had been built by the British in the late nineteenth century, during the Second Anglo-Afghan War.[1] The Army had found itself not just in the same country and the same dis-trict as 130 years earlier, but inside the walls of the self-same fortification from which it had withdrawn in 1880, after the defeat of the outnum-bered First Infantry Brigade at the Battle of Maiwand.[2]

This quirk of history shows how an institution like the Army continually finds itself at the intersection of continuity and change. The two campaigns that brought British soldiers to Nad-e-Ali were separated by more than a century of evolution in tactics, technology and geopolitics. Yet on the ground, the fundamentals of leadership and command for an infantry section patrolling the desert in 2010 would have largely been as recognisable to its prede-cessors of 1880 as their surroundings. As the current Chairman of the Joint Chiefs of Staff General Mark Milley has argued, 'The nature of war is never gonna change. But the character of war is changing before our eyes.'[3] How to manage that change is one of the most pressing, and enduring, challenges of Army leadership. It is enduring because every military, throughout its history, has had to continuously adapt to changes in the technology, economies, culture and society that shape its operating context. And it is chal-lenging because there is not one future to prepare for but several: the near horizon of what is known and likely, the medium frontier of what is possible, and the furthest aspect of what is almost impos-sible to perceive.

As it looks towards these futures, the Army must constantly be aware of its history – determining what traditional strengths need to be maintained, and where breaks with the past are required. Getting ready for what will, may or could happen next is a task that sparks numerous judgement calls and balancing acts. Is recent experience a reliable guide for the future, or simply a reflection of the unique circumstances of a particular operation or campaign? What combination of emerging needs and rising threats should be given priority? How can the limited pool of resources available to the Army at a given time best be organised and deployed? For the Army's senior leaders, the future is a constant test of their ability to distinguish trends from anomalies, weigh experience against uncertainty, and judge not just the direction of change but its probable speed. It demands a series of responses that blend short-term priorities with medium- and long-term requirements, never letting one entirely crowd out the other.

These considerations may culminate on the battlefield – in whatever form and whichever domain that may be – but must also stretch far beyond changes in the business of warfighting. An effective Army must be equally responsive to changes in geopolitics that shift the contours of the threat landscape; changes in society which adjust the expectations of those the Army both serves and recruits; changes in technology which can erode traditional advantages as they empower adversaries; and changes in the global economy and environment which can harbour instability and lead to conflict. The modern Army's stated purposes – to protect the UK, prevent conflict, deal with disaster and fight the nation's enemies – require an institution that is constantly looking forward, evolving its capacity and adapting its methods to remain at peak operational effectiveness in a changing and volatile world. And they require one governed by leaders with the judgement, foresight and risk appetite to steer a complex institution in an unstable environment. 'The litmus test for our leadership is the ability to navigate a new inescapable reality – how to keep up with the pace of change and how to reimagine how it's going to influence our business in the future,' the incumbent CGS, Gen Sir Mark Carleton-Smith, believes.[4]

The future is not just a test for Army leaders but of the principles and practice of Army leadership. An increasingly volatile, technological and fast-paced environment raises the question of what kind of leaders the organisation will require in the future, the skills they will need, and whether these differ fundamentally from those of the past and present. Will the Army leaders of tomorrow require distinct skills and capabilities, what might those look like, and what does it entail for the Army's approach to selecting, training and developing leaders through their military careers? Will navigating the future require a step change in the Army's culture and practice of leadership, or simply an evolution of the enduring principles that have defined it through centuries of past change? How closely or otherwise will the Army leaders of the future resemble those of the past, and how recognisable would their approach be to a Wellington, Slim, Montgomery or Bramall?

As it faces the future, the Army is both equipped with the advantages and confronted with the limitations of being a large, long-standing institution steeped in enduring traditions. It has the experience and perspective of an organisation that has been through numerous generations of development, and the parallel challenge of having accumulated structures, assumptions and institutional biases that can impede the process of change. Like any large organisation, the Army must approach the future with humility about the need for change and recognition of its scale, but also a level of confidence in its core purpose, enduring capabilities and historical legacy. This chapter will examine that balance between change and continuity, looking at what is developing in and around the Army, what elements of its leadership culture are likely or not to endure, and how its leaders can prepare for the challenges and uncertainty the future will bring.

What changes

Writing almost a century ago, while Chief Instructor at Staff College, the British officer and military theorist J. F. C. Fuller set out what he defined as the science of war in what he characterised as a rapidly changing context. 'As regards war, [the reader] must realise that everything is changing. We are faced by air warfare, and mechanical warfare on land, and submarine warfare at sea, and chemical warfare everywhere.'[5] He captured an enduring reality for practitioners of war, who must constantly adapt to new, sometimes dramatic, developments in tactics and technology: a requirement borne out by Fuller's own career. His first campaign had been the Second Anglo-Boer War, whose failings had reopened a long-running dispute over whether cavalry troops were better armed with rifle, sword or lance.[6] He made his name during the First World War as a tactical innovator in the emerging field of armoured warfare, as cavalry gave way to tanks. And in retirement in the 1950s, he pondered how an even more destructive weapon – the atomic bomb – would again change the practice and dynamics of warfare. In the course of half a century, encompassing the career of one individual, the debate about the future of war had evolved from considering which tool to put into the hands of horse-mounted troops to the utility of a remotely delivered weapon that could flatten an entire city.

Witnessing change of such magnitude can be disorienting and confusing, both for an institution and the individuals in it, whether setting policy or being affected by it. The leaders responsible for navigating the organisation through these moments face an acute leadership challenge, with numerous pitfalls. As Fuller outlined, one risk is that change is underappreciated and its long-term significance disregarded.

> After the battle of the Somme in 1916, when tanks first took the field, we were told that it was a mistake to have used them because there were not sufficient [numbers] to warrant success and their surprise effect was consequently lost. After the battle of Cambrai the following year, in which tanks played a decisive part, we were told that a similar surprise could never again be repeated.[7]

Yet, as he pointed out, tanks proved to be the primary agent of surprise in 1940 during the Nazi Blitzkrieg, deploying a weapon that had by then been operational for almost twenty-five years.

At the other end of the spectrum, the first glimpse of change can cause organisations to rush to judgement or into an unwise course of action. 'Just because a new and exciting technology appears doesn't mean it must fit into an emerging warfighting concept,' US Major General (Retd) Robert H. Scales, who led US Army preparations for the future of war in the 1990s, has warned. Reflecting on that work, he suggested that the thinking was correct but the operational application was premature.

> In our study, we concluded that strategic speed necessary to arrive quickly could only be achieved by unburdening the operational force. That meant lighter fighting vehicles, a thin if not missing logistical umbilical cord, and the substitution of aerial systems to replace ground systems [. . .] But we [implemented] too early. The technologies essential for the success of [the strategy] weren't ready for prime time in 2000.

For the Army's leaders, the challenge is how to assimilate the torrents of technological, social, economic and environmental change that surround them, and calibrate both the direction and speed of organisational change. Although the temptation is always to try and move as quickly as the context appears to be changing, this can be a mistake. Transplanting ideas from the more distant horizon into the near future can be as problematic as failing to match the evolving capabilities of allies and adversaries. '[History] shows us that we can't afford to get the thinking part over quickly in order to get a budget line started,' Scales has argued. 'Imagining the future is like making a fine wine. It needs sufficient time for debate, synthesis and second-order thought.'[8]

Operationally, the future is not a linear progress of things yet to come, but a matrix of existing developments maturing and new ones emerging. New threats are not necessarily analogous to new technologies, and the failure to adapt to what is already familiar can be as dangerous as the inability to foresee what has not yet occurred. For the Army, like any large organisation, the question of what changes is multifaceted: encompassing how to adapt in the present to known factors, how to prepare for ongoing shifts that have been anticipated, and how to maintain readiness for what cannot be foreseen. Leadership must be capable of thinking, planning and acting across three time horizons in parallel – taking care not to overemphasise any one dimension. It must avoid the trap of living only in the present and distant future, forgetting the critical middle ground of ideas that are nearing viability. As the technology author Geoffrey Moore argued, writing in 2007, there is often 'little time and management attention for goals that are short of long-term but not contained in the budget year. These projects are strategic but not yet material. Like planes in the Bermuda Triangle, they have a disconcerting tendency to fall off the radar.'[9]

Leaders must juggle these different time horizons in an operating context that is fast evolving – one defined by fluidity in the identity of adversaries, the nature of their activities and the tools at their disposal. A society whose entire functioning has become dependent on digital exchange has become vulnerable, in turn, to attacks on the networks and infrastructure which make that possible. As General Sir Nick Carter, Chief of the Defence Staff from 2018 to 2021, has said: '[The] means to control others – principally through the application of technology – is the crux of the matter. Because control of digital technology allows our rivals to take over our way of life.'[10] Adversaries can mount direct attacks on key systems, whether civil or military, they can spread misinformation and propaganda with unprecedented speed and reach, and they can act indirectly through non-state actors – operating 'sub-threshold' (below the level of armed conflict), in the hope of achieving their aims without recourse to warfighting. In this context, the Army's purpose to defend the UK must extend far beyond combating traditional threats to national security. As the Integrated Operating Concept, the UK's guiding approach to the use of armed force, sets out:

> [. . .] the 'front' no longer lies in some distant theatre of operations, but is within the port, airfield or barracks. It sits across the electromagnetic spectrum; it is in space and inside our networks; it is already loitering in our supply chains. Sub-threshold operations are continuously executed at reach by malign actors who seek to undermine our

military readiness, our critical national infrastructure, our economy, our alliances and our way of life.[11]

The activities of adversaries are only one part of the changing operating context. Equally important are economic, demographic and environmental trends that affect global stability, and in turn determine the Army's roles to prevent conflict and deal with disaster. The factors that shape the world in the coming decades will also do much to determine the Army's role in it. Such mega-trends can have multiple implications spanning the short-, medium- and long-term futures. In the present, climate change is already giving rise to the kind of extreme weather events that require a disaster response, while looking ahead it is set to spur an increased pace of urbanisation, greater competition for resources, and ultimately contribute to political instability that makes military support more likely to be needed. At the time of writing, 80 per cent of personnel on UN peacekeeping operations were deployed in countries regarded as most exposed to the effects of climate change.[12] Empirical research has quantified the impact of global warming as a 14 per cent increase in intergroup conflict for each standard deviation increase in temperatures (of which there are expected to be between two and four by 2050).[13]

A structural, wide-reaching challenge such as climate change highlights how the Army must serve the needs of multiple future time horizons in parallel. Lieutenant General Richard Wardlaw, Chief of Defence Logistics and Support, who has led much of the Army's work on preparing for climate change, has highlighted 'an inevitable tension for the Army which faces short-term imperatives to invest in military capability, imperatives which are currently far more pressing in their manifestation relative to climate change, where the threats will mature over a longer-term timeline.' Resolving this, he has argued, requires leadership that is willing to think and act with a truly long-term perspective:

> [. . .] it became clear to the Army Board that a decision to defer action would be an abrogation of responsibility and would exacerbate the challenge for their successors. It is their responsibility as Board

members to make the best decisions for the long term, and not to make decisions today that compound the future threat.[14]

As the Army adapts to developments in its global environment and operating context, it must also respond to change closer to home, not least among the people it employs and is seeking to recruit. Meeting the needs of its people is a growing challenge at a time when attitudes towards work and career are changing, and divides are opening up between different generations in the workplace. As an organisation that predominantly develops its leaders from the ground up, the Army's future is dependent on its ability to adapt to changing generational mores and expectations, without eroding the structures and systems on which the institution depends. Moreover, as a large employer that brings together those who have been serving for decades with recruits who have just left school, the Army must manage the growing scope for intergenerational tension – something that 59 per cent of employees have experienced according to one study, over issues including use of technology, speed of career progression and workplace culture.[15]

The requirement to embed new generations of officers and soldiers who emerge from a shifting social context is perennial – spurring a balancing act between moulding individuals to fit the institution and adapting it to suit new needs. Equally, some surveyed attitudes of Gen Z – those born after 1997, the Army's primary recruiting pool at the time of writing – represent particular challenges to an organisation that is based around rank, hierarchy and command authority: at least a third of Gen Z said they would never tolerate being forced to work when they don't want to, or having an employer who gave them no say over their work schedule. A clear majority (57 per cent) expect to be promoted at least once a year.[16] This generation is coming of age in a world where individualism is on the rise globally, quantified by researchers through increases in people's propensity to live in smaller households, have been divorced or separated, value friends over family, prize self-expression, and teach their children to be independent.[17] In these contexts, an institution like the Army that has traditionally stressed service before self and the primacy of team must find an accommodation between these enduring philosophies and the growing emphasis that many place on autonomy, self-direction and personal values at work.

As it adapts to changes in the world around it, the Army as an institution is also continuing to undergo change internally. Since the Second World War, the Regular Army has consistently contracted in size, from a headcount of approximately 364,100 in 1950 to 152,800 at the end of the Cold War in 1990, and a target strength of 72,500 by 2025, as more emphasis is placed on technology, data and information systems.[18] As a smaller organisation that is facing a widening threat landscape, the Army also increasingly works in integrated efforts with other Armed Forces, government departments, intelligence agencies and industry partners. The scale and scope of the modern Army's work – responding to health crises at home and around the world, supporting peace enforcement and conflict prevention, assisting allies to develop capacity and expertise, providing disaster response, and remaining ready for future combat operations – requires a response of which the Army can be just one part, lending expertise, resources and capabilities to the integrated operations that define the modern security landscape. That will entail a future in which the Army operates in a different way, providing capacity and specialist skills, working side by side with military and civilian partners to respond to emergencies, as part of what Brigadier John Clark, the Army's head of strategy, has described as 'smaller teams that can go out there and compete beneath the threshold of conflict'.[19]

For Army leaders, this emerging environment creates some distinct challenges. The emphasis on interoperability will require commanders who are comfortable leading without authority, as part of broader teams with contrasting working and leadership cultures. The need for multi-disciplinary teams will depend on leaders who can bring together diverse individuals with contrasting personalities, skillsets and working styles. While the complex, ambiguous threats that are set to arise sub-threshold will need leadership at all levels to navigate with confidence and speed. As they face this future, the Army's leaders must preserve and augment what is best about the institutional approach while recognising that it is no longer operating within a silo of like minds and common experience, nor often facing challenges that can be met with Army knowledge and abilities alone. That raises the question of how Army leaders and leadership can and must change to meet the challenges of the future. What elements of the Army's leadership approach will endure in this emerging landscape and what must evolve in response?

What endures and evolves

A fast-evolving environment poses a strategic dilemma for the leaders of large organisations: how to achieve the institutional adaptation demanded by shifts in context, without losing the core of what made that institution strong in the first place. There are risks of steering too far in the direction of either continuity or change. At one pole is the danger posed by the lure of the familiar. As Professor Rita Gunther McGrath of Columbia Business School has written:

> [. . .] people on the front lines are rarely rewarded for telling powerful senior executives that a competitive advantage is fading away. Better to shore up an existing advantage for as long as possible, until the pain becomes so obvious that there is no choice. That's what happened at IBM, Sony, Nokia, Kodak and a host of other firms that got themselves into terrible trouble, despite ample early warnings from those working with customers.[20]

If institutional reluctance to recognise change and act on its consequences is one trap, another is course-correcting too abruptly, without sufficient explanation to those involved or foresight of unintended consequences. Getting this balance right requires leadership that is as cognisant of the enduring value of an organisation as the challenges that demand its evolution. A. G. Lafley, formerly CEO of the consumer goods giant Procter & Gamble, described his thinking on this question at the beginning of his tenure.

> Focusing first on what would *not* change – the company's core purpose and values – made it easier to ask the organisation to take on what I knew would be fairly dramatic changes elsewhere. [As I rationalised]

the challenge was to understand and embrace the values that had guided P&G over generations – trust, integrity, ownership, leadership, and a passion for winning – while reorienting them towards the outside [context] and translating them for current and future relevance.[21]

The Army faces a similar task as it approaches a period of significant change, one that will demand the best of its leadership, testing the principles it is based on and the capabilities it has traditionally prized in its leaders.

In this process, some aspects will alter but many will endure. One fundamental that will retain its relevance is the centrality of people and the nature of leadership as an essentially human undertaking. As Major General Duncan Capps, Commandant of RMA Sandhurst and Director Leadership for the British Army, reflected:

> Whilst much of the focus for the future British Army is on technology, AI, cyber and space, always remember that what we do is, at its heart, a human endeavour, and our soldiers are that beating heart. They will remain our most critical battle-winning capability, and they need leadership. As I always remind the Officer Cadets at Sandhurst, the fundamentals of that leadership endure, based on human relationships and trust. It is merely the context that changes.[22]

Even an Army that is smaller in headcount and more dependent on technology will remain an organisation reliant on the strength of its people and their ability to guide, inspire, support and challenge those around them. New technologies, tools and operating concepts do not alter the fact that it is people who assess problems, analyse intelligence, operate systems, make decisions, build teams, boost morale, exercise judgement and provide leadership. Equally, the Army cannot be complacent about how it prepares those people for the challenges of the future. The leaders rising through the ranks today are those who will be faced with both the practical and ethical dimensions of technology – artificial intelligence, robotics in warfare, and the extent of meaningful human control over autonomous weapons and systems. Today's tactical commanders – tomorrow's strategic leaders – must be as comfortable with the technical and philosophical aspects of technology in warfare as they have always needed to be with the personal and emotional needs of people on the battlefield.

If the human focus of Army leadership will endure, what will be the fate of the structures it has traditionally rested upon? What is the value of hierarchy in an environment that demands a more regular rhythm of decisions in real time? What is the relevance of the regimental system in an Army whose people will increasingly work outside these organisations, and indeed the Army itself? How does command adapt in a more fluid operating context and to meet the needs of people who expect more independence in their working environment?

One thing that will not change is the essential function fulfilled by command authority in military leadership: providing direction, clarity and accountability in situations where lives can depend on these things. But the exercise of command – a continuous area of development through history, as the gradual emergence and codification of Mission Command has demonstrated – will also evolve to reflect changing conditions. Whether operating at the sub-threshold level, or on modern battlefields that are defined by the dispersion of forces, commanders must take an approach that reflects their relative lack of visibility and consequent reliance on subordinates who are closer to the point of contact, be that physical or virtual.

'I quickly learned that the scale, complexity and intricacy of the modern divisional fight was simply too great for one person to digest in totality,' Major General Nick Borton reflected of his experience commanding 3rd (UK) Division, the Army's primary warfighting formation, on successive large-scale exercises alongside US allies from 2016 to 2018. 'The modern fight requires a much more fluid and collegiate approach, which has been described as collective command. It relies much more heavily on the expertise, advice and the additional decision-making power of those around you.' Commanders, he suggests, must make several adjustments for this approach to succeed. They must become comfortable with a greater level of delegation ('There were almost no decisions that I wasn't comfortable with either my deputy, my artillery commander or my chief of staff taking on my behalf'). They need to prepare their teams to act with a higher degree of independence ('The staff must be used to operating dispersed, and with minimal direction – with good standard operating procedures as a handrail to speed, not a break on initiative'). And they must continue to make themselves available, both to provide encouragement and to facilitate constructive challenge. 'Commanding remotely mustn't mean being a remote commander. You have to find a way on the dispersed battlefield to replicate the personal touch of the commander with their troops. Your people need to get to know you well enough to challenge you.'[23]

Another enduring tenet of the British Army and its leadership culture has been the regimental system which, as previously discussed, has provided a consistent source of ethos, identity and referent power: connecting those who serve today with the generations who came before them, as well as providing a link to the places they represent and from which they recruit. As Lieutenant General Sir Alistair Irwin observed in 2004, when he was Adjutant-General: 'the best of the current regimental system is a sense of belonging to an entity which has an existence, a past, a present and future of its own.'[24] Regimental identity has an enduring power to influence, forge cohesion and inspire morale. Even long past the era in which soldiers followed their regimental colours on to the battlefield, many would still say that pride in the regiment is what they are fighting for: to protect those they serve alongside, uphold the esteem of the cap badge they wear, and honour the tradition handed down by their predecessors.

The regimental system also moulds leadership styles, as those taking on their first command positions learn from mentors in their unit what it means to lead in a distinctive British Army tradition with its own admired leaders, famous achievements and enduring values. Generations of change and consolidation in the Army's regimental structure have not loosened those bonds of loyalty, and there is no reason to believe that the modern operating environment will do differently. Equally, regimental cultures cannot stand still, nor stand apart from an Army whose people are more likely than ever to be working in integrated teams that bring together a range of different organisations and working cultures. As the Army's most avowedly traditional element moves into the future, leaders must work hard to ensure that the advantages of regimental ethos and identity are maintained, in a way that complements and does not compete with the shift towards integration. The future will continue to have a place for the sub-cultures that have been a consistent feature of the British Army through its history, but these must also respond to the wider context in which they operate: a Whole Force environment encompassing military and civilian components, in which there is no room for orders of precedence or distinctions between insiders and outsiders.

As the structures and systems underpinning Army leadership evolve, so too will the principles and philosophies on which it is based. This book has outlined how the Army approach to leadership is values-based, oriented around the action-centred model, shaped by the philosophy of Mission Command and ultimately grounded in the imperative of servant leadership. Some of that terminology is modern, but the underlying ideas are timeless and would have been understood by Army leaders of any era. The question now is how they will evolve into the future, and how leaders should adjust and attune these fundamentals for the emerging operating context.

Values-based leadership will be more important than ever in an environment where people expect to share values with their employer, and may choose between job opportunities on this basis.[25] Equally, in a world that sets more store by personal values, the way leaders communicate those of the institution must develop. It will not be enough for leaders to set the example of what is meant by courage, respect or integrity. They must also be the communicator and translator of what these mean across different contexts, and to individuals with different outlooks. The Army leaders of the future will need to be as adept leading a conversation about its Values and Standards, how these relate to the personal values of their team members, and how they apply in the complex and ambiguous conditions of the modern operating environment, as they are being a symbol and exemplar for others to follow. Similarly, the trinity of action-centred leadership will retain its relevance, but where the Army's historic bias has been towards achieving the task and building the team, tomorrow's leaders are going to have to work equally as hard to meet the needs of the individual.

That speaks to the future articulation of servant leadership, the principle of which does not change but whose practice must evolve as people expect different things from their leaders. People who, as a rule, want to be treated more as individuals, to have greater autonomy in their work, and for their careers to be more closely managed, require in turn leaders with an expanded sense of how to serve their best interests. As has always been the case, leaders must commit the time to truly get to know their people, understand what motivates them and determine the mix of challenge and support each individual needs to do their best work. Those requirements are timeless, but also becoming more complex in a multi-generational Army where leaders must work harder to build common understanding, relying more on interpersonal skills than the legitimate power of rank or generic appeals to service. Being a servant leader in the future will be no more important than it ever has been, but it may become a more complex undertaking, requiring greater investment of time and deeper reserves of emotional intelligence and understanding.

Alongside the imperative to know people is the need to trust them with an appropriate degree of responsibility. Mission Command has been a core component of British Army doctrine for decades, but will never be more relevant than in the fluid, fast-moving future operating environment. Commanders will only be able to rely on the confident decision making of their subordinates if they create a climate that enables Mission Command, provide their people with the necessary resources, and demonstrate the trust and self-confidence to follow and not micro-manage. As Maj Gen Borton suggests: 'Don't rush as a commander to always give your people the right solution. Hold your tongue and see what they come up with. Even if that is mostly right, or good enough, it's probably better than imposing your own solution.'[26] Mission Command is essential to the successful functioning of the modern Army, but can also be a counter-intuitive approach which leaders must work hard to accustom themselves to. It will only thrive when exercised consistently and practised in environments where the stakes are low, allowing a team and its commanders to develop the necessary muscles for when they are most needed. Accordingly, the leaders of the future must be consistent in implementing the Mission Command philosophy in all environments, especially day-to-day in barracks, where the habits of a unit are formed.

Ultimately, the core facets of British Army leadership have endured because they have evolved consistently through changing circumstances. 'Our reforms have been effected – as is our wont – slowly, cautiously, and by degrees, bit by bit,' wrote Field Marshal Viscount Wolseley in 1887, looking back on the previous half-century of change in the Army.[27] As this reflects, evolution is not the process of violent or sudden change, but development through consent, blending the familiar and proven with the novel and newly necessary. In the context of a large and long-standing institution, a consistent drumbeat of small changes can be a more effective path to the future than revolutionary strides into the unknown. Leading the Army into the future will likely require the same – for familiar principles and philosophies to be taken further, their focus adjusted, and their methods more consistently applied.

In the end, the job of a leader is to mould the individuals and build the team towards achieving the mission. The nature of those individuals is changing, as are the complexity of the missions and the composition of the teams. But the fundamental role of leadership in that equation has not. It is still to unite a team of people around a common purpose, set freedoms and constraints, forge an effective climate, and challenge and inspire individuals to do their best work. That role endures: the question for leaders is what form it will take, and how the methods and practices of today must evolve to meet the challenges that tomorrow will bring.

Preparing for the future

'The whole art of war consists of guessing at what is on the other side of that hill [. . .] or, in other words, in learning what we do not know from what we do.'[28] This test, ascribed to the Duke of Wellington, is as true of strategy as battlefield tactics, and as relevant to the Army in the twenty-first century as it was in the nineteenth. It captures the limitations of any effort to prepare a large organisation for a future in which unforeseen threats and unpredictable events are as likely to dominate as forecasted trends and projected vulnerabilities. Unable to see the other side of the hill, an organisation can only endeavour to equip itself for what may lie ahead, focusing on areas of certainty in a much wider landscape of unpredictability, and nurturing an agile, adaptive mentality that will be capable of responding, whatever emerges from the distance. As Professor Sir Michael Howard wrote: 'No matter how clearly one thinks, it is impossible to anticipate precisely the character of future conflict. The key is not to be so far off the mark that it becomes impossible to adjust once that character is revealed.'[29] The future, especially in its more distant horizons, can never be precisely targeted. Instead, the priority must be to invest in leaders and leadership that are sufficiently knowledgeable, adaptable and open-minded to find a way forward.

One challenge for which those leaders must be ready is the speed of change and the pace at which threats requiring a response can now emerge. As the US General Joseph Dunford, who served as Chairman of the Joint Chiefs of Staff from 2015 to 2019, outlined during his tenure, both have increased beyond recognition in recent decades. 'As a lieutenant, I used the same cold weather gear my dad had in Korea 27 years earlier [. . .] The jeeps we drove would have been familiar to veterans of World War II and, to be honest, so would the tactics.' He contrasted this sedate level of change at the beginning of his career with the operating environment he later observed as the US military's most senior general:

> Information operations, space and cyber capabilities, and ballistic missile technology have accelerated the speed of war, making conflict today faster and more complex than at any point in history [. . .] Decision space has collapsed and so our processes must adapt to keep pace with the speed of war.[30]

In that context, one imperative for the future is a continued emphasis on junior leadership, whose influence is continuing to grow as that decision space compresses. In a world of sub-threshold conflict, it is often the junior personnel operating systems, tracking threats and gathering intelligence who are closest to potential points of contact. Everything can rest on the decision-making ability of those who have visibility of the flow of data and information, tracking potentially adverse events in real time. In 1983, Stanislav Petrov, the duty officer at a Soviet command centre monitoring US missile activity, was at his desk when the early-warning system signalled the apparent launch of five nuclear missiles from an American base. He had just minutes to decide whether or not to report the alarm up the chain of command, a message that would likely have triggered a nuclear response. Experience and training told him that a major attack was unlikely to have been launched with only a handful of missiles, and he disregarded the alarm – which had been triggered by sunlight reflecting off clouds – as a malfunction.[31] The stakes may rarely be so high, but the contemporary operating environment revolves around many more information systems whose outputs must be analysed by the often junior personnel who control them. Recent decades have seen a growing emphasis on the influence wielded by junior commanders on the battlefield. Its importance will only grow in the future, as an Army that is reduced in numbers faces a threat landscape that is extending into the emerging domains of space and cyber.

A smaller, more agile and technologically focused Army is one in which the successful development of every single leader, at every level of the rank structure, will take on even greater significance. The Army is already recruiting and training the people who will be leading the organisation into the 2050s. For the distant future about which it knows least, the only certain preparation an organisation can make is in training the people who will be responsible for it. Junior leaders are of great strategic importance not just because of their important role in the present, but in light of the responsibilities they will assume in the future. It has never been more important that the least experienced leaders in an organisation are given the support, the responsibilities and the range of experience that will allow them to shape events both today and tomorrow. Developing these leaders will pay dividends over the short-, medium- and long-term futures that every organisation faces.

Preparing for the future will also require a reassessment of leadership skills, testing whether those that are developed through early experience of tactical command and small team leadership retain their career-long relevance in the emerging environment. If the future is perceived as one in which leaders and their teams will face more complex problems, in a faster-moving context, requiring increased delegation of authority, a breadth of skills will be needed. The future operating environment will still reward those who excel at skills learned at the tip of the spear – imbuing a galvanising sense of purpose, communicating clearly, demanding high standards and taking risks to exploit opportunities. But it will also require leaders to do more than motivate and direct their teams to achieve a fixed task. In a future that will be defined as much by ambiguous problem sets as clear objectives, leaders must also become change agents, helping their teams first to spend sufficient time understanding and defining the problem, then iterating towards solutions as much as organising towards pre-defined goals.

This will require strong interpersonal skills: leaders who can promote initiative, trust ideas and create a climate that fosters experimentation. The Army's best emerging leaders, CGS has suggested, are:

[. . .] undoubtedly independently minded and are inclined to look at problems through first principles, rather than to fit novel problems into set standard templates [. . .] They are people who get to the right and appropriate level of detail because they can ask the right question rather than every question under the sun [. . .] They are people who recognise that actually their job is to create the freedom to exploit for those who work for them and so, fundamentally, their job is to remove barriers and boundaries and create space.[32]

Similarly, Professor Rita Gunther McGrath has argued that fast-moving environments of change demand 'a new kind of leader – one who initiates conversations that question, rather than reinforce, the status quo [and who] seeks contrasting opinions and honest disagreement.'[33]

The growing emphasis on soft skills is changing the perception and articulation of Army leadership. In US Army leadership doctrine, the requirements for character now list empathy and humility alongside the more accustomed attributes of discipline, Army values, warrior ethos and service ethos.[34] These are not new leadership characteristics, in the military or elsewhere, but the emphasis on them has already increased and is set to grow further as leaders engage with an operating environment defined by complexity, ambiguity and speed. Success in that environment will depend on leaders who admit the limits of their knowledge, follow those who are better informed, regardless of rank, and accept the limitations of what a single commander can control in a constantly expanding landscape. And it will rely on their capabilities as team builders, when those teams bring together a wider variety of personal and professional backgrounds than before, and must operate with a greater degree of creativity and independence.

As a major research project by Google into the characteristics of high-performing teams found, empathy and emotional intelligence may be the master skill of team builders in the modern environment. Having studied the behaviour of hundreds of teams within the organisation, its researchers distilled five dynamics of the most effective teams. Top of this list – above the importance of structure and clarity, people being able to depend on each other, doing work that was important to team members and which was seen to have a meaningful impact – was psychological safety: the degree to which people on a team 'feel safe to take risks around their team members [. . .] confident that no one on the team will embarrass or punish anyone else for admitting a mistake, asking a question or offering a new idea.'[35] Teams that ranked highly on this dynamic showed improved retention levels, brought in more revenue and were twice as likely to be highly regarded by senior executives. As this suggests, in a fast-paced, fast-changing environment, teams depend, above all, on the mutual trust between members to take risks and pursue experiments. To reach this point, they rely upon leaders to set an inclusive tone, create space for people to fail and learn, and enable individuals to approach their work and contribute to the team in the way that suits them best. Preparing for the future, therefore, will require Army leaders to understand and embrace a broader set of roles: not just organising, commanding and delegating, but orchestrating, questioning and following.

Adaptive, independent-minded leaders also need structures around them that facilitate their work. The successful organisations of the future will be those that are capable of learning – about the world around them, from others facing the same challenges, and, perhaps most importantly, within their own walls. A learning organisation, wrote the late economist and management academic Professor David Garvin, is one 'skilled at creating, acquiring and transferring knowledge, and at modifying its behavior to reflect new knowledge and insights'.[36] That definition remains as true as when he wrote it in the 1990s, but requires an increasingly bold approach to implement as the volume of information and its speed of circulation continues to increase.

In this context, there can be no institutional barriers between the leaders setting direction from the top down and those implementing initiatives from the bottom up. When the knowledge and perspective of a corporal in their twenties could be as important as that of a general in their fifties, the organisational distance between these individuals needs to be reduced – with middle layers serving to fuse purpose and connect outputs. Adaptability cannot just be an individual trait, but must also become an organisational virtue, hard-wired into institutional systems and processes. Into the more distant future, that may raise questions over how a strictly hierarchical system such as the Army's chain of command needs to change and evolve, so it can blend the timeless advantage of clarity in the orders process with the growing need for organisational flexibility.

The need to prepare for the future does not mean leaders should become seduced by new approaches or lose confidence in those that have been well proven. Being an effective change agent relies as much on the enduring principles of effective command and leadership – providing clarity, direction, focus and inspiration – as it does on softer skills. And it continues to rest upon the appetite for knowledge and professional development that are timeless requirements of Army leadership. The Army has long trained its leaders to be good followers, diligent servants and to have a deep well of empathy and care for the needs of their people. The guiding challenge of the future – across its multiple horizons – is to determine how the established tenets of effective leadership can be utilised, adapted and evolved in recognition of a rapidly changing context.

The answers required may be different, but the questions leaders need to ask themselves remain the same. Do they know the people under their command? Are they serving them effectively and supporting their needs? Have they communicated intent and established clear freedoms and constraints? Is there mutual trust? Have they delegated to the point of discomfort? Are the needs of task, team and individual being held in balance? The leaders of the future may be operating in an environment changed beyond recognition from their forebears, leading teams that look and work differently, and managing individuals with greater needs and increased expectations. But the core leadership approach, if not unaltered, would be familiar to those who held the same rank and occupied the same positions decades or even centuries before. The context changes, the fundamentals endure and the constant art of leadership is to work out the best way of bringing the two together.

Conclusion: Universal Lessons

In the summer of 1705, a year after his victory at the Battle of Blenheim, the Duke of Marlborough was opposed by his Dutch deputies as he sought to mount an opportunistic assault on the French Royal Army in Flanders. Their suggestion that his plan would unnecessarily risk the lives of his soldiers drew a sharp response from the Captain-General. 'I disdain to send troops to dangers which I will not myself encounter. I will lead them where the peril is most imminent.'[1] The plan came to nothing, but the sentiment from one of the British Army's most famous commanders is resonant, capturing much about a leadership tradition that has endured through centuries of change: the necessity of embracing risk to exploit opportunity, the importance of a leader taking responsibility, the centrality of leadership by example.

Much of the strength of the Army's leadership culture can be explained by this tradition, the rich history that offers inspiration and lessons from countless past successes and failures. The Army leaders of present and future may operate in different contexts, with evolving technologies, but they are unlikely to encounter human problems their predecessors have not, or to face tactical situations with no past parallel. The breadth and depth of this experience speaks to its universal relevance. Leadership is, at heart, a human endeavour, whose lessons are applicable to almost any field of life. With respect to differences in context, the essentials of how leadership is done hold true in uniform or out of it.

As Sandhurst's motto of 'Serve to Lead' suggests, the first of those universal lessons will always be about service, the leader's duty and commitment to others. True leaders recognise that the mission depends almost entirely on the actions of the people on their team. By serving those people, challenging them to develop, supporting them when they encounter difficulties and creating an effective climate for them to

work in, the leader makes an important contribution towards collective success. Every leader is just one individual with restricted time,
limited awareness and personal shortcomings. As a servant leader they
can transcend these limitations, acting as a force multiplier for the
effectiveness of their team, meeting the needs of their people and their
mission in equal part.

This service mindset rests on what a leader knows. A leader can
most effectively serve someone they understand as an individual,
appreciating not just their professional strengths and weaknesses but
personal ambitions, desires and pressures faced. A leader needs to
know their people, themselves and their profession, if they are to
build the trust and respect on which their success depends. Even as
they often follow others on their team with greater knowledge, they
must still know enough to ask pertinent questions, grasp key issues
and guide the work that is being done.

Trust also stems from the power of example, an essential asset that
takes many forms. It starts with the leader's example as a practitioner
and professional in their field, demonstrating that they are knowledgeable, capable and willing to do what they ask of others. Their
example as both leader and follower also matters, setting a tone for
others who must do the same, with or without rank. In turn, they are
a critical exemplar of the values, standards and culture of an organisation, which their personal behaviour serves either to uphold or
erode, helping to form the habits of the team they lead. And, perhaps
most importantly, they set an ethical example. In the grey areas that
exist in any organisation or profession, it takes a leader to be clear
about the difference between what is and is not acceptable, establishing and monitoring boundaries only they can set. The multiple forms
of example that a leader provides through their everyday behaviour
do a more important job of communicating intent and influencing
people than any written or verbal communication.

Leaders provide a visible example to their people, but they also stand
apart from them, in both the behaviour that is expected and the work
that is required. A leader will constantly find themselves in the decision
space where there is ambiguity, uncertainty and disagreement about
how to proceed. As President Obama suggested, the easy questions have

been answered on their behalf, meaning only the difficult ones cross their desk.² A working life filled with hard problems demands moral courage: the ability to take good decisions rather than easy ones, and the willingness to confront difficulties rather than duck them. Leadership constantly tests whether an individual has the moral courage to do the right thing in difficult circumstances, with their people watching on. A leader who reinforces their personal integrity through displays of moral courage will forge bonds of trust and respect, just as surely as one who fails to do so will see their authority undermined. An individual's leadership cannot survive on the occasional bold gesture, but must be earned through making a habit of moral courage, difficult decisions and diligence to key responsibilities. Leaders must remember that their every action is being observed, which means their standards and personal example must become habitual.

In parallel, many leaders must grapple with the challenge of limited visibility into the daily business of the organisation or team they lead. A paradox of leadership is that the most responsible figure often has the least direct insight into the work that is being done. There is much that the people in command can never control. Leaders must not fight this reality but find ways to work with it, developing a team that will function well and meet expected standards in their absence. This starts with vision, leaders shaping a positive climate in which people feel valued and are empowered to contribute value, and where expected standards and common purpose are clear to all. It encompasses support, leaders who are willing and able to develop the leadership of others, using their time to mentor and coach people as an investment in the success of the team. And it is crystallised by challenge, leaders using the Mission Command philosophy to delegate responsibility, trusting people to step up and take decisions as the norm. By consistently working at these three levels – communicating vision, offering support, providing challenge – leaders can instil the habits of a cohesive, confident, self-reliant team.

If some leaders may find themselves distant from the everyday workings of their organisation, they are never separated from their responsibility for them. Leaders are responsible for the success of the mission, for the decisions made and actions taken on their behalf, and for the success and well-being of their people. Their responsibilities encompass the need to uphold the legacy of the past, to meet the needs of the present and to set the conditions for success in the future. This creates an intensity to leadership, on which some thrive and from which others may shrink. Every day is important, every decision matters, every action has influence. But alongside these burdens of leadership are its privileges, the power to build careers, shape the success of an organisation and influence lives for the better. Leadership can be as exhilarating as it is exacting, something that has the power to reward as much as it challenges.

To do it well, a leader must constantly be looking towards the needs of others without ever losing sight of themselves. The leader who most effectively serves others is the one who continues to develop and grow. Learning is one of the defining habits of leadership, and even the most seasoned leaders should continue to draw insight from new experiences, challenge themselves with new perspectives, and ask themselves how they should adapt to changes in context. The art of leadership, the balance and judgement that goes into every decision and every human interaction, relies on a leader who is constantly refreshing their knowledge of the context they work in, from the people on their team to the environment that surrounds them. Every situation is unique and every day is different. Experience is an essential guide, but only when combined with the appetite to learn and a continuous desire to understand what is changing.

Good leaders have a bias to action and a tendency to reflection. They lean on tradition and experience, without ever losing sight of what is around them and ahead of them. Most importantly, they recognise that the individual who continues to learn is the one who will continue to lead, inspiring trust and belief in those who follow them. Every leader, of whatever age and role, remains a lifelong work in progress. For those curious and humble enough to seek them out, the most important lessons always lie ahead.

Acknowledgements

For the strength of the pack is the wolf,
and the strength of the wolf is the pack.

Rudyard Kipling,
'The Law of the Jungle'[1]

Throughout my career I have had the honour of serving alongside many great people, men and women of every rank and grade driven by purpose, pride and passion. Any success I have enjoyed has been the result of those very people. This book is no different. It has been a truly collective endeavour, and any success it may have is due to the hard work and dedication of the team. To that end, I would like to say thank you.

To begin, a very special mention for a dear friend and close ally of the Centre for Army Leadership (CAL), Lt Col Jane Hunter. Over a career spanning almost three decades, Jane epitomised the RMAS motto 'Serve to Lead'. It was during the writing of this book, which Jane helped to research, that she tragically lost her final battle. Rest in peace our friend.

To the driving force behind this endeavour, Professor Lloyd Clark, Director of Research at the CAL. Without Lloyd's foresight, dedication, wisdom and mentorship this book would not have been possible. Sincere thanks, Lloyd; it has been quite a journey. To Josh Davis, to whom we are indebted for his insight, creativity and flair; a rare talent indeed. It has been a pleasure working with you. To the Penguin team: first and foremost to Connor Brown our editor, for his professionalism and patience throughout; Leah Boulton, editorial co-ordinator, for all her help in keeping everything on track; Shân Morley Jones, copy-editor, for her diligence and wisdom; Annie Underwood, production manager, for producing such a handsome book; Chris Bentham, designer, for the arresting cover design; Meredith Benson, audiobook editor, for creating a compelling listen; Matthew Crossey and Leo Donlan, communications, for telling the world about this book; Ruth Johnston, Guy Lloyd, Linda Viberg and the rest of the sales team at Penguin and out in the field, for getting the book into the hands of as many people as possible; and to all the other vital, often unseen, contributors at Penguin, thank you. It has been a privilege working with the world's premier publishing company.

To the CAL team who in their own individual way have left their mark on this book and who continue to drive improved leadership across our organisation with such humble commitment: Dr Linda Risso, Maj Ben Acton, WO1 Chris Nicol, WO2 Sheridan Lucas, Cpl Natasha Theodossiadis, CSgt Nick Smith, SSgt Lee Waite, CSgt Rob Hamilton, Capt Toby Eddings, Capt Andy Stephen, Capt Verity Duncan, Maj Paul McFarland, WO1 Mick Latter, Helen Smith and Will Giddings.

To our senior leadership without whose support this book would not have been possible. To the Chief of the General Staff, Gen Sir Mark Carleton-Smith, who has had our back from the very beginning, and to Maj Gen Duncan Capps, Commandant of the Royal Military Academy Sandhurst and Director Leadership for the Army. Leading by example.

To our dedicated team of researchers who volunteered many hours of their own time to bring this book to life, drawing on the richness of our 360 years of history, complemented by their own diverse experience and talent: Dr Chris Kempshall, Dr Aaron Edwards, Capt Gethin Davies, Maj Helen Carter, Capt Lee Rotherham, Lt Col Malcolm Sperrin, Maj Sergio Miller, Mary Hunter, Lt Col Shaun Chandler, Lt Col Jono Palmer, Brig (Retd) Ian Thomas and the dedicated staff of the RMAS Central Library, John Pearce and Sue Lloyd.

Also to all those who kindly gave permission to quote from such authoritative texts: including Rosemary Anderson for Geoffrey Powell's *Men at Arnhem*; and Harriet Fielding at Pen & Sword Books for General Sir Anthony Farrar-Hockley's *The Edge of the Sword*. I have endeavoured to trace copyright holders of all material from which I have quoted but have been unable to trace some, whilst others have not responded to my correspondence. I would, however, be pleased to rectify any omission, as agreed, in future editions should copyright holders contact me.

Our gratitude extends to the soldiers and officers, past and present, who took the time to share their experiences and knowledge, bringing a human reality to this book: Cpl Priscilla Quansah, Cpl Henry Bignell, Cpl Robert Chamberlain, Cpl Oscar Searle, WO2 Andy Pick, WO1 Sarah Cox, WO1 Gav Patton, Lt Charlotte Lord-Sallenave, Capt Den Starkie, Capt Lou Rudd, Sgt Josh Leakey, Capt Theo Jordaan, Padre Jonathon Daniel, Lt Col Will Meddings, Lt Col Andrew Todd, Lt Col Stu McDonald, Brig (Retd) John Ridge, Brig Lizzie Faithfull-Davies, Brig Mike Cornwell, Lt Gen (Retd) James Bashall, Katherine Higgins, Glyn Sheppard, John Acton, Pete Storer, Dr Emily Mayhew and the selected staff of the Infantry Battle School.

To our team of reviewers – our 'critical friends' whose sharp eyes and candid feedback have undoubtedly raised the bar – Prof Chris Gaskell, Lisa Allera and Scott Sherriff, we are most grateful.

Thanks also to Charles Heath-Saunders for his sage advice and diplomacy, finding the path of least resistance through the MOD's bureaucracy, supported by Lt Col Paddy Jackson and Tracy Harrison.

To every soldier and officer I have had the pleasure of serving alongside from over two decades. For your companionship, shared hardships and endless laughter. It is you who make our Army.

My last words go to my family, to whom my gratitude cannot be put into words. To my mum and dad who worked every hour of every day to give me life's opportunities and who taught me right from wrong. To my brother, Spencer, who I have never stopped looking up to (even though I am officially taller than him). To Georgia and Albert who give me purpose and make me smile every day. You are the future. And to my wife, Heather, who has opened my eyes to the sacrifices our families make and the reason for this book's dedication. The very best role model our children could hope for, and my inspiration.

Endnotes

Please note that a full list of the interviewees quoted in this book can be found in the Bibliography.
All websites listed in the notes were accessed in May 2021.

Epigraphs

1 Aristotle (trans. David Ross). 2009. *The Nicomachean Ethics*. Book 1.7. Oxford: OUP, p. 12.
2 Durant, W. 2006. *The Story of Philosophy: The Lives and Opinions of the World's Greatest Philosophers from Plato to John Dewey*. New York, NY: Simon & Schuster, p. 98.

Preface

1 Jock was wounded by mortar fire on 22 June 1944 and evacuated. Swiftly recovering, he rejoined his battalion, going on to fight in the Ardennes (Battle of the Bulge), the Rhine Crossing (Operation Varsity) and advanced across Germany to the Baltic. See https://www.paradata.org.uk/people/john-hutton.

Introduction

1 Davies, F. & Maddocks, G. 2014. *Bloody Red Tabs: General Officer Casualties of the Great War 1914–1918*. Barnsley: Pen & Sword Military, pp. 46–7.
2 For a full account of Bradford's career, see Whitworth, A. 2015. *VCs of the North: Cumbria, Durham & Northumberland*. Barnsley: Pen & Sword Military, pp. 58–66.

3 Anonymous, n.d. *Brigadier-General R. B. Bradford, V.C., M.C. and His Brothers*. Newport: Ray Westlake, pp. 95–6.

4 As outlined in *ADP Army Leadership Doctrine*, AC72029 (first edition, 2016), pp. 14–15.

5 See Taylor, R. L. & Rosenbach, W. E. (eds). 2009. *Military Leadership: In Pursuit of Excellence*. London: Routledge; Wren, J. T. 1995. *The Leader's Companion: Insights on Leadership Through the Ages*. New York, NY: Free Press.

6 As Professor Gary Sheffield argued in his 2010 essay, 'Doctrine and Command in the British Army: An Historical Overview'. *ADP Operations*, E-2.

7 Notable first-hand accounts of Army leadership from different eras include: Harris, B. 2011. *The Recollections of Rifleman Harris*. Plano, TX: Wagram Press; Field Marshal Sir William Slim. 1956. *Defeat into Victory*. London: Cassell; Jary, S. 1987. *18 Platoon*. Carshalton Beeches: Sydney Jary Ltd; Hennessy, P. 2009. *The Junior Officers' Reading Club: Killing Time and Fighting Wars*. London: Allen Lane.

8 As one example, women leaders are playing an increasingly prevalent and influential role in an institution that has historically been predominantly male. Maj Gen (Retd) Susan Ridge became the first woman to be promoted to the rank of two-star general in 2015, and Maj Gen Sharon Nesmith became the first female two-star to hold a command role in 2021, as GOC Army Recruiting and Initial Training Command. (See MOD, 'First female officer to lead Division-level Command of the British Army', army.mod.uk, 5 January 2021). Since 2018, women have been able to apply for all roles in the British Army without exception, including frontline infantry. (See MOD, 'All British Armed Forces roles now open to women', army.mod.uk, 25 October 2018). As of October 2020, women represented 12.1 per cent of officers and 9.8 per cent of all personnel in the Regular Army and 17.8 per cent and 14 per cent respectively in the Army Reserve. (See MOD, 'UK Armed Forces Biannual Diversity Statistics, 1 October 2020', www.gov.uk, 17 December 2020). The use of historical examples in the book explains why soldiers may sometimes be referred to as 'men' by figures representing the realities of their time.

1. In History and Changing Society

1 Quoted in Kirke, C. 2009. *Red Coat, Green Machine: Continuity in Change in the British Army 1700–2000*. London: Bloomsbury Academic, p. 198.

2 *ADP Army Leadership Doctrine*, AC72029 (first edition, 2016), p. 9.

3 As the Army's Land Operations doctrine makes clear: *ADP Land Operations*, AC 71940 (updated March 2017), 3-9, 3-10. See also: Dannatt, R. 2017. *Boots on the Ground: Britain and her Army since 1945*. London: Profile Books; Richards, A. 2021. *After the Wall Came Down: Soldiering Through the Transformation of the British Army, 1990–2020*. Oxford: Casemate Publishing; Mallinson, A. 2011. *The Making of the British Army*. London: Bantam Books.

4 Keegan, J. 2004. *The Mask of Command: A Study of Generalship*. London: Pimlico.

5 Childs, J. 2003. 'The Restoration Army 1660–1702'. In D. Chandler & I. Beckett (eds). *The Oxford History of the British Army*. Oxford: OUP, pp. 54 (Cromwell); 63 (training and pay).

6 Guy, A. 2003. 'The Army of the Georges 1714–1783'. In Chandler & Beckett, *The Oxford History of the British Army*, p. 93.

7 Guy, A. 1985. *Oeconomy and Discipline: Officership and administration in the British Army, 1714–63*. Manchester: Manchester University Press, p. 89.

8 Falkner, J. 2015. *Marlborough's War Machine 1702–1711*. Barnsley: Pen & Sword Military, p. 67.

9 Guy, 'The Army of the Georges', pp. 103 (gentry); 105 (quasi-medieval).

10 Quotations in this chapter are from Simes, T. 1777. *A Military Course for the Government and Conduct of a Battalion*. London, n. p., pp. 217 (junior NCOs); 219 (senior NCOs); 221 (NCO leadership).

11 Crichton, A. 1824. *Life and Diary of Lieut Colonel John Blackader, Deputy Governor of Stirling Castle*. Edinburgh: H. S. Baynes, p. 76.

12 Blanco, R. 1968. 'Attempts to abolish branding and flogging in the Army of Victorian England before 1881'. *Journal of the Society for Army Historical Research*, 46 (187), 137.

13 Gates, D. 2003. 'The Transformation of the Army, 1783–1815'. In Chandler & Beckett, *The Oxford History of the British Army*, p. 145.

14 Macdonald, J. 2016. *Sir John Moore: The Making of a Controversial Hero*. Barnsley: Pen & Sword Military, p. 118.

15 Gen Viscount Wolseley. 1887. 'The Army'. In T. Humphry Ward (ed). *The Reign of Queen Victoria: A Survey of Fifty Years of Progress Vol. I.* London: Smith, Elder & Co, p. 169.

16 See Mallinson, *The Making of the British Army*.

17 See Spiers, E. 2002. 'The Late Victorian Army, 1868–1914'. In D. Chandler (ed). *The Oxford History of the British Army*. Oxford: Oxford University Press, pp. 187–210; Dawson, A. 2014. *Real War Horses: The Experience of the British Cavalry, 1814–1914*. Barnsley: Pen & Sword Military; French, D. 2005. *Military Identities: The Regimental System, the British Army, & the British People c. 1870–2000*. Oxford: Oxford University Press.

18 Quoted in Bond, B. 2016. *The Victorian Army and the Staff College, 1854–1914*. Abingdon: Routledge Library Editions, p. 58.

19 House of Commons. 'Supply – Army Estimates'. In *Hansard*, Vol. 204, Col. 339, 16 February 1871.

20 For an account of the emergence and development of Staff College, see Bond, *The Victorian Army and the Staff College*; for detail on the growing educational requirements of Army officers in the later nineteenth century, see Mahaffey, C. 2004. 'The Fighting Profession: The Professionalization of the British Line Infantry Officer Corps, 1870–1902'. Unpublished PhD thesis, University of Glasgow, pp. 102–64.

21 French, *Military Identities*, p. 152.

22 Mahaffey, 'The Fighting Profession', pp. 16–22.

23 Spiers, E. 1992. *The Late Victorian Army: 1868–1902*. Manchester: Manchester University Press, pp. 113 (Christian gentleman); 97 (60 per cent).

24 Gen Viscount Wolseley. 1886. *The Soldier's Pocket Book for Field-Service*. London: Macmillan and Co., pp. 1–2.

25 Spiers, *The Late Victorian Army*, p. 113.

26 Quoted in Nielsen, N. 2000. 'Industrial Paternalism in the 19th Century: Old or New?' *Ethnologia Europaea*, 30 (1), 59.

27 For more on this, see White, A. S. 2001. *Bibliography of Regimental Histories of the British Army*. 3rd edition. Uckfield: Naval and Military Press; Mallinson, *The Making of the British Army*; Chandler & Beckett, *The Oxford History of the British Army*.

28 Spiers, *The Late Victorian Army*, p. 109.

29 Robertson, W. 2018. *From Private to Field-Marshal: The Autobiography of the First British Private Soldier to Rise to the Highest Rank*. Miami, FL: HardPress, p. 17.

30 Kochanski, H. 1996. 'Field Marshal Wolseley: A Reformer at the War Office, 1871–1900'. Unpublished PhD thesis, King's College London, p. 118.

31 Mahaffey, 'The Fighting Profession', p. 141.

32 Quoted in Riedi, E. 2006. 'Brains or Polo? Equestrian sport, Army reform and the gentlemanly officer tradition, 1900–1914'. *Journal of the Society for Army Historical Research*, 84 (339), 241.

33 Schoy, M. 'General Gerhard Von Scharnhorst: Mentor of Clausewitz and Father of the Prussian-German General Staff'. https://www.cfc.forces.gc.ca/259/181/82_schoy.pdf.

34 Quoted in Jason M. Bender. 'Non-Technical Military Innovation: The Prussian General Staff and Professional Military Education'. *Small Wars Journal*, 14 September 2016.

35 Bendorf, H. 1967. 'Richard Haldane and the British Army reforms 1905–1909'. Unpublished Master's thesis, University of Nebraska at Omaha.

36 House of Commons. 'Supply – Army Estimates'. In *Hansard*, Vol. 153, Col. 672, 8 March 1906.

37 Spiers, 'The Late Victorian Army', pp. 203–5.

38 French, D. 2002. 'Officer Education and Training in the British Regular Army 1919–39'. In G. Kennedy & K. Neilson (eds). *Military Education: Past, Present and Future*. Westport, CT: Praeger, pp. 105–28.

39 Spiers, 'The Late Victorian Army', pp. 209–10.

40 Bond, *The Victorian Army and the Staff College*, p. 239.

41 Gates, 'The Transformation of the Army', p. 132.

42 Spiers, 'The Late Victorian Army', p. 211.

43 Danchev, A. 2003. 'The Army and the Home Front 1939–1945'. In Chandler & Beckett, *The Oxford History of the British Army*, pp. 301–2.

44 Simkins, P. 2003. 'The Four Armies 1914–1918'. In Chandler & Beckett, *The Oxford History of the British Army*, p. 251.

45 Hentel, M. 2017. 'Temporary Gentlemen: The Masculinity of Lower-Middle-Class Temporary British Officers in the First World War'. Unpublished PhD thesis, University of Western Ontario, p. 13.

46 Sheffield, G. 2014. *Command and Morale: The British Army on the Western Front 1914–1918*. Barnsley: Pen & Sword Military, p. 96.

47 Lucy, J. F. 1993. *There's a Devil in the Drum*. Eastbourne: Naval & Military, p. 343.

48 Mallinson, *The Making of the British Army*, p. 424.

49 See 'Queen Mary's Army Auxiliary Corps' at the National Army Museum website. https://www.nam.ac.uk/explore/queen-marys-army-auxiliary-corps.

50 Shipton, E. 2014. *Female Tommies: The Frontline Women of the First World War*. Cheltenham: The History Press, p. 76.

51 Gould, J. 1988. 'The Women's Corps: The Establishment of Women's Military Services in Britain'. Unpublished PhD thesis, University College London, p. 161.

52 Simpson, K. 2014. 'The Officers'. In I. Beckett & K. Simpson (eds). *A Nation at Arms: The British Army in the First World War*. Barnsley: Pen & Sword Select, p. 80.

53 For examples, see Hodgkinson, P. 2013. 'British Infantry Battalion Commanders in the First World War'. Unpublished PhD thesis, University of Birmingham, pp. 179–80. As he also shows (p. 104), the average age of battalion commanders fell from forty-seven at the outbreak of war to thirty-four by the Hundred Days' Offensive in 1918, when the youngest was just twenty-one.

54 Quoted in Hodgkinson, 'British Infantry Battalion Commanders', p. 219.

55 Hodgkinson, P. & Westerman, W. 2015. ' "Fit to Command a Battalion": The Senior Officers' School 1916–18'. *Journal for the Society of Army Historical Research*, 374 (summer), 130.

56 Quoted in Hodgkinson, 'British Infantry Battalion Commanders', p. 215.

57 Spiers, 'The Late Victorian Army', pp. 97–9.

58 See Taylor, R. L. & Rosenbach, W. E. (eds). 2009. *Military Leadership: In Pursuit of Excellence*. London: Routledge.

59 French, 'Officer Education and Training', pp. 106–7.

60 See Otley, C. 1973. 'The Educational Background of British Army Officers'. *Sociology*, 7 (2), 197; Smalley, E. 2015. 'Qualified, but Unprepared: Training for War at the Staff College in the 1930s'. *British Journal for Military History*, 2 (1), 55–72.

61 Crang, J. A. 2000. *The British Army and the People's War 1939–1945*. Manchester: Manchester University Press, pp. 30–31 (WOSBs); p. 61 (Army morale).

62 Summerfield, P. 1981. 'Education and Politics in the British Armed Forces in the Second World War'. *International Review of Social History*, 26 (2), 140.

63 Department of Defense. 2007. *Irregular Warfare (IW) Joint Operation Concept (JOC)*, Version 1.0, p. 6.

64 For more on these topics, see Nolan, V. 2012. *Military Leadership and Counterinsurgency: The British Army and Small War Strategy since World War II*. London: I. B. Tauris.

65 Pugsley, C. 2011. 'We Have Been Here Before: the Evolution of the Doctrine of Decentralised Command in the British Army 1905–1989'. Sandhurst Occasional Papers, No. 9. Camberley: Royal Military Academy Sandhurst, pp. 4; 8–9.

66 Quoted in Nolan, *Military Leadership and Counterinsurgency*, pp. 125 (wide sweeps); 91 (flexibility).

67 Col Norman L. Dodd. 1976. 'The Corporals' War: Internal Security Operations in Northern Ireland'. *Military Review*, 56 (July), 58–68.

68 Gen Charles C. Krulak. 1999. 'The Strategic Corporal: Leadership in the Three-Block War'. *Marines Magazine* (January), pp. 4–5.

69 See Sheffield, G. 2010. 'Doctrine and Command in the British Army: An Historical Overview'. *ADP Operations*, E-2.

70 For a discussion of the Bagnall reforms and their significance, see Mader, M. 2004. *In Pursuit of Conceptual Excellence: The Evolution of British Military-Strategic Doctrine in the Post-Cold War Era, 1989–2002*. Studies in Contemporary History and Security Policy, No. 13. Bern: Peter Lang, pp. 86–98.

71 Pugsley, 'We Have Been Here Before', p. 37.

72 Hirotaka Takeuchi & Ikujiro Nonaka. 'The New New Product Development Game'. *Harvard Business Review*, January 1986.

73 Hoda, R., Grundy, J. & Salleh, N. 2018. 'The Rise and Evolution of Agile Software Development'. *IEEE Software*, PP (99), 1-1.

74 Darrell K. Rigby, Jeff Sutherland & Hirotaka Takeuchi. 'Embracing Agile: How to master the process that's transforming management'. *Harvard Business Review*, May 2016.

75 Sheffield, 'Doctrine and Command in the British Army', E-2.

76 Mader, *In Pursuit of Conceptual Excellence*, p. 89.

77 Sheffield, 'Doctrine and Command in the British Army', E-2.

78 *Values and Standards of the British Army* (2018). https://www.army.mod.uk/media/5219/20180910-values_standards_2018_final.pdf; *ADP Army Leadership Doctrine*.

79 Director Leadership. 2015. *The Army Leadership Code: An Introductory Guide*, AC72021. MOD, pp. 22–3.

2. Challenges of Army Leadership and Uniqueness

1 Gen Sir Charles Guthrie. 'The New British Way in Warfare'. Annual Liddell-Hart Centre for Military Archives Lecture, 12 February 2001. 2001-lecture.pdf (kcl.ac.uk).

2 Mader, M. 2004. *In Pursuit of Conceptual Excellence: The Evolution of British Military-Strategic Doctrine in the Post-Cold War Era, 1989–2002*, Studies in Contemporary History and Security Policy, No. 13. Bern: Peter Lang, pp. 204–8.

3 Lt Gen Sir John Hackett. 1986. '1. Origins of a Profession'. In *The Profession of Arms*. Washington, DC: Center of Military History, p. 3.

4 Huntington, S. 1957. *The Soldier and the State*. Boston, MA: Harvard University Press, pp. 7–9.

5 Tony Ingesson. 'When the Military Profession Isn't'. *The Military Leader*, 2 October 2015; Bélanger, S. A. H. & Lagacé-Roy, D. 2016. *Military Operations and the Mind: War Ethics and Soldiers' Well-being*. Montreal: McGill-Queen's University Press; Toner, J. H. 1995. 'The Profession of Arms: The Full Measure of Devotion'. In *True Faith and Allegiance: The Burden of Military Ethics*. Lexington, KY: University Press of Kentucky, pp. 115–32.

6 See, for example, Center for the Army Profession and Leadership. *America's Army: Our Profession*. Army Profession Pamphlet, October 2018.

7 Quoted in Beckett, I. F. W. 2018. *A British Profession of Arms: The Politics of Command in the Late Victorian Army*. Norman, OK: University of Oklahoma Press, p. 3.

8 Army Doctrine Publication, Volume 5. *Soldiering: The Military Covenant*. MOD. February 2000, p. 1.

9 *ADP Land Operations*, AC 71940 (updated March 2017), 1-4.

10 Huntington, *The Soldier and the State*, p. 15.

11 Shields, P. M. 2020. 'Dynamic Intersection of Military and Society'. In Anders Sookermany (ed). *Handbook of Military Sciences*. New York, NY: Springer, pp. 1–23; Wolfendale, J. 2007. *Torture and the Military Profession*. Basingstoke: Palgrave Macmillan.

12 Holmes, R. 'Soldiers & Society'. Annual Liddell-Hart Centre for Military Archives Lecture, 10 May 2006. Available at liddellhartlecture2006.pdf (kcl.ac.uk).

13 For more on the study of leadership and ethics, see Wolfendale, *Torture and the Military Profession*; Bennis, W. G. 1994. *Beyond Leadership: Balancing Economics, Ethics, and Ecology*. Cambridge, MA: Blackwell Business; Ciulla, J. B. 2004. *Ethics, the Heart of Leadership*. Westport, CT: Praeger; Lawton, A. & Paez, I. 2014. 'Developing a Framework for Ethical Leadership'. *Journal of Business Ethics*, 130 (3), 639–49.

14 Quoted in the British Army's 2013 anthology on leadership, *Serve to Lead*, p. 15.

15 Eyre, G. E. M. *Somme Harvest*. Memories of summer 1916, reprinted 1991. Eastbourne: Antony Rowe Ltd, pp. 120–1.

16 See *Army Field Manual, Command*. MOD.

17 *ADP Land Operations*, 6-2 and 6-3.

18 Ken Turner & Kevin Gentzler. 'Commandership: A Fresh Look at Command'. *Small Wars Journal*, 12 March 2020.

19 British Army. *CLM Policy Handbook*. Version 5.4, March 2018, p. 1.

20 Quoted in Kirke, C. 2009. *Red Coat, Green Machine: Continuity in Change in the British Army 1700–2000*. London: Bloomsbury Academic, pp. 195–6.

21 Quoted in Walker, D. 2018. 'Character in the British Army: A Precarious Professional Practice'. In D. Carr (ed). *Cultivating Moral Character and Virtue in Professional Practice*. Abingdon: Routledge, Chapter 10.

22 *CLM Policy Handbook*, p. 1.

23 See, for example, Grint, K. 2007. *Leadership, Management and Command: Rethinking D-Day*. Basingstoke: Palgrave Macmillan; Grint, K. 2020. 'Leadership, management and command in the time of the Coronavirus'. *Leadership*, 16 (3), 314–19; Pearce, C. L. 2004. 'The Future of Leadership: Combining Vertical and Shared Leadership to Transform

Knowledge Work [and Executive Commentary]'. *Academy of Management Executive*, 18 (1), 47–57.

24 Stephen Bungay. 'The Executive's Trinity: Management, Leadership – and Command'. *The Ashridge Journal*, summer 2011.

25 Quoted in Kirke, *Red Coat, Green Machine*, p. 123.

26 Quoted in Kirke, C. 2002. 'Social Structures in the Regular Combat Arms Units of the British Army: A Model'. Unpublished PhD thesis, Security Studies Institute, Cranfield University, p. 310.

27 French, D. 2005. *Military Identities: The Regimental System, the British Army, & the British People c.1870–2000*. Oxford: Oxford University Press, pp. 14–15.

28 French, D. 2006. 'Templer Medal Winning Essay: The Regimental System: One Historian's Perspective'. *Journal of the Society for Army Historical Research*, 84 (340), 362–79.

29 Logan, D., King, J. & Fischer-Wright, H. 2011. *Tribal Leadership: Leveraging Natural Groups to Build a Thriving Organization*. New York, NY: Harper Business, pp. 4 (building blocks); 23 (Stage 4).

30 MOD. *The Queen's Regulations for the Army 1975*. London: HMSO. Amdt 30, para 8.001.

31 Quoted in French, *Military Identities*, p. 153.

3. Modern British Army Leadership

1 Field Marshal The Viscount Montgomery. 1954. 'The Role of Science in Warfare of the Future', *Engineering and Science*, pp. 28 (roll up our sleeves); 22 (dominant factor).

2 Howard, M. & Guilmartin Jr, J. 1994. Report for the Army War Colleges, 'Two Historians in Technology and War'. Carlisle, PA: Strategic Studies Institute, p. 1.

3 Director Leadership. 'The Army Leadership Review – Final Report'. June 2015.

4 Commander Force Development and Training. *Army Doctrine Primer*, AC 71954, May 2011, p. i.

5 'The Army Leadership Review', p. 7.

6 *Army Doctrine Primer*, para 5-1.

7   *Archbold: Criminal Pleading, Evidence and Practice* is published annually by Sweet & Maxwell. *Erskine May: Parliamentary Practice* is available online at https://erskinemay.parliament.uk/.

8   MOD. 2016. *Household Cavalry Regiment Ethos Booklet*. Version 4.1, p. 2.

9   16 Air Assault Brigade. *The Pegasus Ethos*. April 2016, p. 3.

10 House of Commons Library. 'UK Defence Personnel Statistics' research briefing, 8 March 2021. https://commonslibrary.parliament.uk/research-briefings/cbp-7930/.

11 'The Army Leadership Review', p. 4.

12 For a discussion of the components of fighting power, see *ADP Land Operations*, AC 71940 (updated March 2017); for the leadership framework see *ADP Army Leadership Doctrine*, AC72029 (first edition, 2016), p. 16.

13 *ADP Land Operations* is the British Army's core doctrine which 'provides the framework of understanding for our approach to combat and to operations'. It can be accessed via https://www.gov.uk/government/publications/army-doctrine-publication-operations.

14 Ministry of Defence. *Soldiering: The Military Covenant*, April 2000, para 1-1.

15 Dannatt, R. 2017. *Boots on the Ground: Britain and her Army since 1945*. London: Profile Books, p. 255.

16 Nicholas Blake QC. *The Deepcut Review: A review of the circumstances surrounding the death of four soldiers at Princess Royal Barracks, Deepcut between 1995 and 2002*. House of Commons, HC 795, 29 March 2006.

17 Dannatt, *Boots on the Ground*, p. 256.

18 Army Headquarters. 2018. *Values and Standards of the British Army*, AC 64649. Andover: Army Publications, p. 3.

19 'Values of the NHS Constitution'. https://www.healthcareers.nhs.uk/working-health/working-nhs/nhs-constitution.

20 Committee on Standards in Public Life. 'The Seven Principles of Public Life', issued 31 May 1995.

21 Patty McCord. 'How Netflix Reinvented HR'. *Harvard Business Review*, January-February 2014.

22 Revd Dr P. J. McCormack. 'Grounding British Army Values Upon an Ethical Good'. Executive Committee of the Army Board (ECAB) Paper, March 2015; see p. 7 (Schutzstaffel).

23 Glover, J. 2012. *Humanity: A Moral History of the Twentieth Century*. New Haven, CT: Yale University Press, p. 24.

24 Blake, *The Deepcut Review*, p. 245.

25 *Values and Standards of the British Army*, p. 30.

26 *ADP Land Operations*, i.

27 Ministry of Defence. 2015. 'Strategic Trends Programme: Future Operating Environment 2035', p. 44.

28 See 'Chapter 6: Mission Command' in *ADP Land Operations*; Vandergriff, D. 2019. *Adopting Mission Command: Developing Leaders for a Superior Command Culture*. Annapolis, MD: Naval Institute Press; Master Sgt Fred N. Tolman. 'Mission Command: A Senior Enlisted Leader's Perspective'. *NCO Journal*, May 2020; Col (Retd) James D. Sharpe Jr & Lt Col (Retd) Thomas E. Creviston. 'Understanding Mission Command'. *US Army*, 30 April 2015.

29 Lt Gen Robert L. Caslen. 2011. 'The Army Ethic, Public Trust and the Profession of Arms'. *Military Review*, September, p. 16.

30 *ADP Land Operations*, 6-1.

31 Quoted in Shamir, E. 2011. *Transforming Command: The Pursuit of Mission Command in the U.S., British, and Israeli Armies*. Redwood City, CA: Stanford University Press, p. 112.

32 *ADP Land Operations*, 6-5.

33 Land Operations doctrine outlines the five principles of Mission Command as: unity of effort, freedom of action, trust, mutual understanding, and timely and effective decision making. See *ADP Land Operations*, 6-5 and 6-6.

34 See 'Chapter 6: Mission Command' in *ADP Land Operations*.

35 See Fitz-Gibbon, S. 1995. *Not Mentioned in Despatches: The History and Mythology of the Battle of Goose Green*. Cambridge: The Lutterworth Press, pp. 14–20. The author argues that Lt Col H. Jones, killed in battle while commanding 2 PARA in the Falklands, 'did rather epitomise the philosophy of detailed planning; so much so that a number of officers were left somewhat befuddled by the amount of detail it contained.' By contrast, his 2IC Maj Chris Keeble, who assumed command after his death, had been exposed to *Auftragstaktik* during a posting with the German Army and took a different approach. '[His] first order was to delegate command to the company commander [. . .] the very thing that H had refused to do.' (See Fitz-Gibbon, p. 136.)

36 Lee, S. 1994. 'Deterrence and the Defence of Central Europe: The British Role from the Early 1980s to the End of the Gulf War'. Unpublished PhD thesis, King's College London, p. 339.

37 Major D. Hebditch. 'Planning Fast and Slow: or How to Make Military Planning Work for You'. *2017 School of Armour Papers*, 20 May 2019.

38 Lee, 'Deterrence and the defence of Central Europe', p. 340.

39 Lt Col J. P. Storr. 2004. 'The Command of British Land Forces in Iraq, March to May 2003'. Pewsey: Directorate General of Doctrine and Development, p. 13.

40 Stephen Bungay. 'Mission Command: An Organizational Model for Our Time'. *Harvard Business Review*, 2 November 2010.

41 Berkshire Hathaway. 'Berkshire – Past, Present and Future'. https://www.berkshirehathaway.com/SpecialLetters/WEB%20past%20present%20future%202014.pdf.

42 For key background reading on this topic, see Greenleaf, R. K. 2002. *Servant Leadership: A Journey Into the Nature of Legitimate Power and Greatness*. New York, NY: Paulist Press; Greenleaf, R. K. 1998. *Insights on Leadership: Service, Stewardship, Spirit, and Servant-Leadership*. New York, NY: Wiley; Van Dierendonck, V. 2011. 'Servant Leadership: A Review and Synthesis'. *Journal of Management*, 37 (4), 1228–61; Olesia, W. S., Namusonge, G. S. & Iravo, M. A. 2014. 'Servant Leadership: The Exemplifying Behaviors'. *IOSR Journal of Humanities and Social Science*, 19 (6), 75–80; Greenleaf, R. K. 1998. *The Power of Servant-Leadership: Essays*. San Francisco, CA: Berrett-Koehler Publishers.

43 See Greenleaf's seminal work *The Servant as Leader*. Cambridge, MA: Center for Applied Studies, pp. 6 (material possessions); 3 (new moral principle).

44 British Army's 2013 anthology on leadership, *Serve to Lead*, p. 8.

45 Maj Jennifer O'Connor (RE). 'Where has "Serve to Lead" gone?' CAL Insight, no. 12, February 2019. https://www.army.mod.uk/media/5827/centre-for-army-leadership-leadership-insight-no-12.pdf.

46 Greenleaf, *The Servant as Leader*, p. 6.

47 Jim Heskett. 'Why isn't "Servant Leadership" More Prevalent?' *Working Knowledge*, Harvard Business School, 1 May 2013.

48 Centre for Army Leadership. 'Podcast Episode 11 – Archbishop Justin Welby', 12 May 2021.

49 Pugsley, C. 2011. 'We Have Been Here Before: the Evolution of the Doctrine of Decentralised Command in the British Army 1905–1989'. Sandhurst Occasional Papers, No. 9. Camberley: Royal Military Academy Sandhurst, p. 8.

4. *What British Army Leaders Are*

1 See 'British Dead and Wounded in Afghanistan, Month by Month', *Guardian* datablog, 17 September 2009.

2 Mayhew, E. 2017. *A Heavy Reckoning: War, Medicine and Survival in Afghanistan and Beyond*. London: Profile Books, pp. 145–8.

3 See https://thearmyleader.co.uk/leadership-quotes/.

4 MOD. 'Lieutenant Colonel Rupert Thorneloe and Trooper Joshua Hammond killed in Afghanistan', reported on the GOV.UK website, 2 July 2009.

5 Lt Col (Retd) Charlie Antelme. 'Leadership, Followership and Junior Command'. Centre for Army Leadership JNCO Day, 27 February 2020.

6 See Vidaver-Cohen, D. 1998. 'Moral Climate in Business Firms: A Conceptual Framework for Analysis and Change'. *Journal of Business Ethics*, 17 (11), 1211–26; Chaleff, I. 2009. *The Courageous Follower: Standing Up to & for Our Leaders*. San Francisco, CA: Berrett-Koehler Publishers.

7 Col James B. Stockdale. 1978. 'Machiavelli, Management, and Moral Leadership'. In M. Wakin, K. Wenker & J. Kempf (eds). *Military Ethics*. Washington, DC: National Defense University Press, pp. 33–44.

8 Jonathan Mahler. 'The Lives They Lived; The Prisoner'. *The New York Times*, 25 December 2005.

9 See Hannah, S. T., Avolio, B. J. & Walumbwa, F. O. 2011. 'Relationships between Authentic Leadership, Moral Courage, and Ethical and Pro-Social Behaviors'. *Business Ethics Quarterly*, 21 (4), 555–78; Gahl, L. 1984. 'Moral Courage: The Essence of Leadership'. *Presidential Studies Quarterly*, 14 (1), 43–52.

10 Brian Chesky. 'Don't Fuck Up the Culture'. *Medium*, 20 April 2014.

11 See 'The moral component' in *ADP Land Operations*, 3-8.

12 The Aitken Report. 'An Investigation into Cases of Deliberate Abuse and Unlawful Killing in Iraq in 2003 and 2004', published 25 January 2008, p. 24, para 42.

13 Revd Dr P. J. McCormack. 'Grounding British Army Values Upon an Ethical Good'. Executive Committee of the Army Board (ECAB) Paper, March 2015, p. 10.

14 Lt Col J. G. Shillington. 2011. 'Morale'. *The RUSI Journal*, 156 (2), 96–8.

15 *To Revel in God's Sunshine: The story of RSM J. C. Lord MVO MBE* (as related by former recruits, cadets, comrades). Compiled and published by Richard Alford: 2nd edition, 2013, p. 101.

16 Blake, J. E. 'Key Principles and Components in the Future UK Service Mess System', study published December 2019.

17 Gen Sir Mike Jackson. 2007. *Soldier*. London: Bantam Books, p. 145.

18 Maj Gen (Retd) Chip Chapman, speaking at the Centre for Army Leadership JNCO Day, 27 February 2020.

19 Muir, K. 1992. *Arms and the Woman*. London: Sinclair-Stevenson, p. 13.

20 Centre for Army Leadership. 'Junior Leadership – Army Sergeant Major WO1 G. H. Paton'. Video presentation, 27 May 2020.

21 Quoted in the British Army's 2013 anthology on leadership, *Serve to Lead*, p. 35.

22 *To Revel in God's Sunshine*, p. 40.

5. What British Army Leaders Know

1 'Address by Field Marshal The Viscount Slim on 14 October 1952 to Officer Cadets of the Royal Military Academy Sandhurst'. http://www.pnbhs.school.nz/wp-content/uploads/2015/11/Slim.pdf.

2 Baillergeon, F. A. 2005. 'Field Marshal William Slim and the Power of Leadership'. Unpublished Master's thesis, US Army Command and General Staff College, Kansas.

3 MacDonald Fraser, G. 2000. *Quartered Safe Out Here: A Recollection of the War in Burma*. London: HarperCollins, p. 37.

4 Field Marshal Sir William Slim. 1956. *Defeat Into Victory*. London: Cassell, pp. 537 (flexibility); 209 (better than I).

5 Gen Sir Mark Carleton-Smith. 73rd annual Kermit Roosevelt Lecture at the US Army Command and General Staff College, 7 March 2019.

6 Gen Carl von Clausewitz (trans. J. J. Graham). 1873. *On War*. London: N. Trubner and Co., p. 11.

7 The latter is easily overlooked. Reflecting on experience in Afghanistan, one company commander recalled that so much effort had gone into understanding Afghan culture and assumptions that he had neglected to do the same with a key ally, the Danish Army. Cultural and organisational misunderstandings followed that 'could have been avoided by better preparation'. (See Director General Leadership. *Developing Leaders: A British Army Guide*. Edition 1, January 2014, p. 73.)

8 See Goleman's seminal 1996 work *Emotional Intelligence: Why it can matter more than IQ*. London: Bloomsbury.

9 Daniel Goleman. 'What Makes a Leader?' *Harvard Business Review*, January 2004.

10 Dr J. Quinn. 'How Nazi "fake news" split Allied commanders in 1945'. The National Archives blog, 15 January 2020.

11 Clark, L. 2013. *Arnhem: Jumping the Rhine 1944 and 1945*. London: Headline Publishing, p. 238.

12 Caddick-Adams, P. 2015. *Snow and Steel: The Battle of the Bulge 1944–45*, Oxford: Oxford University Press, pp. 643–4.

13 Gen James Mattis. 2019. *Call Sign Chaos: Learning to Lead*. New York, NY: Random House, p. 42.

14 Murray, W. & Sinnreich, R. (eds). 2006. *The Past as Prologue: The Importance of History to the Military Profession*. Cambridge: Cambridge University Press, p. 7.

15 Field Marshal Lord Alanbrooke. 2001. In A. Danchev & D. Todman (eds). *War Diaries 1939–1945*. London: Weidenfeld & Nicolson, entry for 24 May 1940, p. 68.

16 Writing in 1953, quoted in the introduction to Alanbrooke's *War Diaries*, p. xxv.

17 Alanbrooke's *War Diaries*, entry for 1 June 1944, p. 553.

18 Retrieved from the BBC archives. https://www.bbc.co.uk/search?q=bill+shankly.

19 For the accounts of Private Raven in this chapter, see Jary, S. 1987. *18 Platoon*. Carshalton Beeches: Sydney Jary Ltd, pp. 83–4.

20 Gen Sir Peter de la Billière. 2007. 'Introduction' in Lord Moran. *The Anatomy of Courage: The Classic WW1 Study of the Psychological Effects of War*. London: Constable, p. xiii.

21 See Riggio, R. E., Chaleff, I. & Lipman-Blumen, J. 2008. *The Art of Followership: How Great Followers Create Great Leaders and Organizations*. San Francisco, CA: Jossey-Bass; Chaleff, I. 2009. *The Courageous Follower: Standing Up to & for Our Leaders*. San Francisco, CA: Berrett-Koehler Publishers; Kellerman, B. 2008. *Followership: How Followers Are Creating Change and Changing Leaders*. Boston, MA: Harvard Business Review Press.

22 Quotations in this chapter are taken from Robert E. Kelley. 'In Praise of Followers'. *Harvard Business Review*, November 1988.

23 Observations in this chapter on the relationship between Haig and Lawrence are taken from Harris, P. 2012. 'Soldier Banker: Lieutenant-General Sir Herbert Lawrence as the BEF's Chief of Staff in 1918'. *Journal of the Society for Army Historical Research*, 90 (361), 44–67.

24 Hytner, R. 2014. *Consiglieri: Leading From the Shadows*. London: Profile Books, p. 8.

25 See Chaleff, *The Courageous Follower*.

26 Thomas, T. & Chaleff, I. 2017. 'Moral Courage and Intelligent Disobedience'. *InterAgency Journal*, 8 (1), 58–66.

27 Professor Holmes defined the 10 'diseases of leadership' as: i) Lack of moral courage, ii) Failure to recognise the opposition can be loyal, iii) Consent and evade, iv) 'You don't need to know that', v) 'I've made up my mind', vi) Looking for the perfect solution, vii) Equating the quality of advice with someone's position or experience, viii) 'I'm too busy . . .', ix) 'I can do your job better than you can', and x) Big man, cold shadow. See *ADP Army Leadership Doctrine*, AC72029 (first edition, 2016), pp. 82–3.

28 Russell, B. 2004. *Power: A New Social Analysis*. London: Routledge Classics, p. 4.

29 French, J. R. P. & and Raven, B. 1959. 'The Bases of Social Power' in D. Cartwright (ed). *Studies in Social Power*. Ann Arbor, MI: Institute for Social Research, University of Michigan, pp. 150–67.

30 Subsequently, a sixth base – informational power – was added. See Raven, B. 2008. 'The Bases of Power and the Power/Interaction Model

of Interpersonal Influence'. *Analyses of Social Issues and Public Policy*, 8 (1), 1–22.

31 Director General Leadership. *Developing Leaders*, p. 43.

32 T. E. Lawrence's 'Twenty-Seven Articles', as quoted in this chapter, were first published in *The Arab Bulletin*, 20 August 1917.

33 Schneider, J. J. 2012. 'A Leader's Grief: T. E. Lawrence, Leadership and PTSD'. *Military Review*, January-February, pp. 79–80.

6. *What British Army Leaders Do (and How They Do It)*

1 The account by Sgt Ben Wallis is taken from an interview conducted in June 2005 by Lloyd Clark when researching his 2006 book *Anzio – The Friction of War: Italy and the Battle for Rome, 1944*. London: Headline Publishing.

2 Adair, J. 1973. *Action-Centered Leadership*. New York, NY: McGraw-Hill.

3 *ADP Army Leadership Doctrine*, AC72029 (first edition 2016), p. 42.

4 Robertson, D. & Breen, B. 2013. *Brick by Brick: How LEGO Rewrote the Rules of Innovation and Conquered the Global Toy Industry*. New York, NY: Random House Business, p. 76.

5 Knowledge@Wharton. 'Trouble in Legoland: How Too Much Innovation Almost Destroyed the Toy Company'. *TIME*, 12 July 2013.

6 Field Marshal Sir William Slim. 1956. *Defeat Into Victory*. London: Cassell, pp. 210–11.

7 *ADP Land Operations*, 1A-1.

8 Field Marshal Lord Alanbrooke. 2001. In A. Danchev & D. Todman (eds). *War Diaries 1939–1945*. London: Weidenfeld & Nicolson, entry for 22 November 1939, p. 18.

9 Gen Stanley McChrystal. 2015. *Team of Teams: New Rules of Engagement for a Complex World*. London: Penguin Books, p. 120.

10 WO1 Harley Upham, email to author, 4 September 2020.

11 Schein, E. 1985. *Organizational Culture and Leadership: A Dynamic View*, San Francisco, CA: Jossey-Bass, p. 2.

12 Director General Leadership. *Developing Leaders: A British Army Guide*. Edition 1, January 2014, p. 63.

13 US Army Armor School. 'Order of the Spur'. USAARMS Pamphlet 360-12, February 2019.

14 Lt Charlotte Lord-Sallenave, email to author, 3 September 2020.

15 Centre for Army Leadership. 'Junior Leadership – Army Sergeant Major WO1 G. H. Paton'. Video presentation, 27 May 2020.

16 Reflections of a Company Sergeant Major, WO2 Mike Christian, CSM 150 Pro Coy, 1 RMP, in an email to WO1 Chris Nicol, 14 July 2020.

17 Anita Elberse. 'Ferguson's Formula'. *Harvard Business Review*, October 2013.

7. Officer Leadership

1 Hume, I. 2018. *From the Edge of Empire: A Memoir*. Denver, CO: Outskirts Press, p. 113.

2 Laughlin, C. 1918. *Foch the Man: A Life of the Supreme Commander of the Allied Armies*. Chicago, IL: Fleming H. Revell Company. See Chapter IX: 'The Great Teacher'.

3 Downes, C. 1991. *Special Trust and Confidence: The Making of an Officer*. Portland, OR: Frank Cass, p. 69.

4 Jacobs, A. 2016. 'Teaching IR at Sandhurst: Blended Learning Through an Integrated Approach'. *Military Strategy Magazine*. Special Edition: 'International Relations in Professional Military Education', pp. 50–55.

5 OCdt Steven Cooke, email to Maj Matthew Cary, 12 August 2020.

6 Maj Gen Paul Nanson. 2019. *Stand Up Straight: 10 Life Lessons from the Royal Military Academy Sandhurst*. London: Century, p. 11.

7 Campion Vaughan, E. 2010. *Some Desperate Glory: The Diary of a Young Officer, 1917*. Barnsley: Pen & Sword Military, p. 6.

8 Bellamy, B. 2013. *Troop Leader: A Tank Commander's Story*. Stroud: The History Press, p. 46.

9 Jary, S. 2000. 'Reflections on the Relationship Between the Led and the Leader'. *Journal of the Royal Army Medical Corps*, 146 (1), 54–6.

10 Lt Col (Retd) Charlie Antelme. 'Leadership, Followership and Junior Command'. Centre for Army Leadership JNCO Day, 27 February 2020.

11 Campion Vaughan, *Some Desperate Glory*, p. 8.

12 Hill, L. 2003. *Becoming a Manager: How New Managers Master the Challenges of Leadership*. Boston, MA: Harvard Business School Press, p. 62.

13 The Army Leader Team. 'Do Not Take Leadership for Granted: An Interview with Major General Charlie Collins'. *The Army Leader*, 11 September 2020.

14 The ICSC(L) and all equivalent higher courses are hosted at the Joint Services Command and Staff College in Shrivenham, after the equivalent single Service institutions, including the Army's Staff College at Camberley, were merged in 1997. For background, see National Audit Office. 'Ministry of Defence: The Joint Services Command and Staff College: Report by the Comptroller and Auditor General'. HC 537, Session 2001–2002, 7 February 2002.

15 Maj Al Phillips. 'The Strength of the Clan is in the Clansman: Reflections on Company Command'. *The Army Leader*, 29 August 2019.

16 Maj Gen (Retd) Patrick Marriott. 'My "Lessons Learnt" – Four and a Half Thoughts on Sub-Unit Command'. *The Army Leader*, 20 June 2018.

17 Civil servants play an essential role in the modern Army, not just lending expertise in delivery, but bringing an outside perspective and critical challenge, both at home and on operations. See Richard Johnstone. 'Why the military needs civil servants: incoming chief of defence staff General Sir Nick Carter on the bravery of officials in combat zones'. *Civil Service World*, 11 May 2018.

18 Maj Gen Sir Matthew Gossett. 1891. 'Battalion Command'. *Royal United Service Institution Journal*, 35 (158), 475.

19 Copp, T. & McAndrew, B. 1990. *Battle Exhaustion: Soldiers and Psychiatrists in the Canadian Army, 1939–1945*. Montreal: McGill-Queen's University Press, pp. 81–2.

20 Forty, G. 2013. *Jake Wardrop's Diary: A Tank Regiment Sergeant's Story*. Stroud: Amberley Publishing, p. 54.

21 Sassoon, S. 1972. *The Complete Memoirs of George Sherston*. London: Faber & Faber, pp. 267–8.

22 Seton, G. 1933. *Footslogger*. London: Hutchinson, p. 220.

23 For key background reading, see CIPD Research Insight report. 'Engaging leadership: creating organisations that maximise the potential

of their people'. http://www.cipd.co.uk/shapingthefuture/_leader shipreport.htm; Al-Asfour, A. & Lettau, L. 2014. 'Strategies for Leadership Styles for Multi-Generational Workforce'. *Journal of Leadership, Accountability & Ethics*, 11 (2), 58–69; Senge, P. M. 1990. *The Fifth Discipline: The Art and Practice of a Learning Organization*. New York, NY: Doubleday; Clutterbuck, D. 2004. *Everyone needs a mentor: fostering talent in your organisation*. London: CIPD; Algera, P. M. & Lips-Wiersma, M. 2012. 'Radical Authentic Leadership: Co-creating the Conditions Under Which All Members of the Organization Can be Authentic'. *Leadership Quarterly*, 23 (1), 118–31.

24 General Staff Centre. *General Staff Handbook*. March 2021, p. 59 (clothing); p. 5 (ambassadors).

25 McAleer, G. 2009. 'Leaders in Transition: Advice From Colin Powell and Other Strategic Thinkers'. *Military Psychology*, 15 (4), 313–14.

26 Lindsay, D. 1987. *Forgotten General, A Life of Andrew Thorne*. Salisbury: Michael Russell, p. 74.

27 Quoted in Brown, A. 2017. 'Lions Led by Donkeys? Brigade Commanders of the Australian Imperial Force, 1914–18'. Unpublished PhD thesis, University of New South Wales, p. 15.

28 Fraser, D. 2011. *Alanbrooke*. London: Bloomsbury, p. 215.

29 Peter F. Drucker. 'The American CEO'. *Wall Street Journal*, 30 December 2004.

30 Gen Sir Richard Dannatt. 2010. *Leading From the Front: The Autobiography*. London: Transworld, p. 123.

31 DCLM. 1998. *Strategic Leadership Primer*. Carlisle, PA: US Army War College, p. 1.

32 Field Marshal The Lord Bramall. 2017. *The Bramall Papers: Reflections on War and Peace*. Barnsley: Pen & Sword Military, p. 399.

33 Heuer, R. 1999. *Psychology of Intelligence Analysis*. Fairfax, VA: Center for the Study of Intelligence, p. 5.

34 Max Abelson. 'Warren Buffett's May 1969 Retirement Letter: "Documenting One's Boners"'. *Observer*, 25 August 2010.

35 Gryta, T. & Mann, T. 2020. *Lights Out: Pride, Delusion and the Fall of General Electric*. New York, NY: Houghton Mifflin Harcourt, p. 46.

36 Professor Manfred Kets de Vries. 'The Cure for the Loneliness of Command'. INSEAD Blog, 14 March 2019.

8. Soldier Leadership

1 Sir William Robertson. 2018. *From Private to Field-Marshal*. Miami, FL: HardPress, pp. 28 (backbone); vii (promoted Lance-Corporal); 29 (impartial).

2 MOD. 'UK Armed Forces Quarterly Service Personnel Statistics'. Published 20 February 2020, p. 6, Table 4.

3 Gen Frederick E. Kroesen. 1993. 'The NCO Corps: More than the Backbone'. *The NCO Journal*, winter issue, p. 15.

4 Centre for Army Leadership. 'Junior Leadership — Army Sergeant Major WO1 G. H. Paton'. Video presentation, 27 May 2020.

5 CSgt Aaron Kerin. 'The Unpopular Man: Leading as a Lance Corporal'. *The Army Leader*, 11 May 2018.

6 Cpl Huw Davies. 'Leading as a JNCO: An Army Reserve Perspective'. *The Army Leader*, 2 October 2020.

7 Maj Gen Richard A. Chilcoat. 1996. *The Battalion Commander's Handbook*. Carlisle, PA: US Army War College, Appendix Four.

8 Cardiff Metropolitan University & Bangor University. 2014. ' "Train in, not select out?": Bangor leadership training model decreased the high wastage rates in British army recruits and improved training practices'. Impact case study, REF3b.

9 Quoted in the British Army's 2013 anthology on leadership, *Serve to Lead*, p. 46.

10 Burke, E. 2018. *An Army of Tribes: British Army Cohesion, Deviancy and Murder in Northern Ireland*. Liverpool: Liverpool University Press, p. 172.

11 Gen Charles C. Krulak. 1999. 'The Strategic Corporal: Leadership in the Three-Block War'. *Marine Corps Gazette*. January issue, 4–5.

12 Quoted in Horn, B. 2002. 'A Timeless Strength: The Army's Senior NCO Corps'. *Canadian Military Journal*. Spring issue, 44–5.

13 Human, W. A. 2019. *Arthur: The Great War Memoirs of William Arthur Human*. PublishNation (www.publishnation.co.uk), p. 95.

14 Kirke, C. 2009. *Red Coat, Green Machine: Continuity in Change in the British Army 1700–2000*. London: Bloomsbury Academic, pp. 172–3.

15 Powdrill, E. A. 2009. *In the Face of the Enemy: A Battery Sergeant Major in Action in the Second World War*. Barnsley: Pen & Sword Military, p. 34.

16 Quoted in Dan Ellis. 'Senior Soldier: The Company Sergeant Major'. *The Cove*, 3 September 2019.

17 Gen Sir Mike Jackson. 2007. *Soldier*. London: Bantam Books, p. 284.

18 Capt Doug Beattie (Retd). 2009. *An Ordinary Soldier*. London: Simon & Schuster, pp. 61–2.

19 See Horn, 'A Timeless Strength', p. 42.

9. Leadership in Peace

1   Lord Moran. 2007. *The Anatomy of Courage: The Classic WW1 Study of the Psychological Effects of War*. London: Constable, p. 163.

2   Kirke, C. 2009. *Red Coat, Green Machine: Continuity in Change in the British Army 1700–2000*. London: Bloomsbury Academic, p. 104.

3   Powell, G. 2012. *Men at Arnhem*. Barnsley: Pen & Sword Military, pp. 25 (personal instrument); 38 (fads mattered).

4   Sjt Ben Hayden. 'Get off their backs! A JNCO's Guide to Avoiding Micromanagement'. *The Army Leader*, 22 February 2021.

5   Fitton, R. 1990. *Leadership: Quotations From The Military Tradition*. New York, NY: Avalon Publishing, p. 82.

6   David Novak. 'Follow Indra Nooyi's example: Become a leader people are excited to follow'. *CNBC.com*, 12 September 2018.

7   WO1 Leigh Flanigan. 'Reflections of a Regimental Sergeant Major'. *Cognitio* (The Intelligence Corps Journal), issue 94, summer 2020.

8   The officer, who was interviewed for this book, has asked to remain anonymous.

9   Salesforce UK. 'Leading Through Adverse Conditions: Tips from Boots and the British Army'. *salesforce.com*, 28 October 2020.

10 Speakers Corner. 'Nicky Moffatt Shares the Key Traits a Modern Leader Needs During Change'. YouTube, 26 February 2021.

11 See Col David M. Oberlander. 2013. 'Negative Leadership'. Strategy research project. Carlisle, PA: US Army War College.

12 Lt Col J. Dagless. 'Using Your Rank as an Opportunity and the Threat of Toxic Leadership'. Centre for Army Leadership SNCO Study Day, 24 September 2020.

13 https://www.paradata.org.uk/article/major-chris-keebles-account-goose-green.

14 See King, A. 2006. 'The Word of Command: Communication and Cohesion in the Military'. *Armed Forces & Society*, 32 (4), 493–512.

15 Pugsley, C. 2011. 'We Have Been Here Before: the Evolution of the Doctrine of Decentralised Command in the British Army 1905–1989'. Sandhurst Occasional Papers, No. 9. Camberley: Royal Military Academy Sandhurst, p. 8.

16 Field Marshal The Lord Bramall. 2017. *The Bramall Papers: Reflections on War and Peace*. Barnsley: Pen & Sword Military, p. 438.

17 Gilbert, W. & and Côté, J. 2009. 'An Integrative Definition of Coaching Effectiveness and Expertise'. *International Journal of Sports Science & Coaching*, 4 (3), 307–23.

18 Sgt Mark Davey, email to author, 3 September 2020.

19 McElligott, S. & Seaton, A. 2019. 'Adventurous Training and Leadership: Training for enhanced effectiveness or just a week out of the office?' *Army Mountaineer*, winter issue, p. 10.

10. Leadership in War

1 Maj Gen Roy Urquhart. 2011. *Arnhem*. Barnsley: Pen & Sword Military, p. 131.

2 Descriptions of the events at Hackett's Hollow are taken from Maj Geoffrey Powell. 2012. *Men at Arnhem*. Barnsley: Pen & Sword Military, pp. 107 (stood a chance); 111 (bloody ditch); 112 (proper way); 120 (a fearful sight); 113 (struck back); 119 (our trust).

3 Komer, R. W. 1972. 'The Malayan Emergency in Retrospect: Organization of A Successful Counterinsurgency Effort'. Santa Monica, CA: Rand, pp. 17–18.

4 See Coates, H. 1976. 'An Operational Analysis of the Emergency in Malaya, 1948–1954'. Unpublished PhD thesis, Australian National University, p. 194; Barber, N. 1971. *The War of the Running Dogs: How Malaya Defeated the Communist Guerrillas*. London: William Collins, p. 114.

5 Komer, 'The Malayan Emergency in Retrospect', pp. 26–7.

6 Hack, K. 2009. 'The Malayan Emergency as counter-insurgency para-digm'. *Journal of Strategic Studies*, 32 (3), 383–414.

7 Comber, L. 2015. *Templer and the Road to Malayan Independence: The Man and His Time*. Singapore: ISEAS Publishing, p. 205.

8 Nolan, V. 2012. *Military Leadership and Counterinsurgency: The British Army and Small War Strategy since World War II*. London: I. B. Tauris, p. 94.

9 Ibid., pp. 94–7; Coates, 'An Operational Analysis', p. 130.

10 Komer, 'The Malayan Emergency in Retrospect', p. 20.

11 John P. Kotter. 'Leading Change: Why Transformation Efforts Fail'. *Harvard Business Review*, May-June 1995.

12 McConville, M. 2011. 'General Templer and the Use of Geese As Watchdogs'. *The RUSI Journal*, 156 (5), 95–6.

13 Komer, 'The Malayan Emergency in Retrospect', p. 30.

14 Quotations are taken from Gen Norman Schwarzkopf. 1992. *It Doesn't Take a Hero: The Autobiography*. New York, NY: Bantam Books, pp. 527 (had to mask); 528 (reminding myself); 495 (so complex).

15 Quotations are taken from Gen Sir Peter de la Billière. 2012. *Storm Command: A Personal Account of the Gulf War*. London: HarperCollins, pp. 33 (from scratch); 52 (confused picture); 96 (some guidance).

16 Gen Colin Powell. 1995. *A Soldier's Way: An Autobiography*. London: Random House, p. 475.

17 de la Billière, *Storm Command*, p. 92.

18 Schwarzkopf, *It Doesn't Take a Hero*, p. 607.

19 Frostic, F. 1994. *Air Campaign Against the Iraqi Army in the Kuwaiti Theater of Operations*. Santa Monica, CA: Rand, pp. 63–4.

20 de la Billière, *Storm Command*, pp. 57 (tri-services group); 58 (chain of command); 89–90 ('NOFORN'); 92 (US team leader).

21 Gen Carl von Clausewitz (trans. J. J. Graham). 1873. *On War*. London: N. Trubner and Co., p. 11.

22 Quotations are taken from Farrar-Hockley, A. 2007. *The Edge of the Sword: The Classic Account of Warfare & Captivity in Korea*. Barnsley: Pen & Sword Military, pp. 11 (dry April); 15 (flap on); 17 (a feint); 18 (its outcome); 28 (Castle Hill).

23 Whiting, C. 1999. *Battleground Korea: The British in Korea*. Stroud: Sutton Publishing, p. 155.

24 https://www.nationalarchives.gov.uk/battles/korea/buildup.htm.

25 John Ezard. 'Needless battle caused by uncommon language'. *Guardian*, 14 April 2001.

26 For descriptions of the events at Castle Site, see Farrar-Hockley, *The Edge of the Sword*, pp. 27–8.

27 *The London Gazette*. Supplement 40029, Friday, 27 November 1953, p. 6513.

28 Hastings, M. 2010. *The Korean War: An Epic Conflict*. London: Pan Books, p. 313.

29 Farrar-Hockley, *The Edge of the Sword*, pp. 49–50.

30 Hastings, *The Korean War*, p. 325.

31 Salmon, A. 2009. *To the Last Round: The Epic British Stand on the Imjin River, Korea 1951*. London: Aurum, p. 311.

32 Large, L. 1988. *One Man's War in Korea*. Wellingborough: William Kimber, pp. 45 (habit forming); 60 (roar of the battle).

33 Hastings, *The Korean War*, pp. 322 (Sam Davies); 312 (ammunition dwindled).

34 For Cordingley's comments on the anniversary of the battle, see Forces News. 'Gulf War Commander Recalls Swift Land Battle Against Saddam Hussein'. YouTube, 25 February 2016.

35 de la Billière, *Storm Command*, p. 284.

36 For the switching of the two brigades see Maj Gen Rupert Smith. 1992. 'The Gulf War: The Land Battle'. *The RUSI Journal*, 137 (1), 1–5.

37 de la Billière, *Storm Command*, p. 288.

38 RUSI. 'Gen Sir Rupert Smith – The Evolution of Manoeuvre: RUSILWC18'. YouTube, 21 June 2018.

39 For de la Billière on combat and the aftermath of DESERT SABRE, see *Storm Command*, pp. 289 (unit by unit); 307 (souvenirs).

40 Whiting, *Battleground Korea*, p. 159.

41 Large, *One Man's War in Korea*, p. 81.

42 Quoted in Hastings, *The Korean War*, p. 325.

43 Urquhart, *Arnhem*, pp. 243 (nauseated); 259 (lassitude).

44 Frost, J. 2008. *A Drop Too Many*. Barnsley: Pen & Sword Military, p. 301.

45 Nolan, *Military Leadership and Counterinsurgency*, p. 88.

46 Coates, 'An Operational Analysis', p. 125.

47 Powell, *A Soldier's Way*, p. 475.

48 Gen Colin Powell. 'Town Hall Meeting'. US Department of State, 25 January 2001.

49 Quoted in Salmon, *To the Last Round*, p. 316.

50 Kirstie Brewer. 'Fire fighters' battle with PTSD: "Every day is an anxious day"'. *Guardian*, 23 August 2017.

51 Salmon, *To the Last Round*, pp. 317–18.

52 https://www.britishlegion.org.uk/stories/finding-purpose-in-the-civilian-world.

53 https://www.paradata.org.uk/article/shan-hackett-arnhem-article-john-waddy.

11. *The Future*

1 Bouquet, T. 2012. *617: Going to War with Today's Dambusters*. London: Orion, pp. 86–7.

2 Alistair Bunkall. 'The long goodbye to Afghanistan'. *New Statesman*, 17 October 2013.

3 Robert H. Scales. 'Forecasting the Future of Warfare'. *War on the Rocks*, 9 April 2018.

4 Gen Sir Mark Carleton-Smith. 'Strategic Overview'. Centre for Army Leadership, Remote Leadership Conference, 21 March 2021.

5 Fuller, J. F. C. 1993. *The Foundations of the Science of War*. Fort Leavenworth, KS: US Army Command and General Staff College Press, p. 17.

6 Spiers, E. 1979. 'The British Cavalry, 1902–1914'. *Journal of the Society for Army Historical Research*, 57 (230), 71–9.

7 Fuller, J. F. C. 1953. 'Warfare and the Future'. *Armor*, March-April issue, 48–9.

8 Observations in this and preceding paragraphs are taken from Scales, 'Forecasting the Future of Warfare'.

9 Geoffrey Moore. 'To Succeed in the Long Term, Focus on the Middle Term'. *Harvard Business Review*, July-August 2007.

10 Gen Sir Nick Carter. 'Chief of Defence Staff speech: RUSI Annual Lecture'. MOD. 17 December 2020.

11 MOD. 'Introducing the Integrated Operating Concept', published 30 September 2020.

12 Dr Florian Krampe. 'Why United Nations peace operations cannot ignore climate change'. Stockholm International Peace Research Institute, 22 February 2021.

13 Hsiang, S., Burke, M. & Miguel, E. 2013. 'Quantifying the Influence of Climate on Human Conflict'. *Science*, 341 (6151), 1189–1213.

14 Lt Gen Richard Wardlaw. 'Informing a strategic response to climate change'. University of Cambridge Institute for Sustainability Leadership, briefing for the Board of the British Army, February 2020.

15 Robert Walters. 'Attracting and Retaining Millennial Professionals'. Robert Walters Insight Series whitepaper, August 2017.

16 Workforce Institute @ Kronos. 'Meet Gen Z' report, June 2019.

17 Santos, H., Grossmann, I. & Varnum, M. 2017. 'Global Increases in Individualism'. *Psychological Science*, 28 (9), 1232–3.

18 Rutherford, T. 'Defence Personnel Statistics'. House of Commons Library, SN/SG/02183, 26 September 2014; https://commonslibrary.parliament.uk/uk-army-to-be-reduced-to-72500.

19 See Jonathan Beale. 'Does size matter for Britain's shrinking Army?' *BBC News Online*, 24 February 2021.

20 Professor Rita Gunther McGrath. 'Transient Advantage'. *Harvard Business Review*, June 2013.

21 A. G. Lafley. 'What Only the CEO Can Do'. *Harvard Business Review*, May 2009.

22 Maj Gen Duncan Capps, email to author, 8 June 2021.

23 Maj Gen Nick Borton. 'Leading a Dispersed Division'. Centre for Army Leadership, Remote Leadership Conference, 21 March 2021.

24 Quoted in Holmes, R. 2006. *Dusty Warriors: Modern Soldiers at War*. London: Harper Press, p. 18.

25 Glassdoor. 'Culture over cash? Glassdoor multi-country survey finds more than half of employees prioritize workplace culture over salary', published 10 July 2019.

26 Borton, 'Leading a Dispersed Division'.

27 Gen Viscount Wolseley. 1887. 'The Army'. In T. Humphry Ward (ed). *The Reign of Queen Victoria: A Survey of Fifty Years of Progress Vol. I*. London: Smith, Elder & Co, p. 155.

28 House of Lords. 'The Wellington Statue' in *Hansard*, Vol. 288, Col. 829, 20 May 1884.

29 United States Army Training and Doctrine Command. *The US Army Operating Concept: Win in a Complex World*. TRADOC Pamphlet 525-3-1, 7 October 2014, p. iv.

30 Gen Joseph Dunford Jr. 'From the Chairman: The Pace of Change'. *Joint Force Quarterly* no. 84, National Defense University Press, 26 January 2017.

31 Sewell Chan. 'Stanislav Petrov, Soviet Officer Who Helped Avert Nuclear War, Is Dead at 77'. *The New York Times*, 18 September 2017.

32 Centre for Army Leadership. 'Podcast Episode 1 – General Sir Mark Carleton-Smith KCB CBE ADC Gen', 26 November 2020.

33 McGrath, 'Transient Advantage'.

34 Army Publishing Directorate. 2019. *ADP 6-22: Army Leadership and the Profession*. Washington, DC: Department of the Army, p. vii.

35 https://rework.withgoogle.com/guides/understanding-team-effectiveness/steps/introduction/.

36 Professor David A. Garvin. 'Building a Learning Organization'. *Harvard Business Review*, July-August 1993.

Conclusion: Universal Lessons

1 Falkner, J. 2015. *Marlborough's War Machine 1702–1711*. Barnsley: Pen & Sword Military, p. 62.

2 Transcript: 'Obama's Interview Aboard Air Force One'. *The New York Times*, 7 March 2009.

Acknowledgements

1 Kipling, R. 1998 (first published 1894). *The Jungle Books*. Oxford: OUP World's Classics, p. 165.

Glossary

1 Eldridge, J. & Crombie, A. 1974. *A Sociology of Organizations*. London: Allen and Unwin, pp. 89–90; quoted in Furnham, A. 2004. *The Psychology of Behaviour at Work*. Hove: Psychology Press, p. 555.

Glossary

Army Leadership Code: A set of seven leadership behaviours applied through a spectrum of leadership styles. The behaviours are nested in academic research on high-performance teams and are designed to translate the Army's Values and Standards into learned behaviours.

Army Leadership Doctrine: A publication that codifies the British Army's thinking on leadership, drawing together ideas, principles and methods that have been proven to work throughout history. It is the capstone document for the British Army on leadership.

Army Reserve: This provides support to the Regular Army at home and overseas. Army Reserve soldiers come from all walks of life and work part-time as soldiers for the British Army alongside full-time regular soldiers.

Cap badge: The badge worn on the headdress of all soldiers, distinguishing the individual's unit or organisation. Each regiment and corps has their own cap badge.

Climate: Climate is the environment experienced in specific teams or units within an organisation. Being inherently less stable than culture, a climate can change relatively quickly as it is highly dependent upon the context and the people involved. The smaller the team, the more quickly this change may occur.

Command responsibility: The duty invested in an individual to supervise subordinates, and liability for the failure to do so, both in government and military law.

Commanding Officer: Held in the rank of lieutenant colonel commanding a unit of around 650 soldiers, comprising between four and six sub-units.

They are responsible for the overall operational effectiveness of their unit in terms of military capability, welfare, discipline and administration.

Counter-insurgency (COIN): Defined as comprehensive civilian and military efforts to defeat an insurgency and to address core grievances. It encompasses those military, paramilitary, political, economic, psychological and civil actions taken by government or its partners to defeat an insurgency.

Counter-terrorism (CT): Counter-terrorism describes all preventive, defensive and offensive measures taken to reduce the vulnerability of forces, individuals and property against terrorist threats and/or acts to respond to terrorist acts.

Culture: The culture of an organisation refers to the unique configuration of norms, values, beliefs, ways of behaving and so on that characterise the manner in which groups and individuals combine to get things done. This distinctiveness of a particular organisation is intimately bound up with its history and the character-building effects of past decisions and past leaders.[1]

Followership: The act of willingly following a leader. Leadership and followership not only coexist, they are mutually supporting. A 'follower', like a 'leader', is a role but not an assigned position or authority. Followership refers to the actions of one person or a team in a subordinate role to that of the leader. It is not a lesser role and it is not a preparation to become a leader. Followership is an intentional act and it plays an essential individual and collective role in defining leadership failures and successes.

Improvised explosive device (IED): A bomb constructed and deployed in ways other than in conventional military action. It may be constructed of conventional military explosives, such as an artillery shell, or using improvised materials, attached to a detonating mechanism.

JNCO: A junior non-commissioned officer refers to the ranks of lance corporal (LCpl) and corporal (Cpl); they hold a rank but have not been commissioned. This is the lowest level of command. A corporal would be responsible for between 8 and 12 soldiers.

Logistics: The science of planning and carrying out the movement and maintenance of forces. Logistics comprises the development, acquisition, storage, movement, distribution, maintenance, recovery and disposal of material; transport of personnel, acquisition and construction; maintenance, operation and disposal of facilities; acquisition of furnishing of services; medical and health services.

Mission Command: The British Army's command philosophy. This is an approach which empowers subordinate commanders and promotes initiative as well as freedom and speed of action. Critically, it focuses on achievement of higher intent through mission-type orders. It empowers leaders at every level and is intended to generate agility and tempo.

Non-commissioned officers (NCOs): Soldiers who have gained a position of authority through promotion. They range from lance corporal to warrant officer class one (WO1). The role of an NCO is critical as they are the primary leaders responsible for carrying out and executing the mission and, for some, the training of British Army personnel.

Officer Commanding (OC): An OC is in command of a company comprising 3 platoons and an average of 120 soldiers. The OC is the lead for decision making in that company, with the support of platoon commanders and senior soldiers. OCs hold the rank of major.

Operational level: The level at which campaigns and major operations are planned, conducted and sustained to accomplish strategic objectives within theatres or areas of operations.

Regular Army: This term refers to the professional-standing army, consisting of full-time soldiers.

Servant leadership: A concept that promotes the leader as a servant of those they lead, whereby the leader puts the needs of others, specifically the individuals within their team, before themselves. Such an approach provides a foundation for developing trust and loyalty between leader and follower.

SJAR: A Servicepersons' Joint Appraisal Report is an annual report for soldiers. Each individual receives an assessment of both their performance and potential from a 1st reporting officer (1RO – in most cases their immediate line manager) and a more senior 2nd reporting officer (2RO). Both assessments make recommendations for employability and promotion. An officers' equivalent is called an OJAR.

SNCO: A senior non-commissioned officer refers to the ranks of sergeant (Sgt) and colour/staff sergeant (CSgt/SSgt). Like JNCOs and warrant officers, SNCOs hold a rank but have not been commissioned. A Sgt is second-in-command (2IC) of a platoon of approximately 30 soldiers. CSgts/SSgts fulfil a variety of roles but typically support the management of a company/squadron, e.g. as a company quartermaster sergeant, managing all equipment and stores.

Staff College: A British military academic establishment that provides periodic formal training and education to officers throughout their career. Its purpose is to intellectually develop officers, by giving them the skills they need to address the current and future security and defence challenges.

Strategic level: The level at which a nation or group of nations determines national or multinational security objectives, and deploys national, including military, resources to achieve them.

Sub-threshold operations: Operational activities that are designed to remain below the threshold of conventional military conflict and open interstate war. Such operations are intended to achieve gains without escalating to overt warfare, without crossing established red lines, and thus without exposing the practitioner to the penalties and risks that such escalation might bring.

Tactical level: The level at which activities, battles and engagements are planned and executed to accomplish military objectives assigned to tactical formations and units. It is at the tactical level that troops are deployed directly in offensive or defensive activities.

Transactional leadership: A style of leadership in which leaders promote compliance by followers through both rewards and punishments.

Transformational leadership: A process that changes and transforms individuals and teams for the better. It requires leaders to connect with the emotions, motives and needs of those they lead. Transformational leadership is empowering, and motivates individuals to place the needs of the team before their own. It requires the creation of a vision, which becomes a focal point, a conceptual map of where the organisation is heading. The vision gives a unifying purpose for all, and helps create a sense of identity for individuals and team. Transformational leadership is often said to produce performance beyond expectations.

Unlimited liability: A term coined by General Sir John Hackett in 1983. It describes the fact that, on becoming a soldier, one gives up individual rights, accepts collective standards which contribute to the common good, and undertakes, in the last analysis, to kill or be killed for a purpose in which one may have no personal interest.

Values and Standards: The British Army's Values (courage, discipline, respect for others, integrity, loyalty and selfless commitment) are the moral principles which define who British soldiers are as individuals and what the British Army stands for as an organisation. Standards (lawful, acceptable behaviour and totally professional) are the authoritative benchmarks against which we judge our conduct.

Warrant Officer: Warrant Officers (WO) are the senior ranks within the NCO cohort, holding a Queen's (or King's) warrant. A warrant officer class two (WO2) typically holds the appointment of company/squadron sergeant major or regimental quartermaster sergeant. Warrant officer class one (WO1), the more senior, is the highest rank an NCO can attain and holds appointments such as regimental sergeant major, command sergeant major and, the most senior WO1 in the Army, the Army sergeant major.

Whole Force: An amalgamation of all personnel required to deliver Defence outputs, including non-operational roles, covering regular and reserve service personnel, civil servants and other civilians and contractors.

Appendices

Appendix 1: Unit Sizes and Grouping⋆

Type of unit (a)	Contains (b)	Personnel (c)	Officers (d)	NCOs (e)
Fire Team	4 soldiers	4		Lance Corporal
Section	2 fire teams	8–10		Corporal
Platoon/Troop	3 sections	30	Second Lieutenant, Lieutenant or Captain	Sergeant
Company/ Squadron	HQ + 3 platoons	120	Major	Warrant Officer Class 2
Battalion/ Regiment	HQ + 4–6 companies	650	Lieutenant Colonel	Warrant Officer Class 1
Battlegroup	Battalion + supporting arms	700–1,000	Lieutenant Colonel	Warrant Officer Class 1
Brigade	3–5 battalions	5,000	Brigadier	Command Sergeant Major
Division	3 brigades	10,000+	Major General	Command Sergeant Major

⋆ Source: https://www.army.mod.uk/who-we-are/

Appendix 2: Army Rank Structure

Soldiers/non-commissioned officers

Rank	Insignia
Private	
Lance Corporal	
Corporal	
Sergeant	
Colour Sergeant/Staff Sergeant	
Warrant Officer Class 2	
Warrant Officer Class 1	

Commissioned officers

Rank	Insignia
Second Lieutenant	
Lieutenant	
Captain	
Major	
Lieutenant Colonel	

Colonel	
Brigadier	
Major General	
Lieutenant General	
General	

Bibliography

All websites listed in the Bibliography were accessed in May 2021.

Books

Alanbrooke, Field Marshal Lord (eds A. Danchev and D. Todman). 2001. *War Diaries 1939–1945*. London: Weidenfeld and Nicolson

Alford, Richard (ed). 1981. *To Revel in God's Sunshine: The story of RSM J C Lord MVO MBE*. R. Alford (n. p.)

Bass, Bernard M. 1990. *Bass & Stogdill's Handbook of Leadership: Theory, Research, and Managerial Applications*. New York, NY: Free Press

Beattie, Doug. 2009. *An Ordinary Soldier*. London: Simon & Schuster

Beckett, I. F. W. 2018. *A British Profession of Arms: The Politics of Command in the Late Victorian Army*. Norman, OK: University of Oklahoma Press

Bélanger, Stéphanie A. H. and Lagacé-Roy, Daniel. 2016. *Military Operations and the Mind: War Ethics and Soldiers' Well-being*. Montreal: McGill-Queen's University Press

Bennis, Warren G. 1994. *Beyond Leadership: Balancing Economics, Ethics, and Ecology*. Cambridge, MA: Blackwell Business

Bouquet, Tim. 2012. *617: Going to War with Today's Dambusters*. London: Orion

Bramall, Field Marshal Lord (ed. Robin Brodhurst). 2017. *The Bramall Papers: Reflections on War and Peace*. Barnsley: Pen & Sword Military

Burke, Edward. 2018. *An Army of Tribes: British Army Cohesion, Deviancy and Murder in Northern Ireland*. Liverpool: Liverpool University Press

Caddick-Adams, Peter. 2015. *Snow and Steel: The Battle of the Bulge 1944-45*. Oxford: OUP

Chandler, David and Beckett, Ian (eds). 2003. *The Oxford History of the British Army*. Oxford: OUP

Ciulla, Joanne B. 2004. *Ethics, the Heart of Leadership*. Westport, CT: Praeger

Clark, Lloyd. 2006. *Anzio – The Friction of War: Italy and the Battle for Rome, 1944*. London: Headline Publishing.

Clark, Lloyd. 2013. *Arnhem: Jumping the Rhine 1944 and 1945*. London: Headline Publishing Group

Comber, Leon. 2015. *Templer and the Road to Malayan Independence*. Singapore: Institute of Southeast Asian Studies

Copp, Terry and McAndrew, Bill. 1990. *Battle Exhaustion: Soldiers and Psychiatrists in the Canadian Army, 1939–1945*. Montreal: McGill-Queen's University Press

Covey, Stephen R. 1992. *Principle-Centered Leadership*. New York, NY: Simon & Schuster

Crang, Jeremy. 2000. *The British Army and the People's War 1939–1945*. Manchester: Manchester University Press

Crichton, Andrew. 1824. *The Life and Diary of Lieut. Col. J. Blackader*. Edinburgh: H. S. Baynes

Cushion, Nigel. 2019. *Undefeatable Spirit: The story of 11 days, of Albert, and the lads from the yards. The Norfolk Regiment. 1909–1919*. Norwich: Nelsonspirit Publishing

Dannatt, Richard. 2010. *Leading From the Front: The Autobiography*. London: Transworld

Dannatt, Richard. 2017. *Boots on the Ground: Britain and Her Army since 1945*. London: Profile Books

Davies, Frank and Maddocks, Graham. 1995. *Bloody Red Tabs: General Officer Casualties of the Great War 1914–1918*. Barnsley: Pen & Sword Military

Dawson, Anthony. 2014. *Real War Horses: The Experience of the British Cavalry, 1814–1914*. Barnsley: Pen & Sword Military

Downes, Cathy. 1991. *Special Trust and Confidence: The Making of an Officer*. Portland, OR: Frank Cass

Fairholm, Gilbert W. 1991. *Values Leadership: Toward a New Philosophy of Leadership*. New York, NY: Praeger

Falkner, James. 2015. *Marlborough's War Machine 1702–1711*. Barnsley: Pen & Sword Military

Fitton, Robert. 1990. *Leadership: Quotations From The Military Tradition*. New York, NY: Avalon Publishing

Forty, George. 2013. *Jake Wardrop's Diary: A Tank Regiment Sergeant's Story*. Stroud: Amberley Publishing

Fraser, David. 1982. *Alanbrooke*. London: William Collins

French, David. 2005. *Military Identities: The Regimental System, the British Army, & the British People c.1870–2000*. Oxford: OUP

Fuller, J. F. C. 1926. *The Foundations of the Science of War*. London: Hutchinson & Co

Furnham, A. 2004. *The Psychology of Behaviour at Work*. Hove: Psychology Press

Glover, Jonathan. 2012. *Humanity: A Moral History of the Twentieth Century*. London: Yale University Press

Greenleaf, Robert K. 1970. *The Servant as Leader*. Cambridge, MA: Center for Applied Studies

Grint, Keith. 2007. *Leadership, Management and Command: Rethinking D-Day*. Basingstoke: Palgrave Macmillan

Guy, Alan J. 1985. *Oeconomy and Discipline: Officer and Administration in the British Army, 1714-63*. Manchester: Manchester University Press

Hastings, Max. 2010. *The Korean War: An Epic Conflict.* London: Pan Books

Holmes, Richard. 2007. *Dusty Warriors: Modern Soldiers at War.* London: Harper Perennial

Huntington, Samuel. 1957. *The Soldier and the State.* Boston, MA: Harvard University Press

Hytner, Richard. 2014. *Consiglieri: Leading From the Shadows.* London: Profile Books

Keegan, John. 2004. *The Mask of Command: A Study of Generalship.* London: Pimlico

Kirke, Charles. 2009. *Red Coat, Green Machine: Continuity in Change in the British Army 1700–2000.* London: Bloomsbury Academic

Laughlin, Clara E. 2008. *Foch the Man: A Life of the Supreme Commander of the Allied Armies.* BiblioLife (n. p.)

Laver, Harry S. and Matthews, Jeffry J. (eds). 2008. *The Art of Command: Leadership from George Washington to Colin Powell.* Lexington, KY: University Press of Kentucky

Lindsay, Donald. 1987. *Forgotten General, A Life of Andrew Thorne.* Salisbury: Michael Russell

McChrystal, Stanley. 2015. *Team of Teams: New Rules of Engagement for a Complex World.* London: Penguin

Macdonald, Janet. 2016. *Sir John Moore: The Making of a Controversial Hero.* Barnsley: Pen & Sword Military

MacDonald Fraser, George. 2000. *Quartered Safe out Here: A Recollection of the War in Burma.* London: HarperCollins

Mäder, Markus. 2004. *In Pursuit of Conceptual Excellence: The Evolution of British Military-strategic Doctrine in the Post-Cold War Era, 1989–2002.* Oxford: Peter Lang

Mallinson, Allan. 2011. *The Making of the British Army.* London: Bantam Books

Mayhew, Emily. 2017. *A Heavy Reckoning: War, Medicine and Survival in Afghanistan and Beyond.* London: Profile Books

Moran, Lord. 2007. *The Anatomy of Courage: The Classic WW1 Study of the Psychological Effects of War.* London: Constable

Muir, Kate. 1992. *Arms and the Woman.* London: Sinclair Stephenson

Nanson, Maj Gen Paul. 2019. *Stand Up Straight: 10 Life Lessons from the Royal Military Academy Sandhurst.* London: Century

Newsinger, John. 2015. *British Counterinsurgency.* Basingstoke: Palgrave Macmillan

Nolan, Victoria. 2012. *Military Leadership and Counterinsurgency: The British Army and Small War Strategy since World War II.* London: I. B. Tauris

Parker, Peter. 2007. *The Old Lie: The Great War and the Public-School Ethos.* London: Continuum

Powdrill, Ernest. 2009. *In the Face of the Enemy: A Battery Sergeant Major in Action in the Second World War.* Barnsley: Pen & Sword Military

Richards, Andrew. 2021. *After the Wall Came Down: Soldiering through the Transformation of the British Army, 1990–2020.* Oxford: Casemate Publishing

Russell, Bertram. 2004. *Power: A New Social Analysis*. London: Routledge Classics

Salmon, Andrew. 2009. *To the Last Round: The Epic British Stand on the Imjin River, Korea 1951*. London: Aurum

Shamir, Eitan. 2011. *Transforming Command: The Pursuit of Mission Command in the U.S., British, and Israeli Armies*. Redwood City, CA: Stanford University Press

Sheffield, Gary. 2014. *Command and Morale: The British Army on the Western Front, 1914–18*. Barnsley: Pen & Sword Military

Shipton, Elisabeth. 2014. *Female Tommies: The Frontline Women of the First World War*. Cheltenham: The History Press

Simes, Thomas. 1777. *A Military Course for the Government and Conduct of a Battalion*. London (n.p.)

Spiers, Edward. 1992. *The Late Victorian Army: 1868–1902*. Manchester: Manchester University Press

Taylor, Robert L. and Rosenbach, William E. (eds). 2009. *Military Leadership: In Pursuit of Excellence*. Oxford: Routledge

Vandergriff, Don. 2019. *Adopting Mission Command: Developing Leaders for a Superior Command Culture*. Annapolis, MD: Naval Institute Press

Vandergriff, Don and Webber, Stephen (eds). 2017. *Mission Command: The Who, What, Where, When and Why: An Anthology*. Volume I. Kabul, Afghanistan

Vandergriff, Don and Webber, Stephen (eds). 2019. *Mission Command: The Who, What, Where, When and Why: An Anthology*. Volume II. Virginia, USA

Westlake, R. *Brigadier-General R. B. Bradford, V.C., M.C. and His Brothers*. Ray Westlake (Newport: n.d.)

White, Arthur S. 2001. (3rd edition). *Bibliography of Regimental Histories of the British Army*. Uckfield: Naval and Military Press

Whiting, Charles. 1999. *Battleground Korea: The British in Korea*. Stroud: Sutton Publishing

Wolfendale, Jessica. 2007. *Torture and the Military Profession*. Basingstoke: Palgrave Macmillan

Wolseley, Gen Viscount. 1886. *The Soldier's Pocket Book for Field-Service*. London: Macmillan and Co.

Wren, J. Thomas. 1995. *The Leader's Companion: Insights on Leadership Through the Ages*. New York, NY: Free Press

Articles, chapters, reports and papers

Bender, Jason M. 'Non-Technical Military Innovation: The Prussian General Staff and Professional Military Education'. *Small Wars Journal*, 14 September 2016. https://smallwarsjournal.com/jrnl/art/non-technical-military-innovation-the-prussian-general-staff-and-professional-military-educ#_edn10

Blanco, R. 1968. 'Attempts to Abolish Branding and Flogging in the Army of Victorian England before 1881'. *Journal of the Society for Army Historical Research*, 46 (187), 137–45

Bungay, Stephen. 'The Executive's Trinity: Management, Leadership – and Command'. *The Ashridge Journal*, summer 2011

Caslen, Lt Gen Robert L. 2011. 'The Army Ethic, Public Trust and the Profession of Arms'. *Military Review* (September issue)

Childs, John. 2003. 'The Restoration Army 1660–1702'. In D. Chandler and I. Beckett (eds). *The Oxford History of the British Army*. Oxford: OUP, pp. 46–66

Copeland, Mary Kay. 2014. 'The Emerging Significance of Values Based Leadership: A Literature Review'. *International Journal of Leadership Studies* 8 (2), 105–35

Dodd, Norman L. 1976. 'The Corporals' War: Internal Security Operations in Northern Ireland'. *Military Review*, 56(7), 58–68

Dunford Jr, Gen J. 'From the Chairman: The Pace of Change'. *Joint Force Quarterly* no. 84, National Defense University Press, 26 January 2017

Fielder, Dave. 2011. 'Defining Command, Leadership, and Management Success Factors Within Stability Operations'. Report for Strategic Studies Institute, US Army War College

French, David. 2002. 'Officer Education and Training in the British Regular Army 1919–39'. In G. Kennedy and K. Neilson (eds). *Military Education: Past, Present and Future*. Westport, CT: Praeger, pp. 105–28

French, David. 2006. 'The Regimental System: One Historian's Perspective'. *Journal of the Society for Army Historical Research*, 84 (340), 362–79

French, John R. and Raven, Bertram. 1959. 'The Bases of Social Power' in D. Cartwright (ed). *Studies in Social Power*. Ann Arbor, MI: Institute for Social Research, University of Michigan, pp. 150–67

Frostic, Fred L. 1994. *Air Campaign Against the Iraqi Army in the Kuwaiti Theater of Operations*. Santa Monica, CA: Rand

Fuller, Maj Gen J.F.C. 1953. 'Warfare and the Future'. *Armor*, March-April issue, 48–9

Gossett, Maj Gen Sir M. 1891. 'Battalion Command'. *Royal United Service Institution Journal*, 35 (158), 469–86

Grint, Keith. 2020. 'Leadership, management and command in the time of the Coronavirus'. *Leadership*, 16 (3), 314–19

Guy, Alan J. 2003. 'The Army of the Georges 1714–1783'. In D. Chandler and I. Beckett (eds). *The Oxford History of the British Army*. Oxford: OUP, pp. 92–111

Hack, Karl. 2009. 'The Malayan Emergency as counter-insurgency paradigm'. *Journal of Strategic Studies*, 32 (3), 383–414

Hackett, Lt Gen Sir John. 1986. '1. Origins of a Profession'. In *The Profession of Arms*. Washington, DC: Center of Military History, pp. 3–8

Harris, P. 2012. 'Soldier Banker: Lieutenant-General Sir Herbert Lawrence as the BEF's Chief of Staff in 1918'. *Journal of the Society for Army Historical Research*, 90 (361), 44–67

Horn, Lt Col B. 2002. 'A Timeless Strength: The Army's Senior NCO Corps'. *Canadian Military Journal* (spring issue)

Howard, Sir Michael and Guilmartin. John F. 1994. 'Two Historians in Technology and War'. Report for the Army War College. Carlisle, PA: Strategic Studies Institute

Hsiang, Solomon M., Burke, Marshall and Miguel, Edward. 2013. 'Quantifying the Influence of Climate on Human Conflict'. *Science*, 341 (6151), 1189–1213

Jary, Sydney. 2000. 'Reflections on the Relationship Between the Led and the Leader'. *Journal of the Royal Army Medical Corps*, 146 (1), 54–6

King, Anthony. 2006. 'The Word of Command: Communication and Cohesion in the Military'. *Armed Forces & Society*, 32 (4), 493–512

Komer, R. W. 1972. 'The Malayan Emergency in Retrospect: Organization of A Successful Counterinsurgency Effort'. Santa Monica, CA: Rand

Kroesen, Gen Frederick E. 1993. 'The NCO Corps: More than the Backbone'. *NCO Journal* (winter issue)

Krulak, Gen Charles C. 1999. 'The Strategic Corporal: Leadership in the Three-Block War'. *Marine Corps Gazette* (January issue)

Lawton, Alan and Paez, Iliana. 2014. 'Developing a Framework for Ethical Leadership'. *Journal of Business Ethics*, 130 (3), 639–49

McAleer, George. 2009. 'Leaders in Transition: Advice from Colin Powell and Other Strategic Thinkers'. *Military Psychology*, 15 (4), 313–14

McConville, Michael. 2011. 'General Templer and the Use of Geese as Watchdogs'. *The RUSI Journal*, 156 (5), 94–101

McCormack, Rev Dr P. J. 'Grounding British Army Values Upon an Ethical Good'. 30 March 2015. https://www.cgscfoundation.org/wp-content/uploads/2015/04/McCormack-GroundingBritishArmyValues.pdf

McElligott, Sheila and Seaton, Sgt A. 2019. 'Adventurous Training and Leadership: Training for enhanced effectiveness or just a week out of the office?' *Army Mountaineer* (winter issue)

Montgomery, Field Marshal The Viscount. 1954. 'The Role of Science in Warfare of the Future'. *Engineering and Science*, 20–28

Otley, C. B. 1973. 'The Educational Background of British Army Officers'. *Sociology*, 7 (2), 191–209

Pearce, Craig L. 2004. 'The Future of Leadership: Combining Vertical and Shared Leadership to Transform Knowledge Work [and Executive Commentary]'. *Academy of Management Executive*, 18 (1), 47–57

Pugsley, Christopher. 2011. 'We Have Been Here Before: the Evolution of the Doctrine of Decentralised Command in the British Army, 1905–1989'. Sandhurst Occasional Papers No. 9. Camberley: Royal Military Academy Sandhurst

Riedi, Eliza. 2006. 'Brains or Polo? Equestrian Sport, Army Reform and the Gentlemanly Officer Tradition, 1900–1914'. *Journal of the Society for Army Historical Research*, 84 (339), 236–53

Santos, Henri C., Varnum, Michael E. W. and Grossmann, Igor. 2017. 'Global Increases in Individualism'. *Psychological Science*, 28 (9), 1228–39

Schneider, J. J. 2012. 'A Leader's Grief: T. E. Lawrence, Leadership and PTSD'. *Military Review* (January-February issue)

Shields, Patricia M. 2020. 'Dynamic Intersection of Military and Society'. In Anders Sookermany (ed). *Handbook of Military Sciences*. New York, NY: Springer, pp. 1–23.

Shillington, Lt Col J. G. 2011. 'Morale'. *The RUSI Journal*, 156 (2), 96–8

Smalley, Edward. 2015. 'Qualified, but Unprepared: Training for War at the Staff College in the 1930s'. *British Journal for Military History*, 2 (1), 55–72

Smith, Maj Gen Rupert. 1992. 'The Gulf War: The Land Battle'. *The RUSI Journal*, 137 (1), 1–5

Spiers, Edward. 1979. 'The British Cavalry, 1902–1914'. *Journal of the Society for Army Historical Research*, 57 (230), 71–9

Spiers, Edward. 2003. 'The Late Victorian Army, 1868–1914'. In David Chandler & Ian Beckett (eds). *The Oxford History of the British Army*. Oxford: OUP, pp. 187–210

Storr, Lt Col J. P. 2004. 'The Command of British Land Forces in Iraq, March to May 2003'. Pewsey: Directorate General of Doctrine and Development

Strachan, Hew. 2007. 'British Counter-Insurgency from Malaya to Iraq'. *The RUSI Journal*, 152 (6), 8–11

Thomas, Ted and Chaleff, Ira. 2017. 'Moral Courage and Intelligent Disobedience'. *InterAgency Journal*, 8 (1), 58–66

Toner, James H. 1995. 'The Profession of Arms: The Full Measure of Devotion'. In *True Faith And Allegiance: The Burden of Military Ethics*. Lexington, KY: University Press of Kentucky, pp. 115–32

Walker, David. 2020. 'Character in the British Army: A Precarious Professional Practice'. In D. Carr (ed). *Cultivating Moral Character and Virtue in Professional Practice*. Abingdon: Routledge, Chapter 10

Wolseley, Gen Viscount. 1887. 'The Army'. In T. Humphry Ward (ed). *The Reign of Queen Victoria: A Survey of Fifty Years of Progress Vol. I*. London: Smith, Elder & Co, pp. 155–225

Unpublished PhDs and MAs

Baillergeon, F. A. 2005. 'Field Marshal William Slim and the Power of Leadership' (MA, US Army Command and General Staff College, Kansas)

Bendorf, Harry H. 1967. 'Richard Haldane and the British Army Reforms, 1905–1909' (MA, University of Nebraska at Omaha)

Brown, Ashleigh. 2017. 'Lions Led by Donkeys? Brigade Commanders of the Australian Imperial Force, 1914–18' (PhD, University of New South Wales)

Coates, H. 1976. 'An Operational Analysis of the Emergency in Malaya, 1948–1954' (PhD, Australian National University)

Gould, Jenny. 1988. 'The Women's Corps: The Establishment of Women's Military Services in Britain' (PhD, University College London)

Hentel, Magdalena J. 2017. 'Temporary Gentlemen: The Masculinity of Lower-Middle-Class Temporary British Officers in the First World War' (PhD, University of Western Ontario)

Hodgkinson, Peter. 2013. 'British Infantry Battalion Commanders in the First World War' (PhD, University of Birmingham)

Kirke, Charles. 2002. 'Social Structures in the Regular Combat Arms Units of the British Army: A Model' (PhD, Cranfield University)

Kochanski, H. 1996. 'Field Marshal Wolseley: A Reformer at the War Office, 1871–1900' (PhD, King's College London)

Lee, Sangho. 1994. 'Deterrence and the Defence of Central Europe: The British Role from the Early 1980s to the End of the Gulf War' (PhD, King's College London)

Mahaffey, C. L. 2004. 'The Fighting Profession: The Professionalization of the British Line Infantry Officer Corps, 1870–1902' (PhD, University of Glasgow)

Memoirs

Campion Vaughan, Edwin. 2010. *Some Desperate Glory: The Diary of a Young Officer, 1917*. Barnsley: Pen & Sword Military

de la Billière, Peter. 2012. *Storm Command: A Personal Account of the Gulf War*. London: HarperCollins

Eyre, Giles. 1991. *Somme Harvest*. Eastbourne: Antony Rowe

Farrar-Hockley, Anthony. 2007. *The Edge of the Sword: The Classic Account of Warfare & Captivity in Korea*. Barnsley: Pen & Sword Military

Frost, John. 2008. *A Drop Too Many*. Barnsley: Pen & Sword Military

Human, William Arthur. 2019. *Arthur: The Great War Memoirs of William Arthur Human*. PublishNation (www.publishnation.co.uk)

Hume, Ian. 2018. *From the Edge of Empire: A Memoir*. Denver, CO: Outskirts Press

Jary, Sydney. 1987. *18 Platoon*. Carshalton Beeches: Sydney Jary Ltd

Lucy, J. F. 1993. *There's a Devil in the Drum*. Eastbourne: Naval & Military

Powell, Colin. 1995. *A Soldier's Way: An Autobiography*. London: Random House

Powell, Geoffrey. 2012. *Men at Arnhem*. Barnsley: Pen & Sword Military

Robertson, Field Marshal Sir William. *From Private to Field-Marshal: The Autobiography of the First British Private Soldier to Rise to the Highest Rank*. Miami, FL: HardPress

Sassoon, Siegfried. 1972. *The Complete Memoirs of George Sherston*. London: Faber & Faber

Schwarzkopf, Norman H. 1992. *It Doesn't Take a Hero: The Autobiography*. New York, NY: Bantam Books

Seton, Graham. 1933. *Footslogger*. London: Hutchinson

Slim, Field Marshal Sir William. 1956. *Defeat Into Victory*. London: Cassell

Urquhart, R. E. 2011. *Arnhem*. Barnsley: Pen & Sword Military

Magazine, newspaper and news site articles

BBC News

Lila Allen. 'Afghanistan makes army training "longer and tougher"', 11 January 2011
https://www.bbc.co.uk/news/newsbeat-12156808

Jonathan Beale. 'Does size matter for Britain's shrinking Army?', 24 February 2021
https://www.bbc.co.uk/news/uk-56007073

Guardian

Kirstie Brewer. 'Fire Fighters' Battle with PTSD: "Every day is an anxious day"', 23 August 2017
https://www.theguardian.com/public-leaders-network/2017/aug/23/mental-health-fire-service-government-cuts-grenfell-firefighters-charity

DataBlog. 'British Dead and Wounded in Afghanistan, Month by Month', 17 September 2009
https://www.theguardian.com/news/datablog/2009/sep/17/afghanistan-casualties-dead-wounded-british-data

John Ezard. 'Needless battle caused by uncommon language'. 14 April 2001
https://www.theguardian.com/uk/2001/apr/14/johnezard

Harvard Business Review

Anita Elberse. 'Ferguson's Formula', October 2013
https://hbr.org/2013/10/fergusons-formula

David A. Garvin. 'Building a Learning Organization', July-August 1993
https://hbr.org/1993/07/building-a-learning-organization

Daniel Goleman. 'What Makes a Leader?', January 2004
https://hbr.org/2004/01/what-makes-a-leader

Robert E. Kelley. 'In Praise of Followers', November 1988

https://hbr.org/1988/11/in-praise-of-followers

John P. Kotter. 'Leading Change: Why Transformation Efforts Fail', May-June 1995

https://hbr.org/1995/05/leading-change-why-transformation-efforts-fail-2

A. G. Lafley. 'What Only the CEO Can Do', May 2009

https://hbr.org/2009/05/what-only-the-ceo-can-do

Rita Gunther McGrath. 'Transient Advantage', June 2013

https://hbr.org/2013/06/transient-advantage

Geoffrey Moore. 'To Succeed in the Long Term, Focus on the Middle Term', July-August 2007

https://hbr.org/2007/07/to-succeed-in-the-long-term-focus-on-the-middle-term

Military Strategy Magazine

An Jacobs. 'Teaching IR at Sandhurst: Blended Learning through an Integrated Approach', winter 2016

https://www.militarystrategymagazine.com/article/teaching-ir-at-sandhurst-blended-learning-through-an-integrated-approach/

New Statesman

Alistair Bunkall. 'The Long Goodbye to Afghanistan', 17 October 2013

https://www.newstatesman.com/2013/10/what-brits-are-leaving-behind-helmand

Wall Street Journal

Peter F. Drucker. 'The American CEO', 30 December 2004

https://www.wsj.com/articles/SB110436476581112426

Primary sources

Speeches

Carter, Gen Sir Nick. 'Chief of the Defence Staff speech RUSI Annual Lecture', 17 December 2020 https://www.gov.uk/government/speeches/chief-of-defence-staff-at-rusi-annual-lecture

Guthrie, Gen Sir Charles. 'The New British Way in Warfare'. Annual Liddell-Hart Centre for Military Archives Lecture, 12 February 2001 https://www.kcl.ac.uk/library/assets/archives/2001-lecture.pdf

Holmes, Professor Richard. 'Soldiers & Society'. Annual Liddell-Hart Centre for Military Archives Lecture, 10 May 2006 https://www.kcl.ac.uk/library/assets/archives/liddellhartlecture2006.pdf

Powell, Gen Colin. 'Town Hall Meeting'. US Department of State, 25 January 2001 https://2001-2009.state.gov/secretary/former/powell/remarks/2001/24.htm

Sanders, Gen Sir Patrick. Speech at RMAS Sovereign's Parade, 12 December 2020 https://www.facebook.com/RoyalMilitaryAcademySandhurst/videos/rmas-sovereigns-parade-live-stream/1314094822301198/

Slim, Field Marshal The Viscount. Address to Officer Cadets of the Royal Military Academy Sandhurst, October 1952 http://www.pnbhs.school.nz/wp-content/uploads/2015/11/Slim.pdf

Official Army publications/documents

16 Air Assault Brigade. *The Pegasus Ethos* (April 2016)

ADP. *Soldiering: The Military Covenant*. Army Doctrine Publication Vol. 5 (February 2000)

Army Headquarters. 2018. *Values and Standards of the British Army*. AC 64649. Andover: Army Publications

The Battalion Commander's Handbook. 1996. Carlisle, PA: US Army War College

Commander Force Development and Training. *Army Doctrine Primer*. AC 71954 (May 2011)

Director Leadership. 2015. *The Army Leadership Code: An Introductory Guide*. MOD

Director Leadership. 'The Army Leadership Review – Final Report' (June 2015)

General Staff Centre. *General Staff Handbook* (March 2021)

Irregular Warfare (IW) Joint Operating Concept (JOC) V.1 (11 September 2007) https://www.jcs.mil/Portals/36/Documents/Doctrine/concepts/joc_iw_v1.pdf?ver=2017-12-28-162020-260

Land Warfare Development Centre. *ADP Land Operations*. AC 71940 (March 2017)

MOD. 'Introducing the Integrated Operating Concept', 30 September 2020

Royal Military Academy Sandhurst. *Serve to Lead* (2nd Edition). 2013

Strategic Leadership: Primer for Senior Leaders (4th Edition). Department of Command, Leadership, and Management, United States Army War College (n.d.) https://ssl.armywarcollege.edu/dclm/pubs/Strategic_Leadership_Primer.pdf

US Army Armor School. 'Order of the Spur'. USAARMS Pamphlet 360-12, Feb 2019 https://www.benning.army.mil/Armor/OCoA/Content/PDF/USAARMS%20Pam%20360-12%20Example%20Spur%20Ride%20SOP.pdf?07FEB2019

The US Army Operating Concept:'Win in a Complex World'. TRADOC Pamphlet 525-3-1, 7 October 2014

Other

The Aitken Report. 'An Investigation into Cases of Deliberate Abuse and Unlawful Killing in Iraq in 2003 and 2004', 25 January 2008 http://data.parliament.uk/DepositedPapers/Files/DEP2008-0229/DEP2008-0229.pdf

Archbold: Criminal Pleading, Evidence and Practice. London: Sweet & Maxwell

British Army Newsletter. *In Front*, Summer 2019, Issue 3 https://www.army.mod.uk/media/6481/adr008449_in_front_issue_31.pdf

Cardiff Metropolitan University and Bangor University. 2014. ' "Train in, not select out?": Bangor leadership training model decreased the high wastage rates in British army recruits and improved training practices'. Research Excellence Framework Impact Case Studies https://impact.ref.ac.uk/casestudies/CaseStudy.aspx?Id=32269

Department of the Army. 1996. *Command, Leadership, And Effective Staff Support.* Washington, DC: The Information Management Support Center Pentagon

Erskine May: Parliamentary Practice. https://erskinemay.parliament.uk/

Government Announcement. 'Lt Col Rupert Thorneloe and Tpr Joshua Hammond killed in Afghanistan', 2 July 2009. https://www.gov.uk/government/fatalities/lieutenant-colonel-rupert-thorneloe-and-trooper-joshua-hammond-killed-in-afghanistan

House of Commons. 'Supply – Army Estimates'. *Hansard*, Vol 204: Debated on Thursday 16 February 1871 https://hansard.parliament.uk/Commons/1871-02-16/debates/88ec4080-7ec8-4514-a8fe-a47827330093/Supply—ArmyEstimates

House of Commons. 'UK Defence Personnel Statistics', 8 March 2021. https://commonslibrary.parliament.uk/research-briefings/cbp-7930/

Lawrence, T. E. 'Twenty-Seven Articles', *The Arab Bulletin*, 20 August 1917 https://wwi.lib.byu.edu/index.php/The_27_Articles_of_T.E._Lawrence

The London Gazette: Supplement, Friday, 27 November 1953 https://www.thegazette.co.uk/London/issue/40029/supplement/6513

Ministry of Defence Guidance. 'Future Operating Environment, 2035', 14 December 2015 https://www.gov.uk/government/publications/future-operating-environment-2035

National Statistics. 'Quarterly Service Personnel Statistics: 2020', 20 February 2020 https://www.gov.uk/government/statistics/quarterly-service-personnel-statistics-2020

Col (Retd) James D. Sharpe Jr and Lt Col (Retd) Thomas E. Creviston, 'Understanding Mission Command'. *US Army*, 30 April 2015 https://www.army.mil/article/106872/Understanding_mission_command/

Internet sources

Videos

Centre for Army Leadership – Army Sergeant Major WO1 G. H. Paton, 27 May 2020 https://www.youtube.com/watch?v=93zbU4jR3BI

Centre for Army Leadership – Remote Leadership Conference, 21 March 2021 https://www.youtube.com/watch?v=jCsD3V783L8

Centre for Army Leadership JNCO Day, 27 February 2020 https://www.youtube.com/watch?v=Pa6GsMglFRA

Cordingley, Maj Gen Patrick. *Gulf War Commander Recalls Swift Land Battle Against Saddam Hussein* https://www.youtube.com/watch?v=8AYZ340Iqmk

Smith, Gen Sir Rupert. *Are the Principles of Manoeuvre Valid in the 21st Century? RUSI* Land Warfare Conference, 2018 https://www.youtube.com/watch?v=fRkYiUrQYy4

'Nicky Moffat Shares the Key Traits a Modern Leader Needs During Change', 26 February 2021 https://www.youtube.com/watch?v=M7LCArACOG8

Articles

Army Leadership Team. 'Do Not Take Leadership for Granted: An Interview with General Charlie Collins' https://thearmyleader.co.uk/major-general-charlie-collins-interview/

Berkshire Hathaway. 'Berkshire – Past, Present and Future' https://www.berkshirehathaway.com/SpecialLetters/WEB%20past%20present%20future%202014.pdf

Cambridge Institute for Sustainability Leadership. 'Informing a Strategic Response to Climate Change: A Review of a Workshop for the British Army'

Huw Davies. 'Leading as a JNCO: An Army Reserve Perspective' https://thearmyleader.co.uk/reserve-jnco-leadership/

Dan Ellis. 'Senior Soldier: The Company Sergeant Major' https://cove.army.gov.au/article/senior-soldier-the-company-sergeant-major

Glassdoor. 'Culture over Cash? Glassdoor Multi-Country Survey Finds more than Half of Employees Prioritize Workplace Culture over Salary' https://www.glassdoor.com/about-us/workplace-culture-over-salary/

Ben Hayden. 'Get off Their Backs! A JNCO's Guide to Avoiding Micromanagement' https://thearmyleader.co.uk/jncos-guide-to-avoiding-micromanagement/

Hebditch, Maj Daniel. 'Planning, Fast and Slow: Or How to Make Military Planning Work for You' https://cove.army.gov.au/sites/default/files/10-12/12/MAJ-Hebditch-Planning-Fast-and-Slow.pdf

Jim Heskett. 'Why Isn't "Servant Leadership" More Prevalent?' Harvard Business School https://hbswk.hbs.edu/item/why-isnt-servant-leadership-more-prevalent

Tony Ingesson. 'When the Military Profession Isn't' https://themilitaryleader.com/when-military-profession-isnt/

CSgt Aaron Kerin. 'The Unpopular Man: Leading as a Lance Corporal' https://thearmyleader.co.uk/lead-as-a-lance-corporal/

Dr Florian Krampe. 'Why United Nations Peace Operations Cannot Ignore Climate Change'. Stockholm International Peace Research Institute https://www.sipri.org/commentary/topical-backgrounder/2021/why-united-nations-peace-operations-cannot-ignore-climate-change

Maj Gen (Retd) Patrick Marriott. 'My "Lessons Learnt" – Four and a Half Thoughts on Sub-Unit Command' https://thearmyleader.co.uk/lessons-learnt-sub-unit-command/

Andrew Marshall. 'The Other Side of the Hill' https://bootcampmilitaryfitnessinstitute.com/2019/03/12/the-other-side-of-the-hill/

Al Philips. 'The Strength of the Clan is in The Clansman: Reflections on Company Command' https://thearmyleader.co.uk/reflections-on-company-command/

Salesforce UK. 'Leading Through Adverse Conditions: Tips from Boots and the British Army' https://www.salesforce.com/uk/blog/2020/10/leading-through-change-boots-army.html

Scales, Robert H. 'Forecasting the Future of Warfare' https://warontherocks.com/2018/04/forecasting-the-future-of-warfare/

John Waddy. 'Shan Hackett at Arnhem' https://www.paradata.org.uk/article/shan-hackett-arnhem-article-john-waddy

Robert Walters. Whitepaper 'Attracting and Retaining Millennial Professionals' https://www.robertwalters.co.uk/content/dam/robert-walters/country/united-kingdom/files/whitepapers/robert-walters-whitepaper-millennials.pdf

Workforce Institute. 'Meet Gen Z' https://workforceinstitute.org/wp-content/uploads/2019/05/Meet-Gen-Z-Hopeful-Anxious-Hardworking-and-Searching-for-Inspiration.pdf

'Major Chris Keeble's Account of Goose Green' https://www.paradata.org.uk/article/major-chris-keebles-account-goose-green

'Queen Mary's Army Auxiliary Corps' https://www.nam.ac.uk/explore/queen-marys-army-auxiliary-corps

Podcasts

The Centre for Army Leadership Podcast Episode 11 – Archbishop Justin Welby, 12 May 2021 https://armyleadership.podbean.com/e/episode-11-archbishop-justin-welby/

The Centre for Army Leadership Podcast Special Edition – General Sir Mark Carleton-Smith, 26 December 2020 https://armyleadership.podbean.com/e/special-edition-general-sir-mark-carleton-smith-kcb-cbe-adc-gen/

Interviews

Maj Ben Acton, 2 April 2021
Lt Gen (Retd) James Bashall, 2 March 2021
Cpl Henry Bignell, 17 March 2021
Gen Sir Mark Carleton-Smith (CGS), 21 July 2020
Cpl Robert Chamberlain, 17 March 2021
Brig Lizzie Faithfull-Davies, 9 March 2021
Sgt Josh Leakey, 18 May 2021
Lt Col Will Meddings, 23 February 2021
WO1 Chris Nicol, 18 March 2021
Brig (Retd) John Ridge, 16 October 2020
Capt Lou Rudd, 5 April 2021
Cpl Oscar Searle, 17 March 2021
Maj (Retd) Glyn Sheppard, 4 March 2021
Capt Den Starkie, 10 April 2021
Capt Andy Stephen, 18 March 2021
Cpl Natasha Theodossiadis, 17 March 2021
SSgt Lee Waite, 21 December 2020

Index

Page references in *italics* indicate images.